Historic
Canada

North Vancouver's Lonsdale Neighbourhood

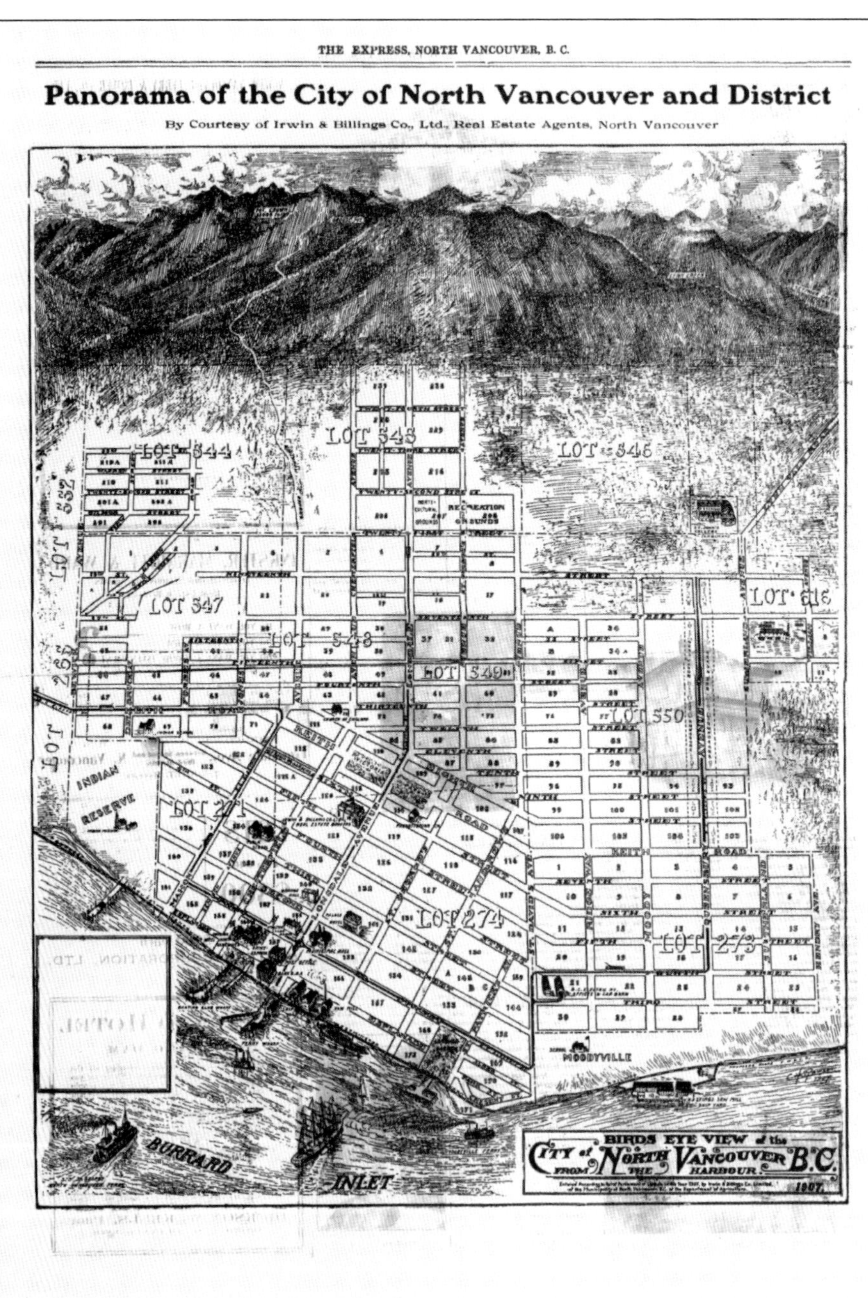

This map was taken from an Irwin & Billings advertisement in the June 28, 1907, edition of the *Express*, North Vancouver's first newspaper. It is part bird's-eye view and part street map. Lonsdale Avenue is shown running from the ferry dock on the north side of Burrard Inlet to the Coast Mountains of the North Shore. (Courtesy of the North Vancouver Museum & Archives.)

On the cover: This photograph, taken from a ferry, shows Lonsdale Avenue, the ferry wharf, streetcars, horses and wagon, women with a baby buggy, and businesses in the Lower Lonsdale area in 1908. (Courtesy of the North Vancouver Museum & Archives.)

Historic
Canada

North Vancouver's Lonsdale Neighbourhood

Shervin Shahriari

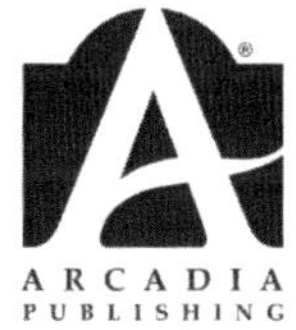

ARCADIA
PUBLISHING

ISBN 978-0-7385-7211-6

Published by Arcadia Publishing
Charleston SC, Chicago IL, Portsmouth NH, San Francisco CA

Printed in the United States of America

Library of Congress Control Number:2009927937

For all general information contact Arcadia Publishing at:
Telephone 843-853-2070
Fax 843-853-0044
E-mail sales@arcadiapublishing.com
For customer service and orders:
Toll-Free 1-888-313-2665

Visit us on the Internet at www.arcadiapublishing.com

Contents

Acknowledgements

I would like to thank the individuals, families, and organizations that over the years have kindly donated their valuable photographs and documents to the North Vancouver Museum & Archives (NVMA). Nancy Kirkpatrick, NVMA Director, has generously supported me since day one, provided lots of useful advice, and wrote the foreword; Janet Turner, NVMA archivist, provided me with valuable research insights; Daien Ide, NVMA reference historian, provided helpful research assistance. In addition to them, I would also like to thank Robin Inglis, former Director of NVMA, for providing perceptive comments; June Thompson, former NVMA archivist, who provided thorough and detailed feedback; and Shannon Craver, for scanning many of the photographs. I would also like to thank Sharon Fortney, Bob Heywood, Jan Manaton, Michael McCarthy, Cindy McLellan, Bonnie Miller, Magdalena Moore, Shirley Sutherland, John Stuart, and Joan Thornley for their assistance and support. Finally, I would like to thank mom, dad, my daughter Noosha who made sure I took frequent "play breaks," and my wife Homa for being a source of abundant encouragement and support.

A portion of the proceeds from this book will go to the Friends of the North Vancouver Museum & Archives Society.

Unless otherwise noted, all photographs are from the North Vancouver Museum & Archives photograph collection.

FOREWORD

Lonsdale Avenue forms the backbone of North Vancouver. For over a century, this major artery has connected the waters of Burrard Inlet to the mountains of the Coast Range, bisected two municipalities—the City of North Vancouver and the District of North Vancouver—and served as the region's main street.

Lonsdale Avenue is the spine along which North Vancouver originally developed. Main civic institutions located within several blocks of the street include schools, a hospital, both municipal halls, a library, a courthouse, police and fire stations, parks, and public recreation facilities. Lonsdale Avenue is a major transit corridor, served first by streetcars (1906–1946) and later by buses (1946–present). It is also a thriving commercial corridor whose lower and central sections are lined by shops and offices. Unlike the main streets of communities elsewhere in North America that declined in the post–World War II era when people and commerce moved to suburban areas, Lonsdale Avenue retained a strong commercial and civic focus. Today Lower Lonsdale and Central Lonsdale are designated by Metro Vancouver as a regional town centre, and thousands of people live in nearby houses and apartments.

A main artery for commercial, political, and social life, Lonsdale Avenue provides people with a way to get to work, go to school, attend a place of worship, enjoy recreation, partake in entertainment, and purchase household necessities. These essential activities are revealed in this book's unique photographs, most of which date from the first half of the 20th century. The photographs show children at play and at school, parents at work, shopkeepers in their stores, families attending social gatherings, and friends enjoying recreational activities.

The North Vancouver Museum & Archives thanks Arcadia Publishing for their invitation to participate in the Historic Canada book series. We are grateful to Shervin Shahriari for proposing, researching, and writing the book. We also want to recognize the contributions of Archivist Janet Turner and Reference Historian Daien Ide whose knowledge of the people, stories, and photographs represented in the archives collections have made this book possible.

Nancy Kirkpatrick
Director, North Vancouver Museum & Archives

INTRODUCTION

The Coast Salish aboriginal people lived in southwestern British Columbia for generations prior to the arrival of European settlers. Their descendants, members of today's Squamish Nation, were by 1886 established on the "Mission Reserve," located two and a half blocks west of the foot of today's Lonsdale Avenue. This site, at the mouth of a creek, is where the French order of Oblate Fathers had built a mission church. The land and environment of the traditional native territories on the north shore of Burrard Inlet were by then being transformed. Logging activities were razing some of North Vancouver's old growth rainforest; and some early settlers nurtured visions of North Vancouver becoming a great port city.

In the early years of the 20th century, North Vancouver's Lonsdale neighbourhood was beginning to take form. Across the Burrard Inlet, Vancouver had the significant advantage of being linked to the rest of Canada by a railway. However, those who were planning and designing North Vancouver had the confidence necessary to envision and develop a remarkable neighbourhood.

The ferry system provided a crucial transportation link to Vancouver, and, indirectly, to the rest of Canada via the Canadian Pacific Railway, as the ferries carried people and goods back and forth across Burrard Inlet. Early businesses in North Vancouver realized that the local environment, with its mountains, canyons, and many creeks, offered an unparalleled natural setting. A scenic ferry ride away, North Vancouver was attractive to visitors wanting to get away from the hustle and bustle of Vancouver.

One of the businessmen who recognized the potential of the ferry service was Pete Larson, who built North Vancouver's first hotel, the Hotel North Vancouver, in 1902. Located on West Esplanade near the corner of Lonsdale Avenue, it had a pleasant setting on grassy grounds near the beach. The hotel quickly became popular for picnics and for celebrations. The Dominion Day festivities attracted over 10,000 local residents and visitors from the south shore who arrived in North Vancouver via a scenic ferry ride.

When Alfred St. George Hamersley purchased a substantial parcel of land from Henry Heywood-Lonsdale and James Pemberton Fell's Lonsdale Estate in early 1903 and named the area the Town of Lonsdale, only a small number of people lived in this area. Significant improvements to infrastructure were needed to make it attractive for people to come, clear and purchase land, build houses, and live in the neighbourhood permanently.

Pockets of settlement also needed to be connected farther east and west of Lonsdale Avenue. James Cooper Keith's loan to the municipality enabled the construction of a road, bearing his name, which had started in 1893 and ran roughly parallel to the waterfront. Lonsdale Avenue bridged the outside world, through the North Vancouver Ferry Wharf and Lower Lonsdale, to Central Lonsdale, Upper Lonsdale, and the mountains. In time, Lonsdale Avenue was extended to reach the higher elevations and became a sea to mountain artery. These two intersecting arteries, Keith Road and Lonsdale Avenue, acted as a matrix around which most of the north shore's early development coalesced.

In 1905, the Bank of British North America opened a branch on Lonsdale signalling growing financial activities in the area. City lights were turned on in 1906, at which point Arnold A. Kealy, District of North Vancouver reeve and first City of North Vancouver mayor, said, "These lights glitter tonight for the first time . . . [and] are a prophecy of greater things that will make us more than a second to the city across the Inlet."

Another significant investment further established Lonsdale Avenue as the backbone of the North Vancouver community. In 1906, the streetcar system, made possible by the arrival of electrical service in North Vancouver, was officially inaugurated. The streetcar was a major investment, and it connected communities such as Central and North Lonsdale, Lynn Valley and Capilano to the Lonsdale core and to the North Vancouver Ferry Wharf at the foot of Lonsdale. With the streetcar and the ferries providing transportation, people were able to live on more affordable lots farther from Lower Lonsdale and ride back and forth to work.

In 1907, the City of North Vancouver, seceded from the District of North Vancouver and was incorporated. The District, which was incorporated in 1891, retained a larger land mass that included Upper Lonsdale, Capilano, Deep Cove, and Lynn Valley. The City, essentially a townsite built around Lower and Central Lonsdale, was then able to focus its efforts in a smaller area. This focus resulted in a concentration of amenities, such as hospitals, police, and educational institutions, around the Lonsdale core.

The waterfront at Lower Lonsdale was an ideal location for a shipbuilding and repair industry that lasted for generations. At one point, during World War II, as many as 13,000 men and 1,000 women worked at the Burrard Dry Dock shipbuilding and repair facilities. These figures are remarkable even by today's measures. The two world wars affected North Vancouver in other ways as well. The 6th Field Company, headquartered at a drill hall on Forbes Avenue, participated in both world wars and built mock trenches at Mahon Park. A regrettable historical fact is the treatment of Japanese Canadians during World War II, who lived and worked in North Vancouver and, through forced displacement by the federal authorities, ended up losing their livelihoods, properties, and belongings.

In North Vancouver's early years, most buildings were made of wood, as this was readily available in abundance. However, buildings such as the Bank of Hamilton stood out with its impressive brick siding and structure. Other grand statements were made with the construction of architectural landmarks such as Ridgeway and Queen Mary schools that have been providing educational services to generations of students. Perhaps the most noteworthy landmark remaining today, however, is St. Paul's Catholic Church on the Mission Reserve, which is prominent in some of the oldest images of North Vancouver and is the oldest surviving Catholic church in Greater Vancouver.

There were challenges that had to be overcome as well. In 1913, the western world was in an economic depression that also affected North Vancouver and put a damper on its real estate boom. The Depression years starting in 1929 eventually bankrupted both the District and the City. The Province intervened by appointing commissioners to run the affairs of the municipalities, and elections resumed once the financial situation was under control. After a long service, the streetcars were decommissioned in the late 1940s and replaced by buses. The old cars were literally discarded. It was years later when one of North Vancouver's streetcars, No. 153, was rescued after having been deployed as a chicken coop and a restoration project was begun. However, perhaps the most devastating setback was a decision to shut down the ferry service at the foot of Lonsdale in 1958, as by then most people owned cars and were able to access Vancouver via bridges at the first narrows (Lions Gate Bridge) and the second narrows (Ironworkers Memorial Crossing). The ferry service was to Lonsdale Avenue as a root is to a tree.

Once the ferries shut down, Lonsdale Avenue lost its footing and went into a local economic slump that lasted until 1977. That year the Seabus went into operation, Lower Lonsdale was re-established as a transit hub, and the revitalization of the area began.

North Vancouver's original planners had the foresight to include a series of parks and greenways throughout the community. Although the Hotel North Vancouver had sizeable grounds, which were used as a public park at times, other parks and green areas were envisioned. A work bee was organized and community volunteers cleared Victoria Park around 1905. In 1908, the Grand Boulevard was cleared. Promoters boasted that it would be to North Vancouver "what the Champs Elysees is to Paris." Mahon Park, to the west, was created as a site for athletic activities, celebrations, and events. The city fathers envisioned a community that would inspire residents with its beauty and splendid views of the mountains and the inlet. Today the Lonsdale neighbourhood retains much of its original "green necklace" set of parks including Ottawa Gardens, Victoria Park on Keith Road, Mahon Park, and Grand Boulevard.

The Lower Lonsdale area, anchored by the Seabus (1977) and the Lonsdale Quay Market (1986), has seen a dramatic transformation. A number of trendy high-rise condominiums offer fabulous city, water, and mountain views and have brought in an upscale generation of residents. The neighbourhood is increasingly multicultural. Today many people of non-European origin, including Iranians, Koreans, Chinese, and Filipinos, call North Vancouver their home, and their presence is reflected in a variety of shops, bakeries, and restaurants on Lonsdale Avenue.

When Lonsdale Avenue was first drawn on a map, it linked the waterfront, near Tom Turner's farm, to the heavily forested slopes of the North Shore mountains. A vibrant community with Lonsdale Avenue operating as its spine was envisioned. Today's lively Lonsdale Avenue and its surrounding neighbourhood is the realization of that vision. Since its determined and confident beginning in the early 1900s, North Vancouver—with Lonsdale Avenue as its major artery—has successfully responded to the many challenges of the times and is a desired place to live, work, and visit.

One

EARLY RESIDENTS AND PIONEERS

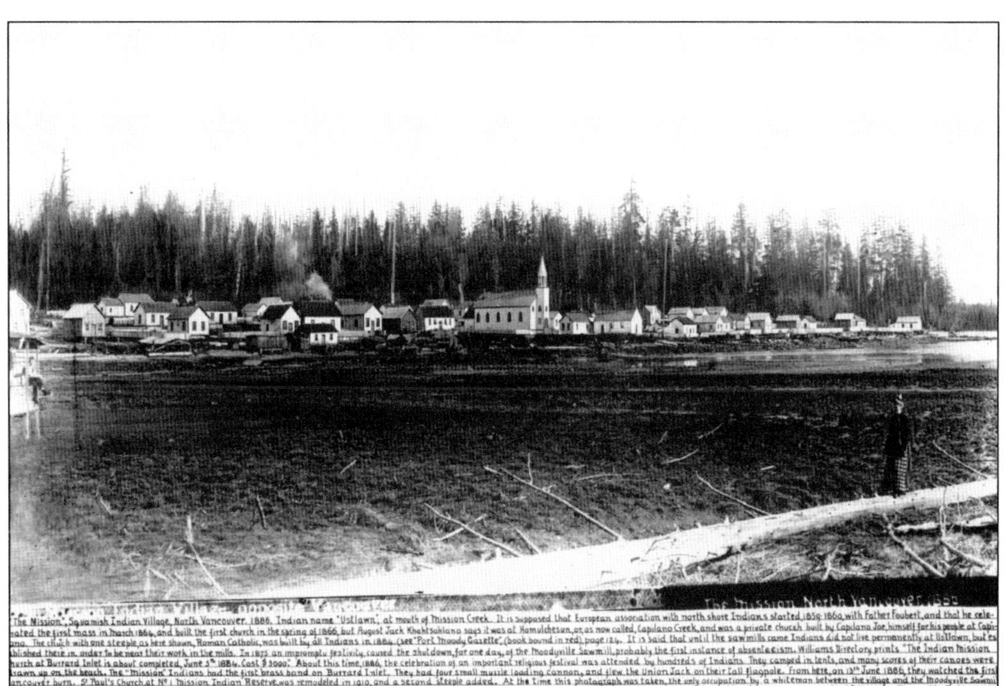

The Coast Salish people lived in southwestern British Columbia for generations before Europeans and other settlers arrived. By 1886, many Squamish people had settled on the Mission Reserve, located two and a half blocks west of the foot of today's Lonsdale Avenue, where the French order of Oblate Fathers had built the St. Paul's Catholic Church. During the 1880s, First Nations people living on the Reserve made up a substantial portion of the workforce at Moodyville sawmill.

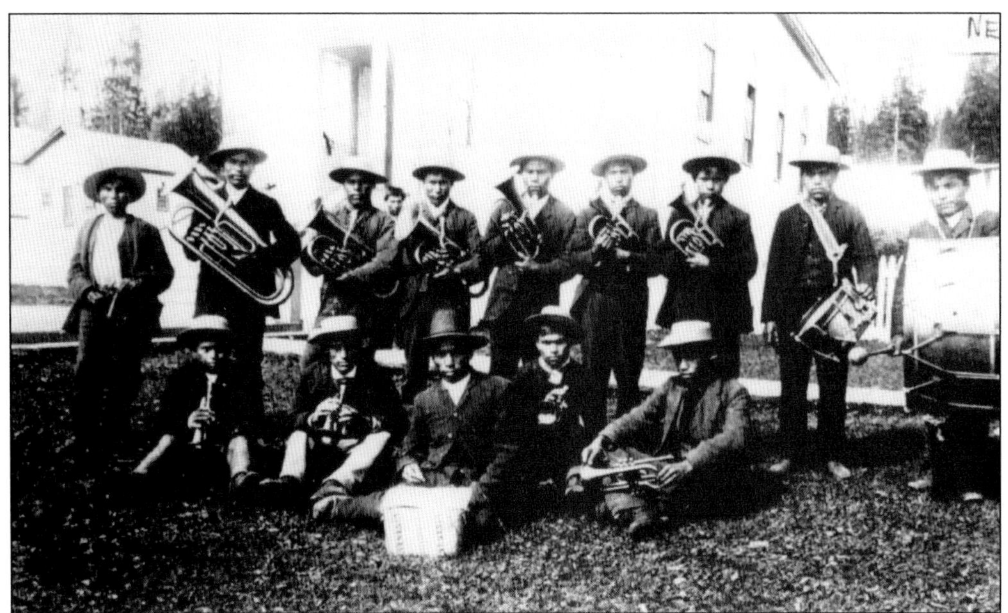

Members of a Squamish Nation Brass Band are seen in front of St. Paul's Catholic Church, now the oldest surviving Catholic church in Greater Vancouver, in 1889. Between 1898 and 1959, cultural traditions that had been passed on from one generation to another for hundreds of years were restricted by the existence of St. Paul's Indian Residential School north of the Reserve.

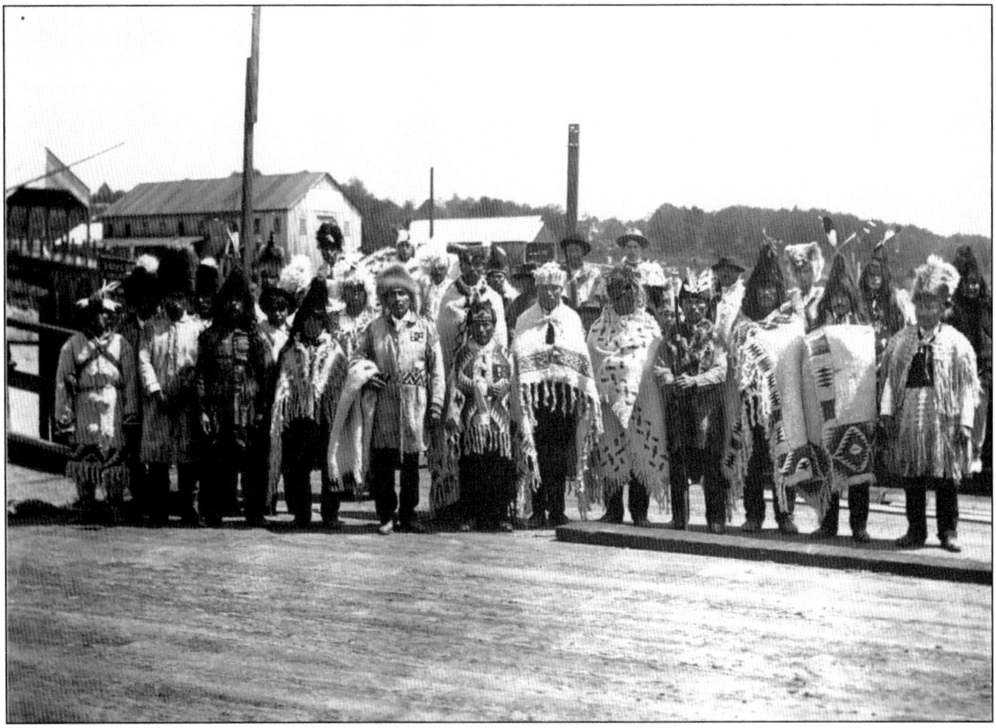

Chief Joe Capilano of the Squamish Nation, fifth from the left, leads a delegation of Coast Salish leaders in May 1908 on the North Vancouver Ferry Wharf prior to leaving for Ottawa to meet with Prime Minister Wilfred Laurier.

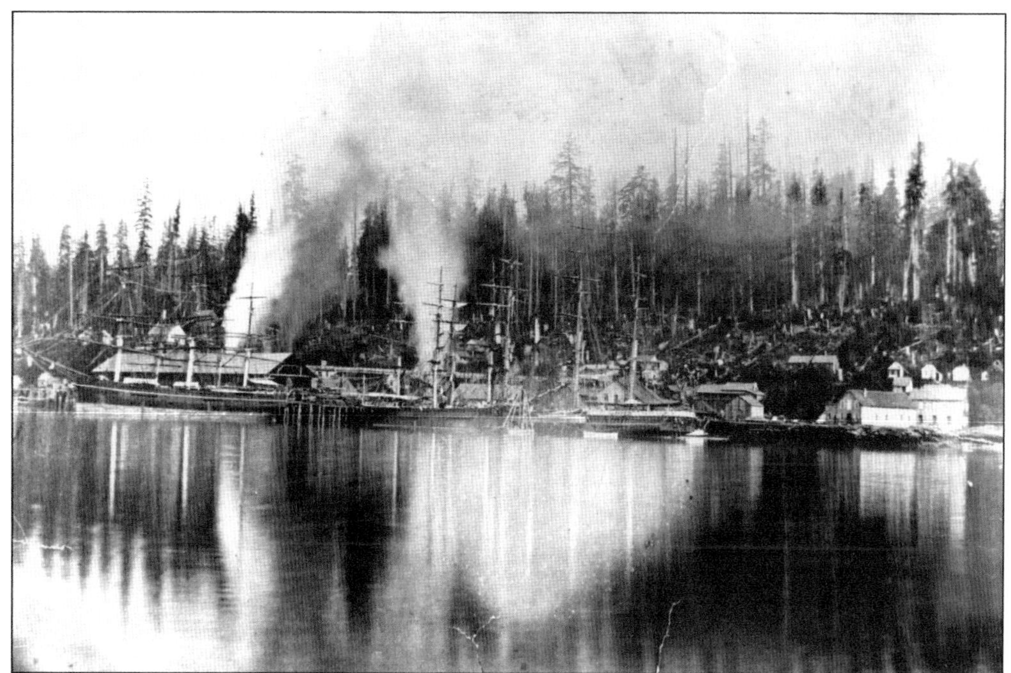

Moodyville village, to the east of the Lonsdale townsite and near where the Saskatchewan Wheat Pool grain elevators now stand, housed a major sawmill in the 1860s, until it closed down in 1901. While in operation, it milled and shipped the old-growth trees of the coastal rainforest to local and off-shore customers.

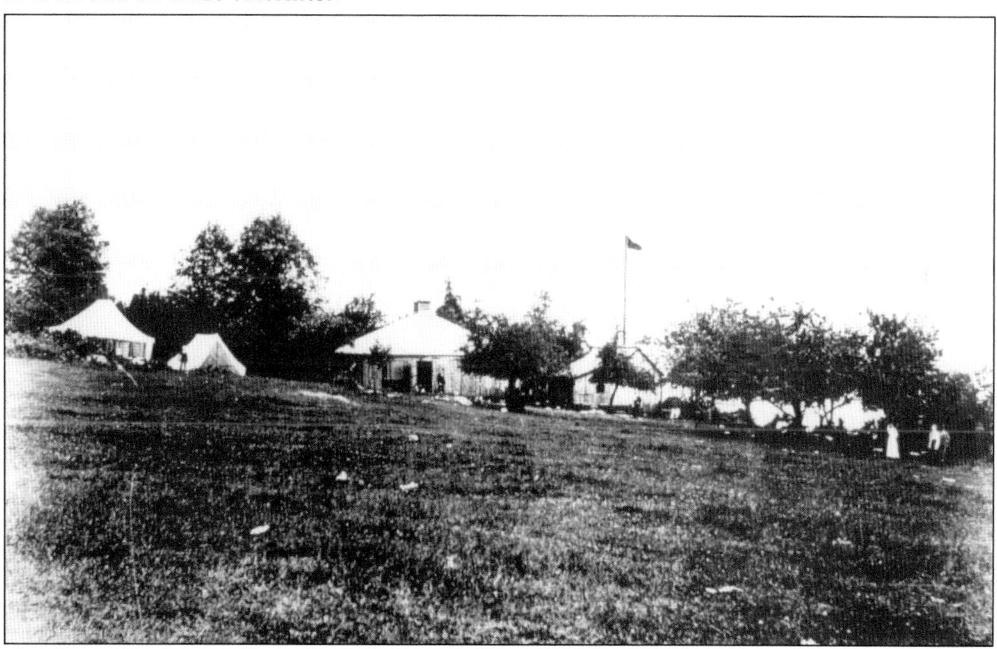

Tom Turner's ranch, seen here around 1892 and located at the foot of today's Chesterfield Avenue, is arguably the birthplace of the Lonsdale neighbourhood. In the early days, Tom Turner's ranch offered the only grass field in North Vancouver and became a picnic destination for residents. Turner supplied Moodyville with vegetables.

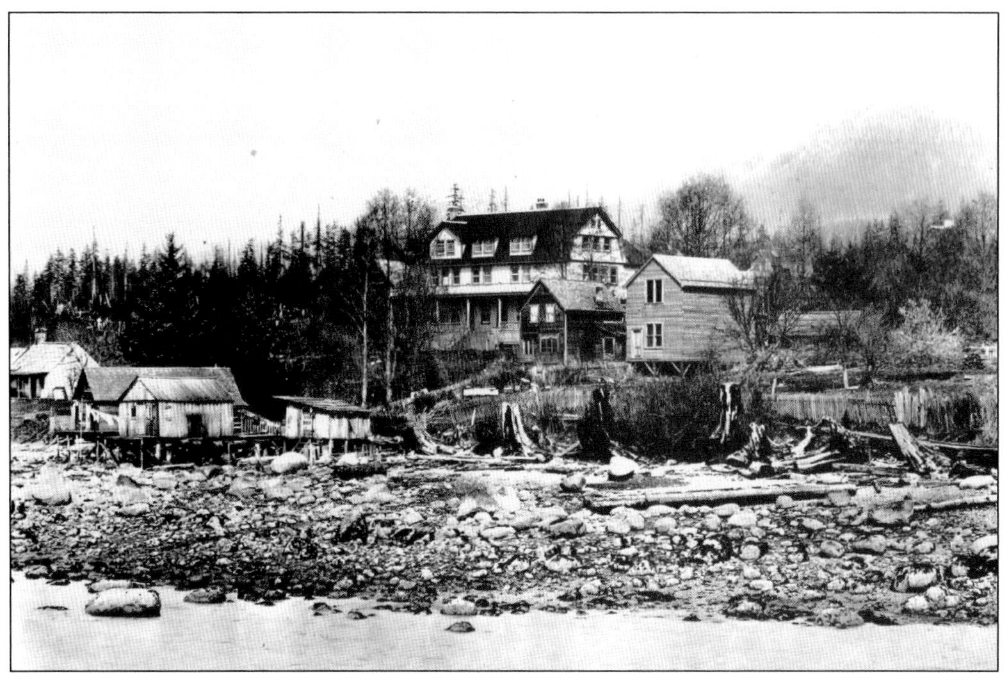

In 1902, Pete Larson built a hotel above Tom Turner's orchard. In this photograph, Tom Turner's ranch is on the extreme left in relation to Larson's hotel. In this 1905 picture, the home of another pioneer, Charles Mee, is in front of the hotel. In 1907, hotel rooms were advertised at a daily rate of $2 and up.

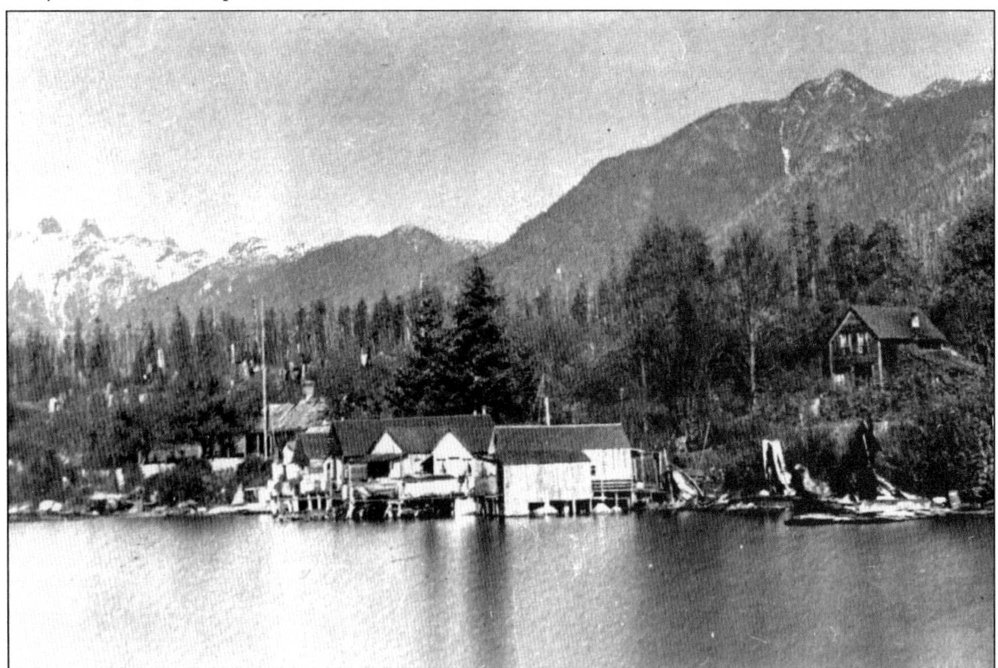

This 1898 photograph shows the waterfront west of the ferry landing with Tom Turner's house at left centre and Charlie Mee's house at extreme right. The Lions, the North Shore's most recognizable natural landmark, are partially covered in snow and can be seen on the left.

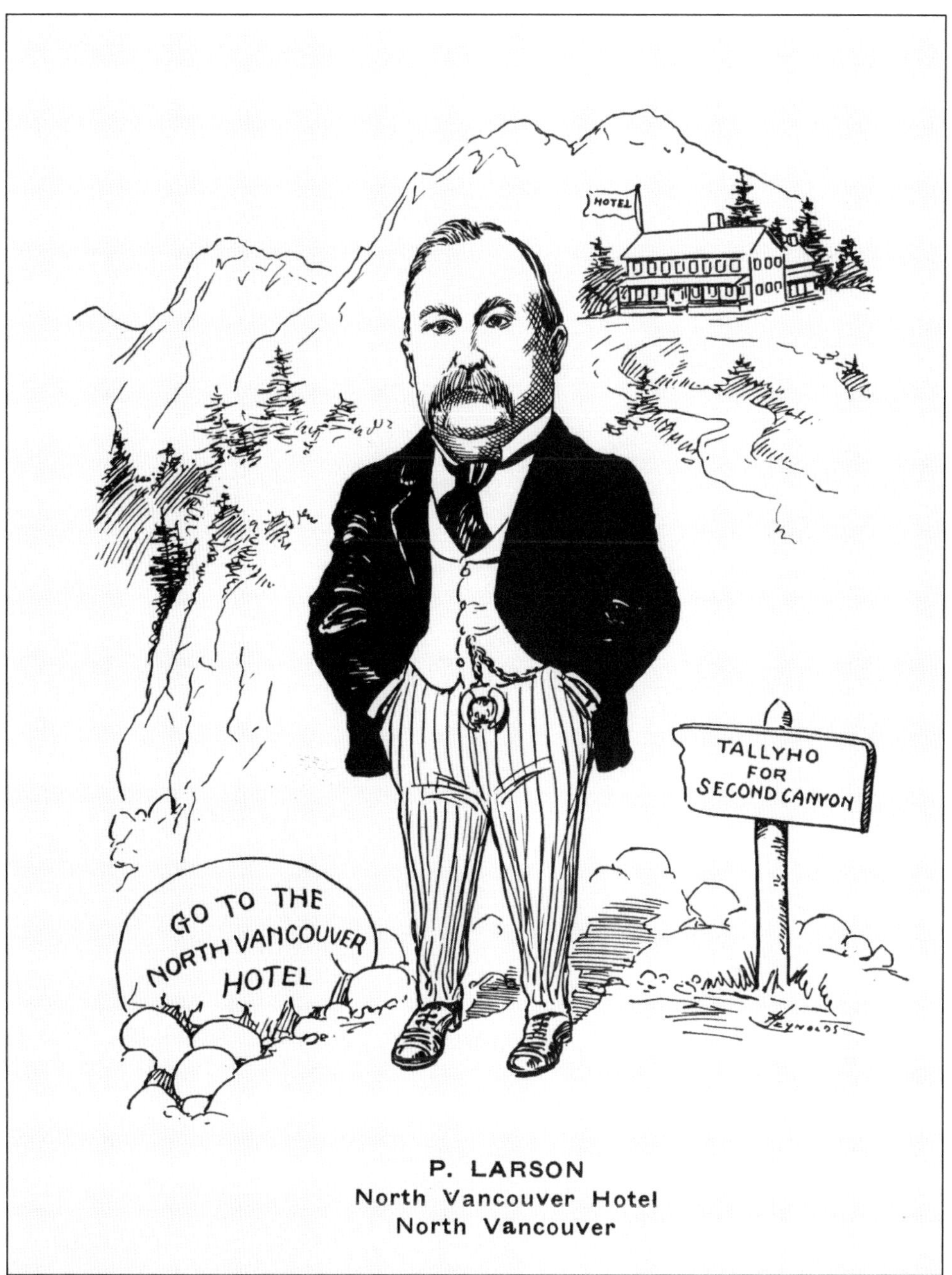

P. LARSON
North Vancouver Hotel
North Vancouver

Pete Larson came to British Columbia from Sweden on a ship as a sailor. He left his ship, worked for some time, saved money, and started a hotel in Vancouver. He then came to North Vancouver, a townsite with only about 365 residents in 1901, and built a hotel and called it Hotel North Vancouver. The hotel had a profound impact in shaping North Vancouver's status as first a resort destination and later as a place to live. In the early years, Pete Larson brought in many attractions such as band concerts, balloon flights, and tight-rope walking, which created business for the ferry. The grounds of Hotel North Vancouver were also often used for political gatherings. Later Pete Larson built another hotel at the Second Canyon of Capilano, as drawn in this caricature, and operated the two hotels until 1915.

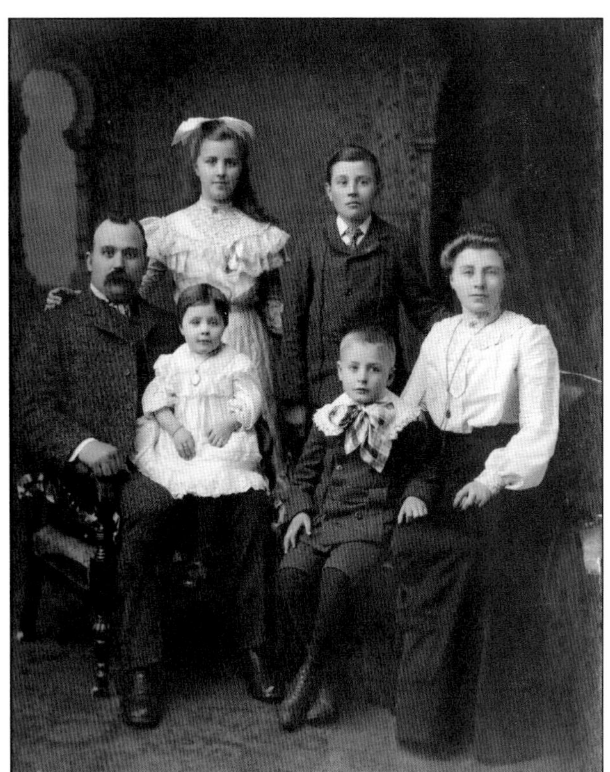

This picture was taken a year after Hotel North Vancouver was built. The Larson family is shown. From left to right are Pete Larson, Alma, Rudolph, Gerda Larson, Olga, and Henry standing.

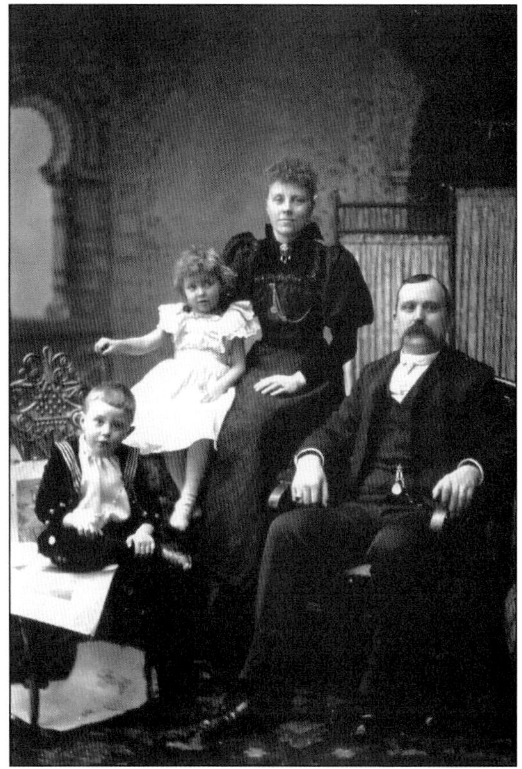

Pete Larson, with wife Gerda and children Henry and Olga, is shown in this picture, which was taken in the 1890s before they came to North Vancouver from Sweden.

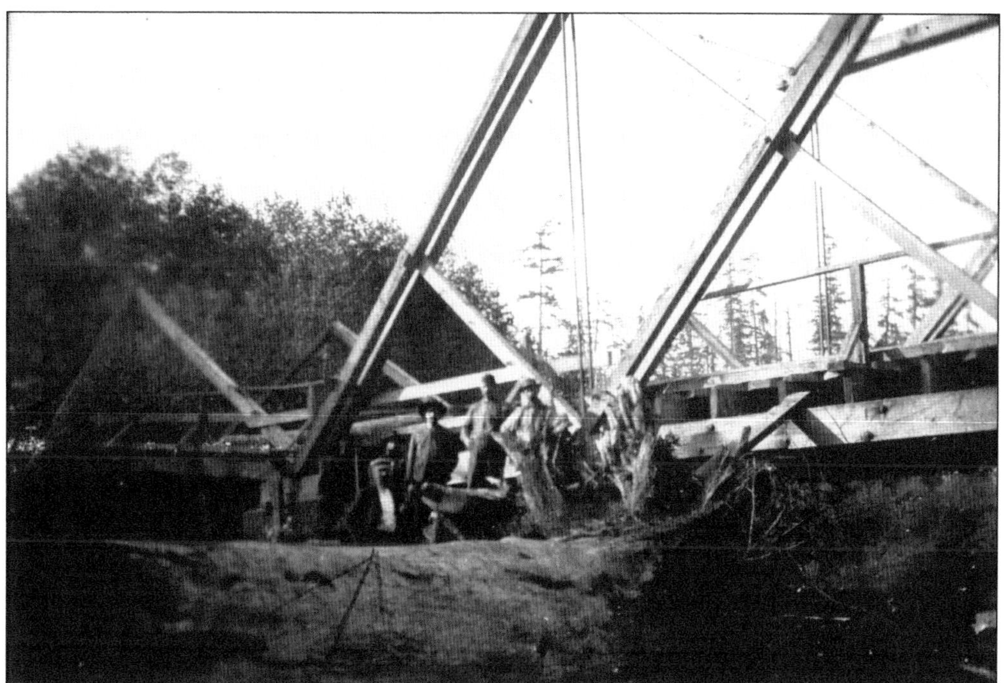

Charlie Mee was in charge of the repair of the Lynn Creek Bridge at Keith Road. He is pictured in this September 1902 photograph, at the left, wearing a white shirt. In the photograph below, early pioneers (from left to right) Charlie Mee and Pete Larson flank an unidentified man displaying the day's catch. The Hotel North Vancouver is in the background.

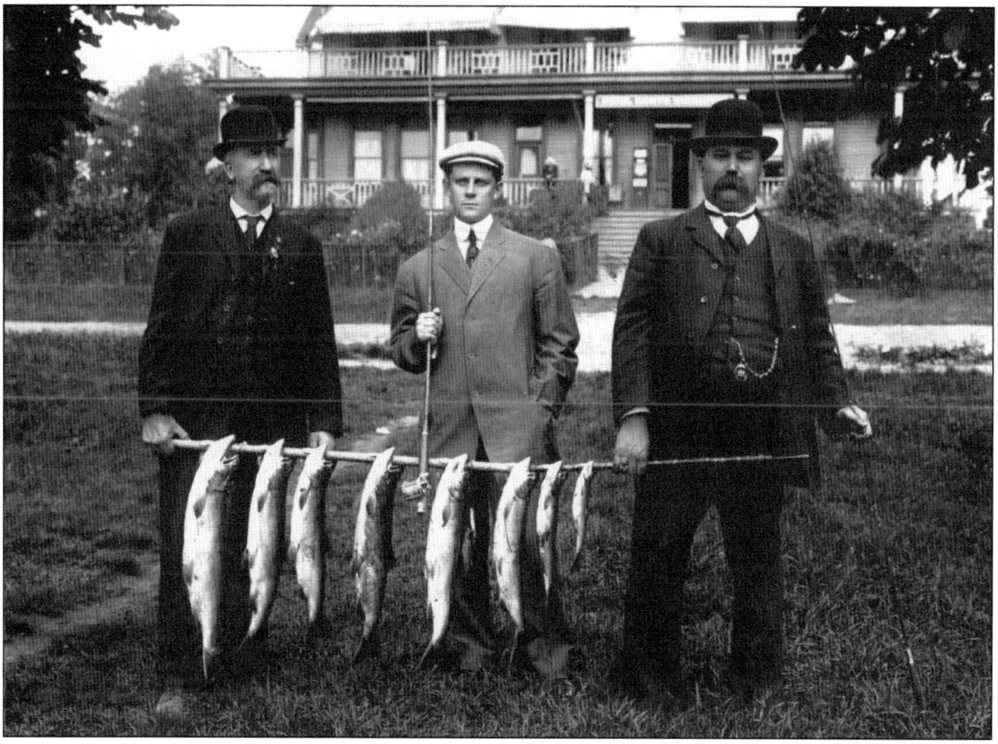

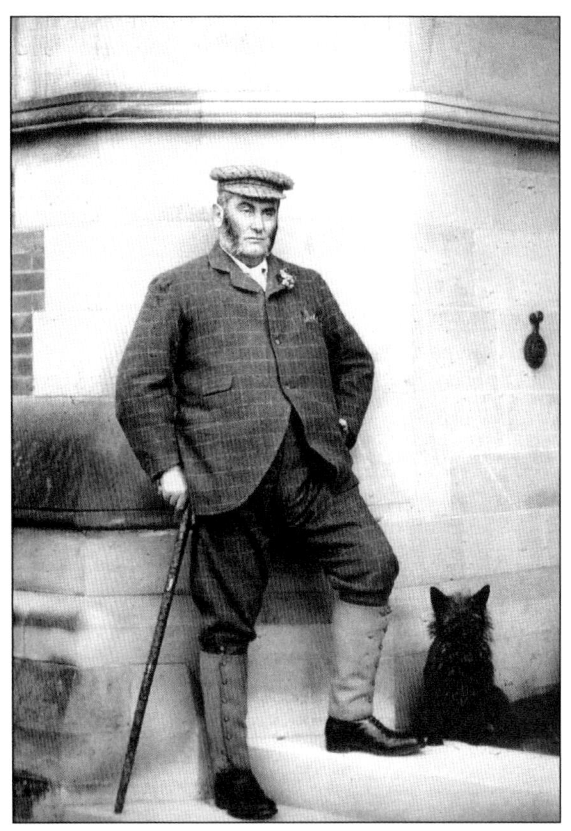

Arthur Pemberton Heywood-Lonsdale (1835–1897) stands on the steps of Shavington Hall in England, which he purchased. A number of street names in the Lonsdale neighbourhood are derived from Heywood-Lonsdale's English associations. His uncle John Pemberton Heywood built Cloverly Estate in England, also the name of a street in North Vancouver. Heywood-Lonsdale was a major investor in the Moodyville Lands and Sawmill Company. His son Henry Heywood-Lonsdale (not shown) co-owned the Lonsdale Estate, which had inherited the Moodyville assets. The Lonsdale Estate later named one of the city streets Shavington Street when submitting plans for a parcel of land. (Courtesy of Bob Heywood.)

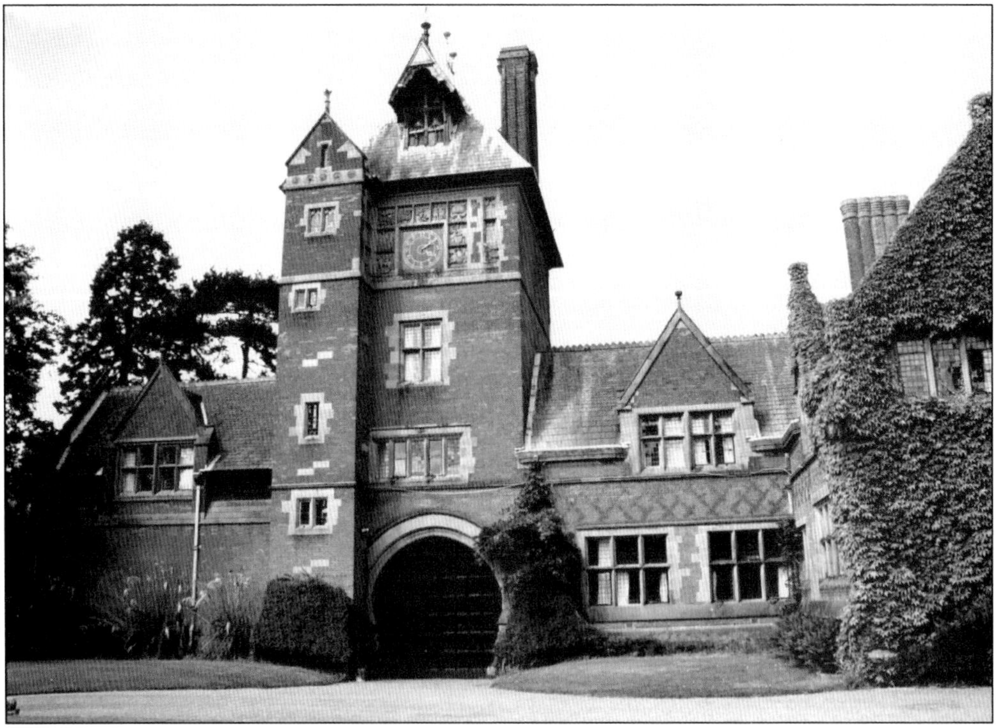

When Henry Heywood-Lonsdale looked for someone to help manage his Lonsdale Estate, his cousin Maj. James Pemberton Fell (pictured here) was the ideal choice. Arrangements were made and Fell became a co-owner of the Lonsdale Estate and an agent of the company in North Vancouver. In 1912 Fell became the first commander of the 6th Field Company, for which a drill hall was built in 1914–1915. It still stands today on Forbes Avenue.

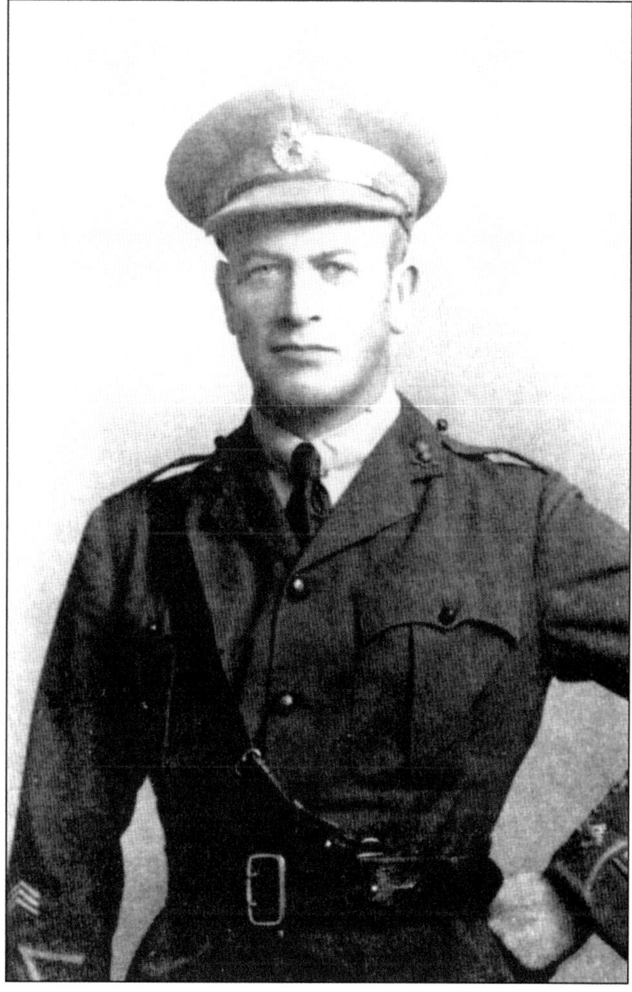

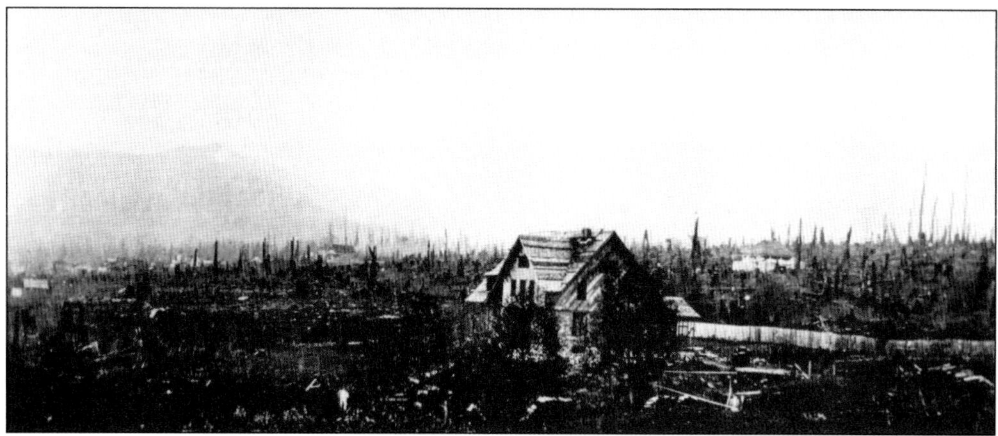

Around the year 1904, Sir Alfred Hamersley started construction of his home at 350 East Second Street. Hamersley's decision to build a house and move his family to North Vancouver made it easier for other influential and wealthy people to make a similar choice. The Hamersley house, preserved as a heritage building, still stands today and at one point was a private hospital.

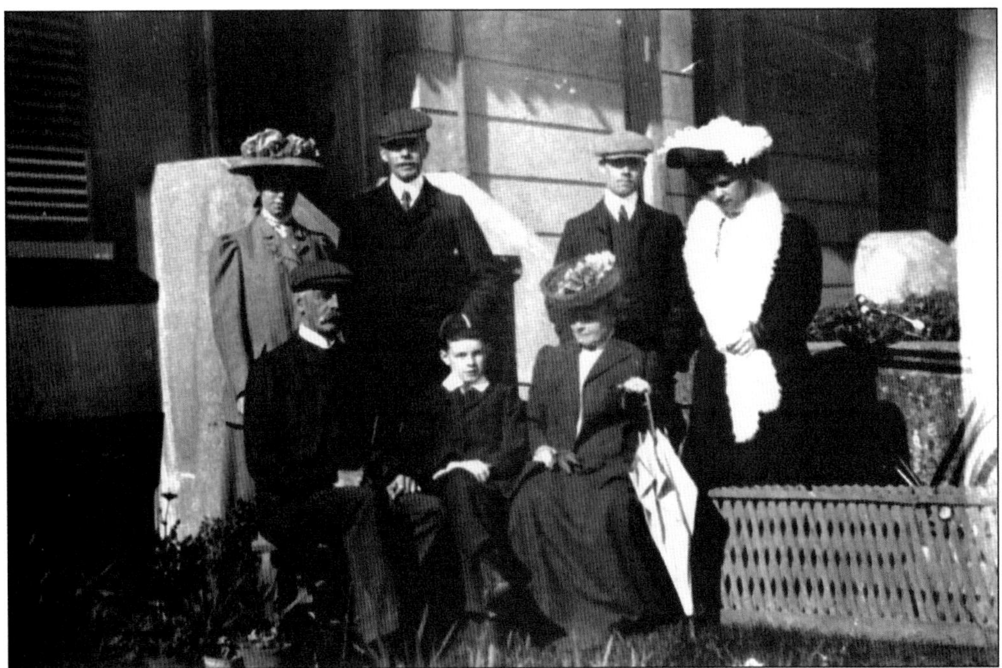

The Hamersley family (around 1907), in front of their home, from left to right includes (first row) Sir Alfred St. George Hamersley, Alfred Tommy, and Maud Hamersley; (second row) Martha, Hugh, Harold, and Connie. In early 1903 Alfred St. George Hamersley purchased a substantial parcel of land from Henry Heywood-Lonsdale and James Pemberton Fell's Lonsdale Estate. Once subdivided, the property was named the Town of Lonsdale but would soon be called North Vancouver. By 1904 a commercial townsite had formed near the waterfront, and suburban homes were being built in the areas around Lonsdale Avenue.

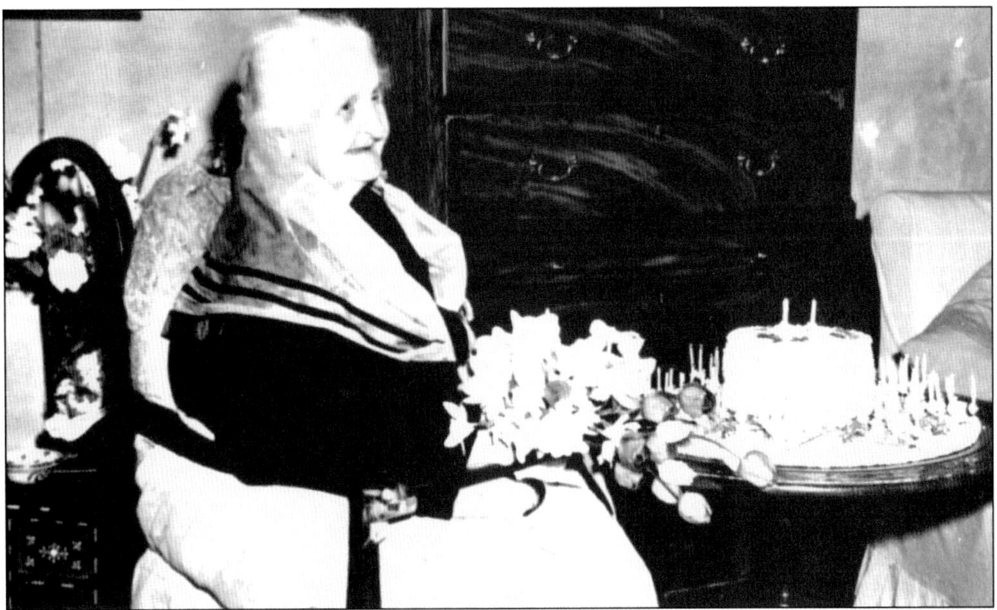

Maud Hamersley is seen on her 100th birthday, in England, on April 29, 1953. In her lifetime, North Vancouver grew from a small confident townsite to a vital port city.

James Cooper Keith owned extensive properties on either side of the North Shore. He underwrote a loan for $40,000 on behalf of the first district council elected in 1891, which led to the construction of what was later named Keith Road, running east to west throughout the municipality. James Cooper Keith was also District of North Vancouver reeve from 1892 to 1894. Concurrent engagements in both business dealings and politics were not unusual in those days.

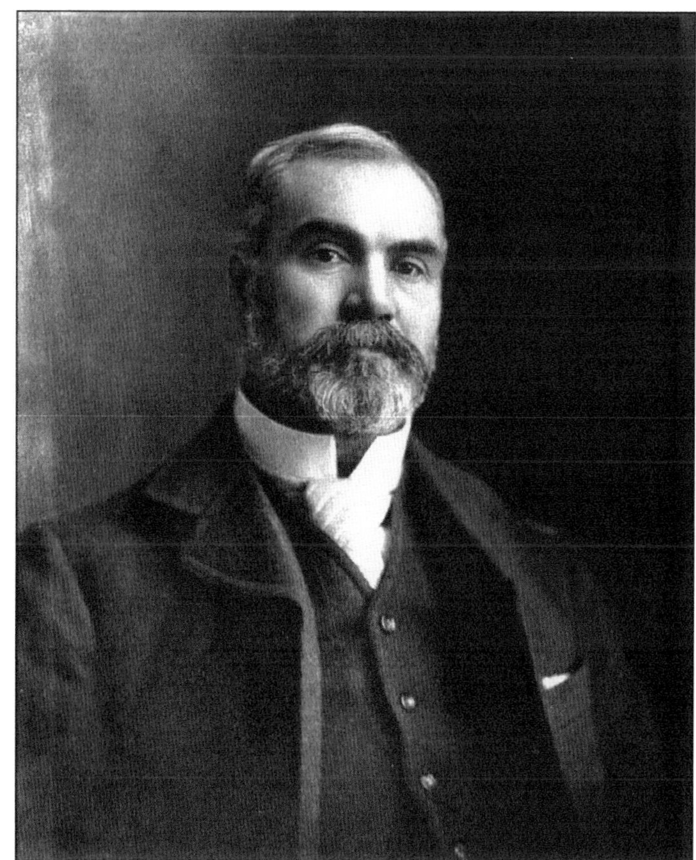

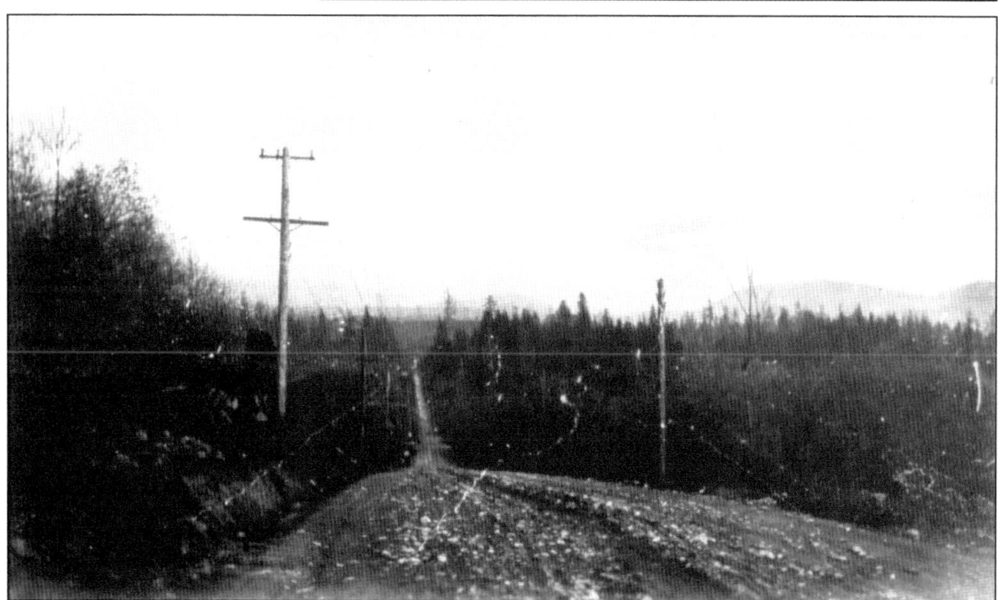

This photograph taken in the 1920s shows a section of Keith Road. When the road was constructed, it literally cut through the forest in most cases, linking otherwise disjointed properties with the Lonsdale area and paving the way for development in more remote areas.

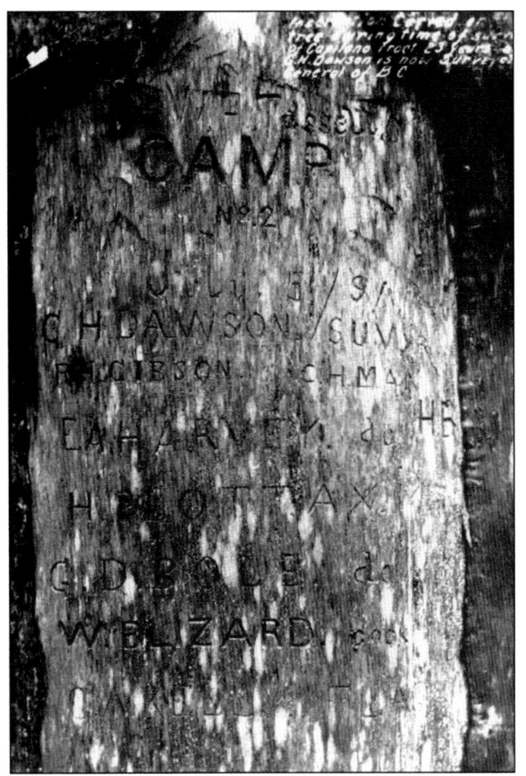

Surveyor George Herbert Dawson came to Vancouver in 1890. He later completed several land surveying and civil engineering projects in North Vancouver, and he is associated with the location of Keith Road and the survey of the North Vancouver townsite (much of today's City of North Vancouver). From 1911 to 1917, Dawson served as surveyor general of British Columbia. This photograph shows a tree marker, now in the North Vancouver Museum collection, that was carved on July 5, 1914, during a survey of the Capilano area.

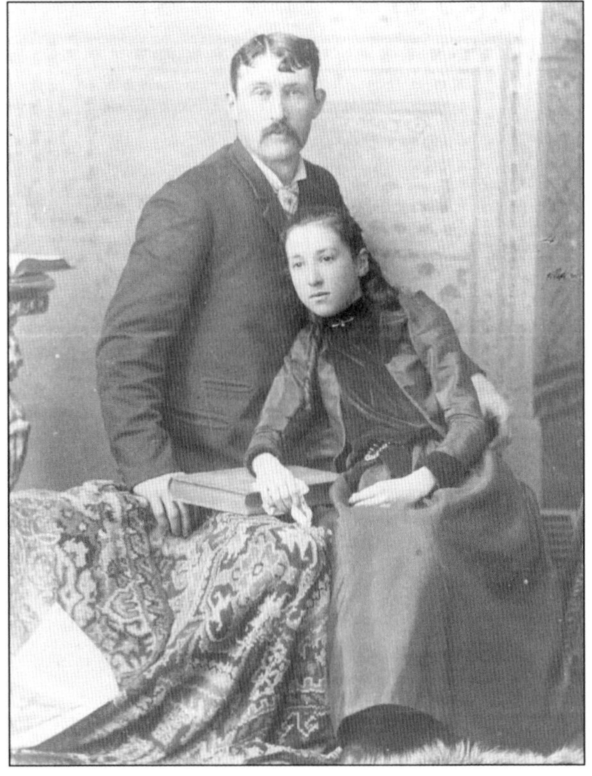

This 1890s picture shows Capt. Charles H. Cates with his sister Lillian. Cates settled in Moodyville in 1885 and became involved with the tugboat business in 1890. He established the first waterfront business at the North Vancouver townsite at the foot of Lonsdale Avenue in 1904 and formed the company of C. H. Cates in 1913. With his three sons, John, Charles, and James, he incorporated the firm of C. H. Cates & Sons in 1921.

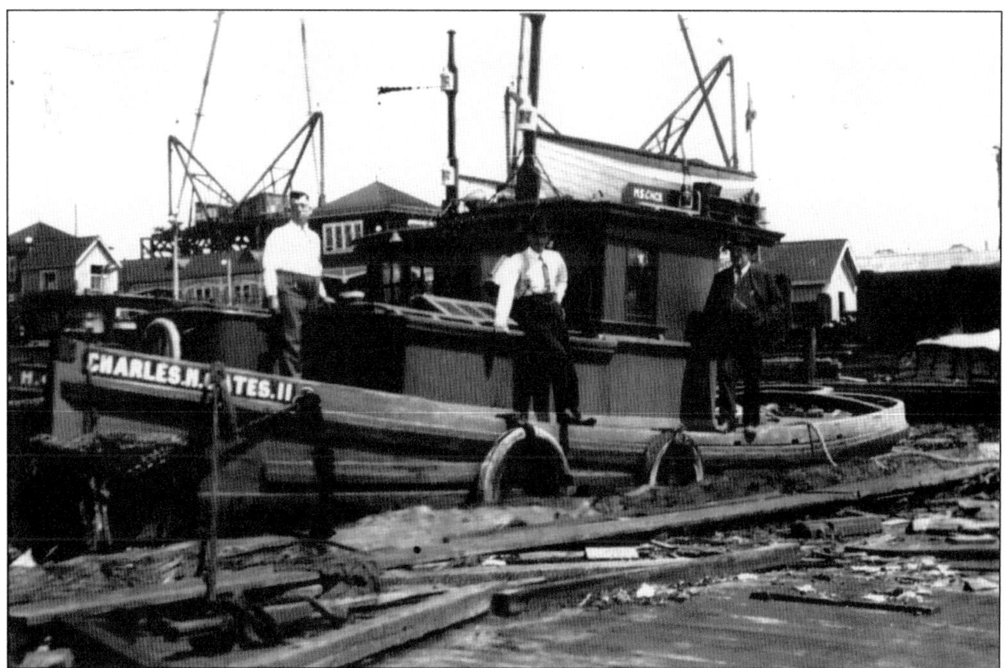

This 1925 photograph shows (from left to right) an unidentified man, Dan King, and Charles H. Cates with the tugboat *Charles H. Cates II*. This was primarily a ship-berthing firm, but it also fought fires and salvaged wrecks. It handled logs and lumber and scow materials for many firms. Cates Tugs later amalgamated with Seaspan International and is now owned by the Washington Marine Group. It still operates from a base at the foot of Lonsdale Avenue adjacent to Lonsdale Quay.

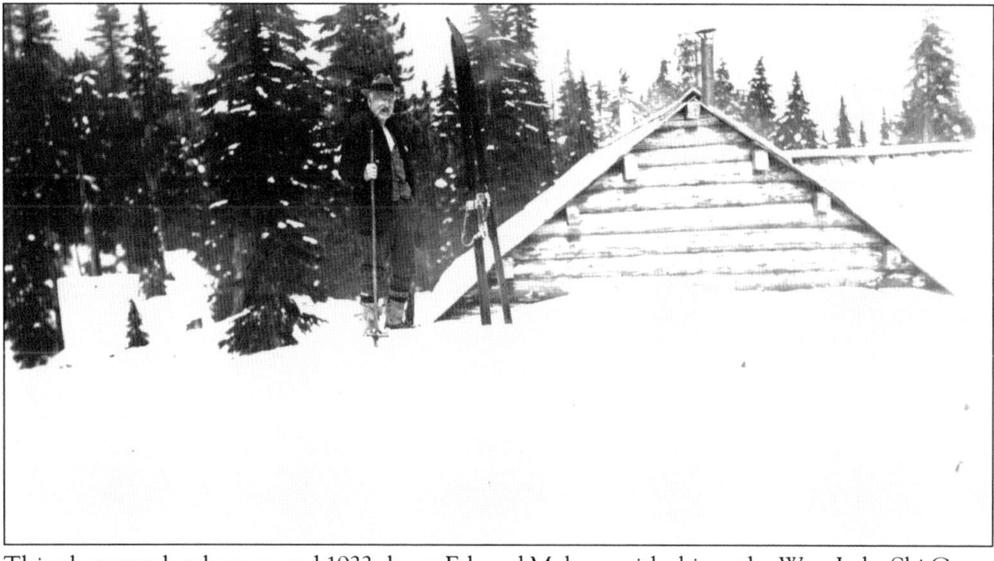

This photograph taken around 1933 shows Edward Mahon, with skis at the West Lake Ski Camp on Hollyburn Mountain. He was one of the founding trustees of the North Vancouver Land and Improvement Company, a firm that was among the most powerful real estate companies in the early years of North Vancouver. He also became an active member of Mahon, McFarland and Mahon, which sold much of the company's land.

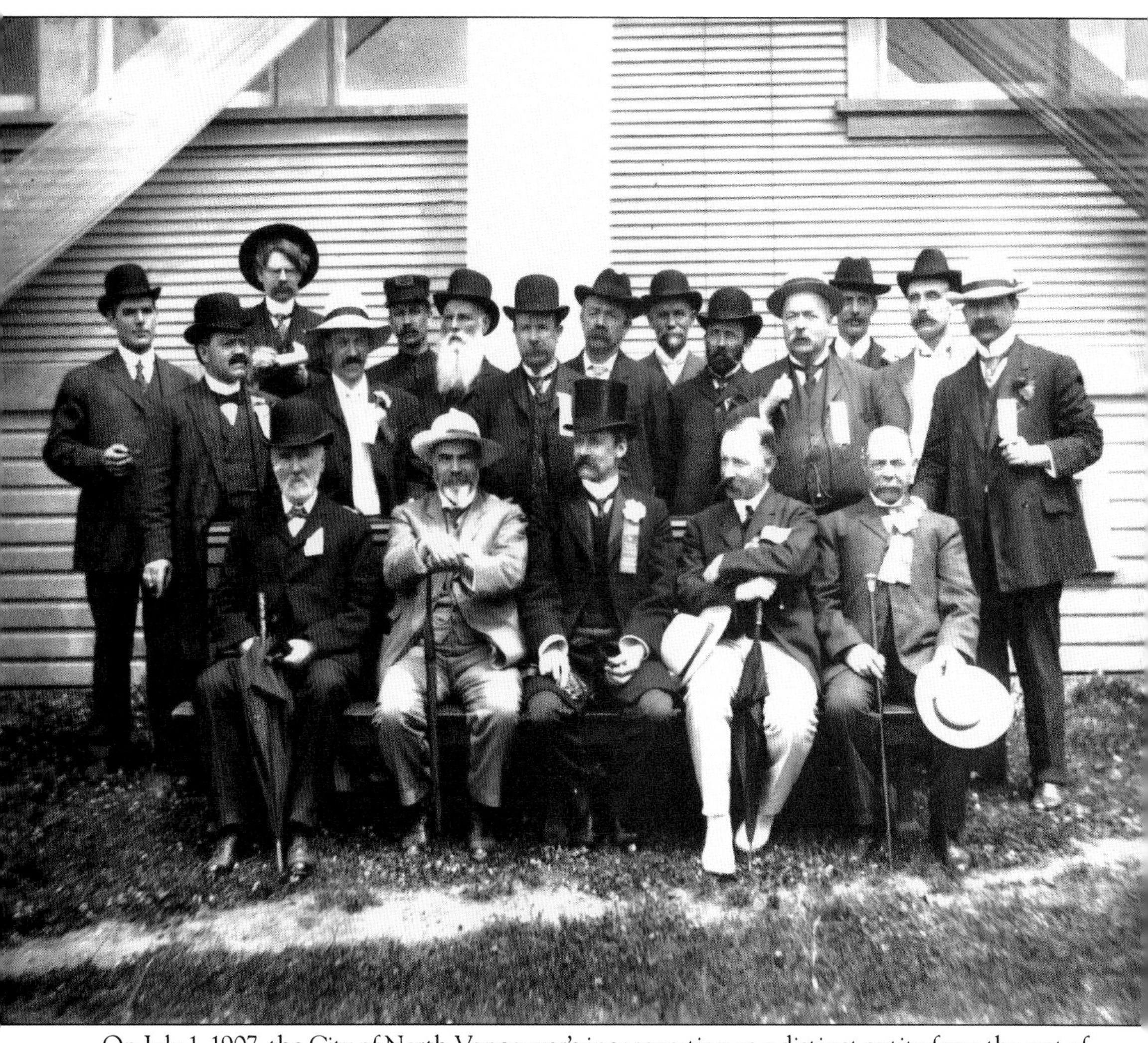

On July 1, 1907, the City of North Vancouver's incorporation as a distinct entity from the rest of the municipality was celebrated. City fathers and dignitaries who assembled for a picture outside the city hall are, from left to right, (first row) F. Carter-Cotton, member of the legislative assembly of British Columbia; J. C. Keith, a pioneer citizen and landowner; Arnold E. Kealy, reeve of the District of North Vancouver and first mayor of the City of North Vancouver; Edward Mahon, President of the North Vancouver Land and Improvement Company; Alderman William May, former reeve of the District, and subsequently mayor of the City; (second row) W. J. Dick, who served on the city council; A. McKay Jordan, a scientist and longtime alderman; Mr. Robb, a reporter; D. G. Dick, longtime alderman; Alexander Bethune, Vancouver mayor; Reeve Byrne, municipality of Burnaby; Alderman Alexander Smith; Alderman William F. Emery, who served on the city council; Ex-Mayor of Vancouver Garden, who served on the city council; J. J. Woods, assessor for both the District and City; Alderman W. J. Irwin, councillor for District of North Vancouver and mayor of the City; and Honourable Macpherson, MLA and postmaster for the City of Vancouver.

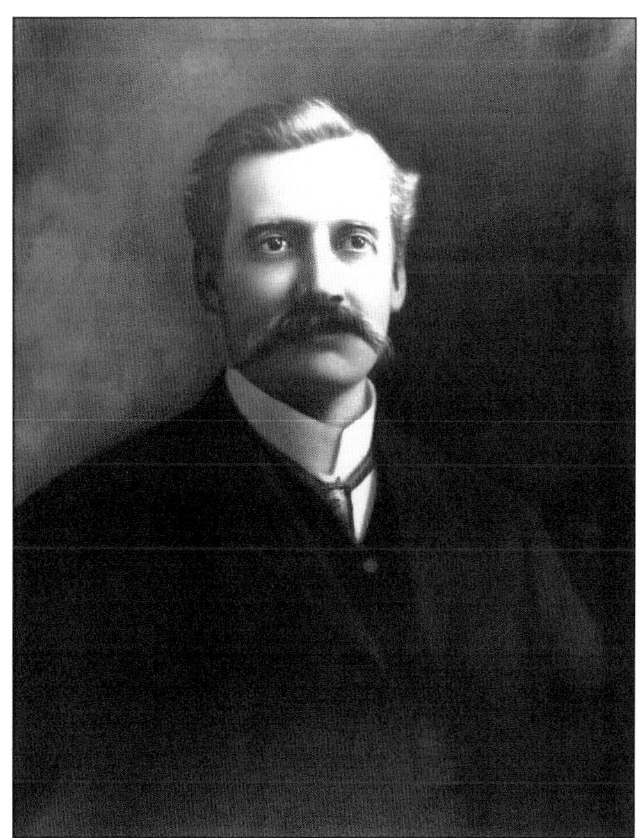

Arnold A. Kealy, Western Corporation secretary, chaired the original committee to review the idea of a new city distinct from the 15-year-old District of North Vancouver. Kealy, who was district reeve from 1905 to June 1907, was acclaimed North Vancouver City's first mayor and served from 1907 to 1908. The other council members were elected by a group of male British subjects over the age of 21, as those were the only individuals legally entitled to vote. Arnold A. Kealy lived in the house shown, on the corner of St. Andrews and East Fifteenth Street.

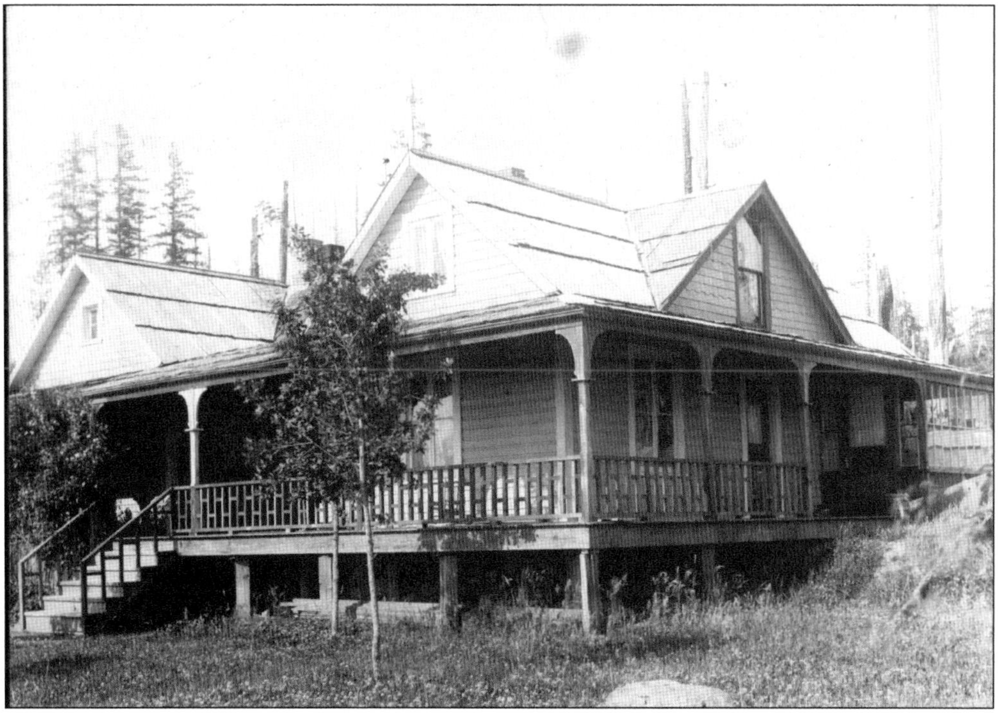

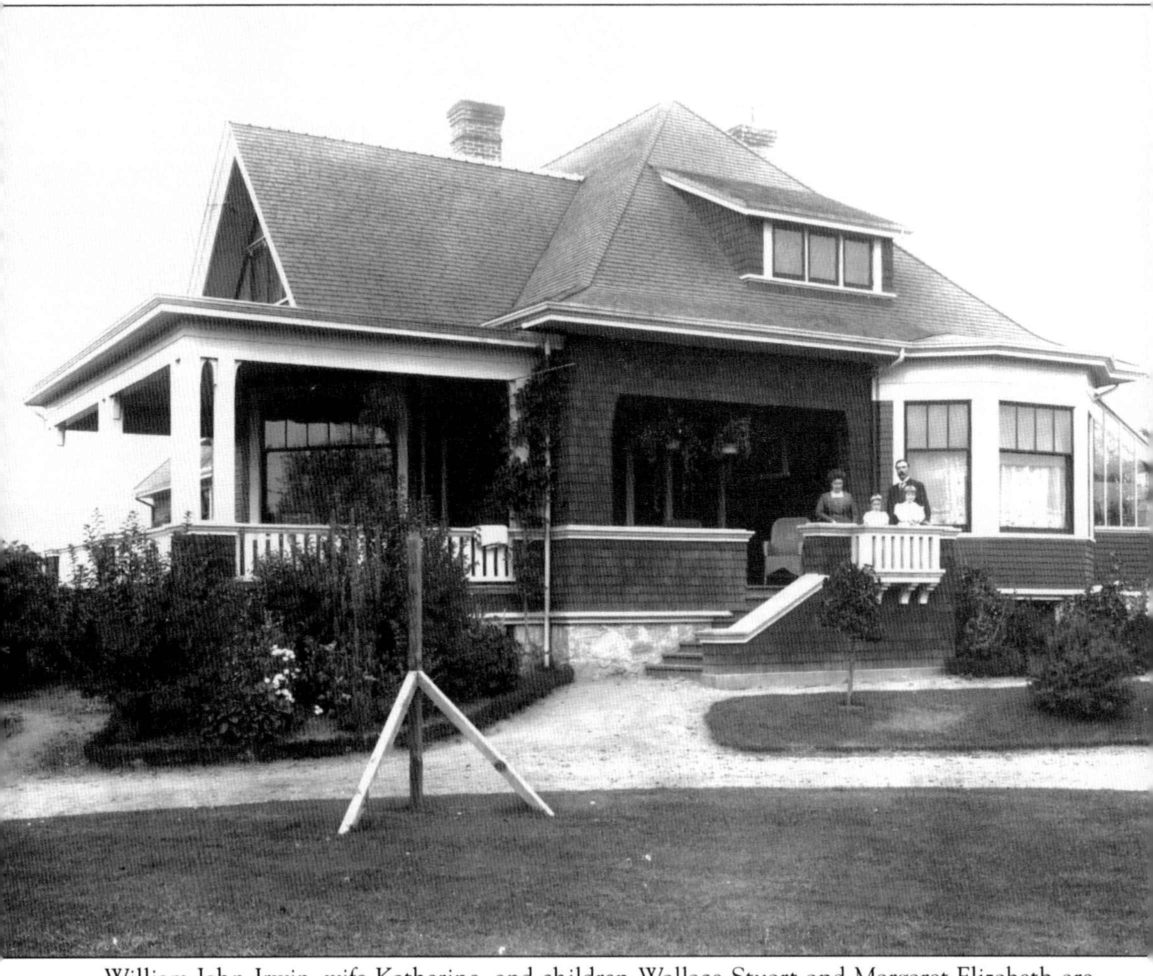

William John Irwin, wife Katherine, and children Wallace Stuart and Margaret Elizabeth are seen standing on the veranda of their home at 114 East Fifteenth Street in 1910. John and Katherine Irwin were married in Los Angeles in 1905; the couple took a trip to Vancouver for their honeymoon and never left North Vancouver. After arriving with her husband, Katherine Irwin was at different times the first president of the Lonsdale Elementary School Parent Teachers Association and the American Women's Club. She was also an avid gardener, winning a silver trophy at a horticultural show in 1912. William John Irwin served one term as North Vancouver City's mayor and was an alderman for 10 years. He founded the Irwin & Billings real estate firm and the North Vancouver Board of Trade in 1906.

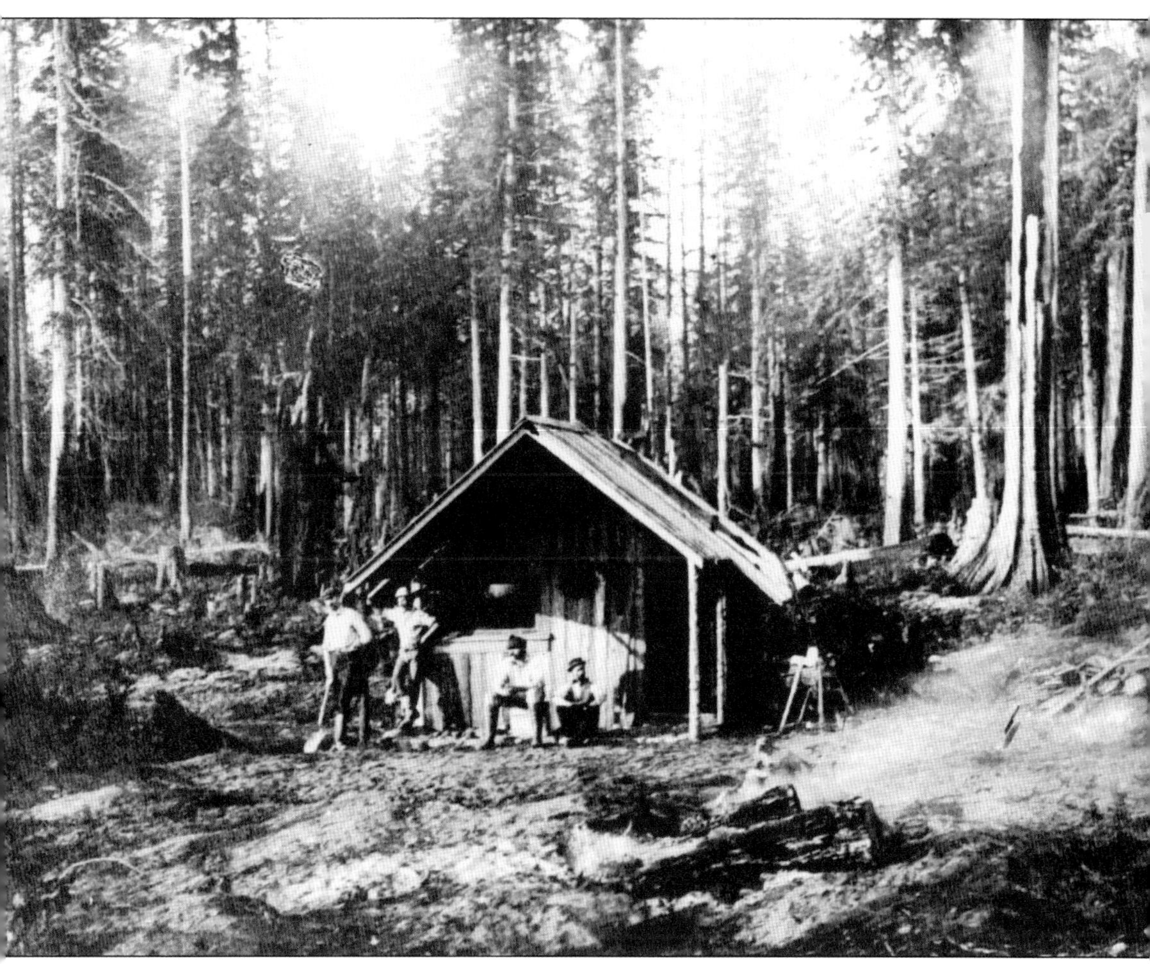

In 1897 and 1898 five families, called the "founding five" by Warren Sommer in *The Ambitious City: a History of the City of North Vancouver*, purchased some 20 acres of land near today's Lonsdale Avenue and East Fifteenth Street. One of these early settlers was Alfred Edward Crickmay, a customs broker in North Vancouver. This 1897 photograph shows his house between East Fifteenth and East Seventeenth, east of St. Georges Avenue. People in front of the house are identified as (from left to right) F. G. Keeley, A. E. Crickmay, Ben J. Cornish, and W. L. Keene. Crickmay, Cornish, and Keene were three of the founding five.

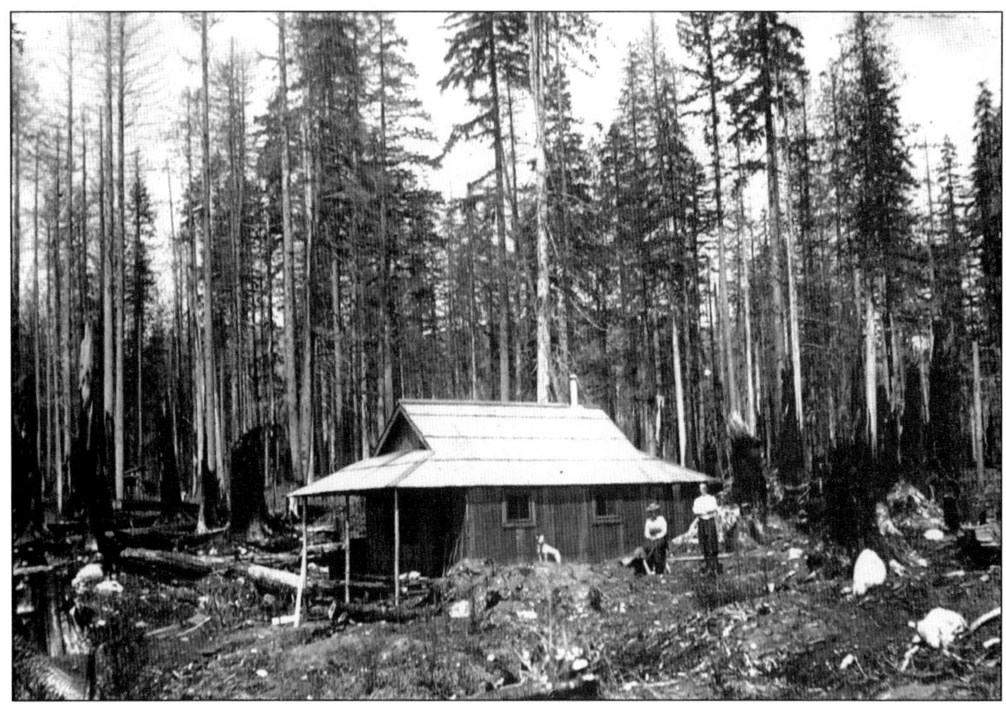

William L. Keene was another of the founding five, and in 1884 he married Catherine Crickmay, the sister of A. E. Crickmay. The Keenes moved to North Vancouver in 1888 and lived in the house photographed here. The people in front of the above 1896 photograph are unidentified. In the 1900 photograph below, the Keenes are pictured with their calves near the barn. Keene became the third municipal clerk and formed the first horticultural society.

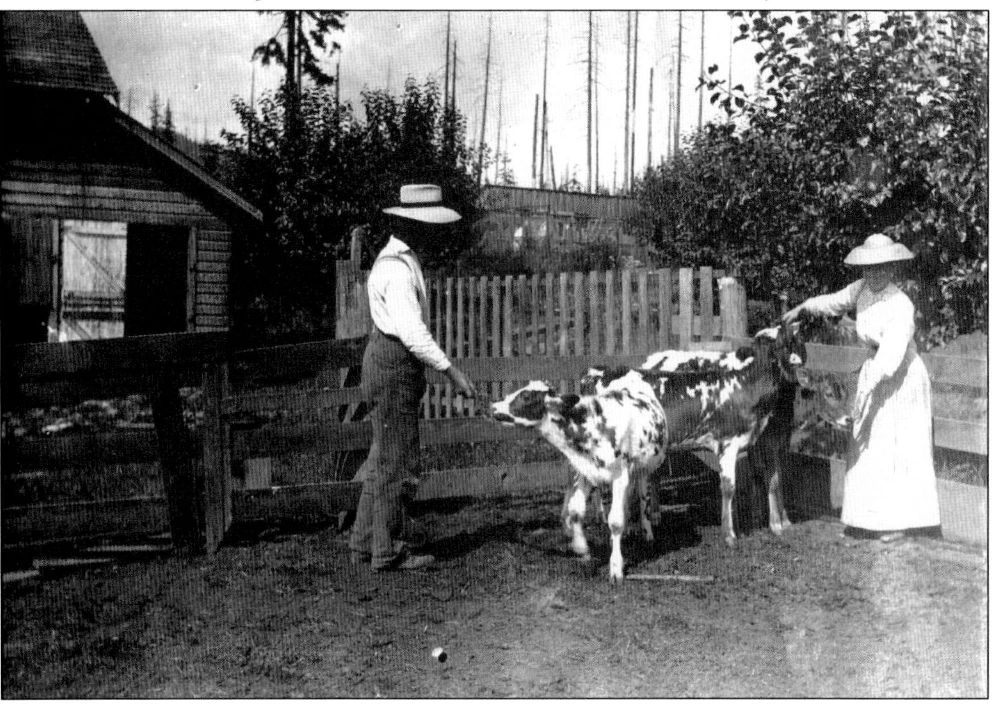

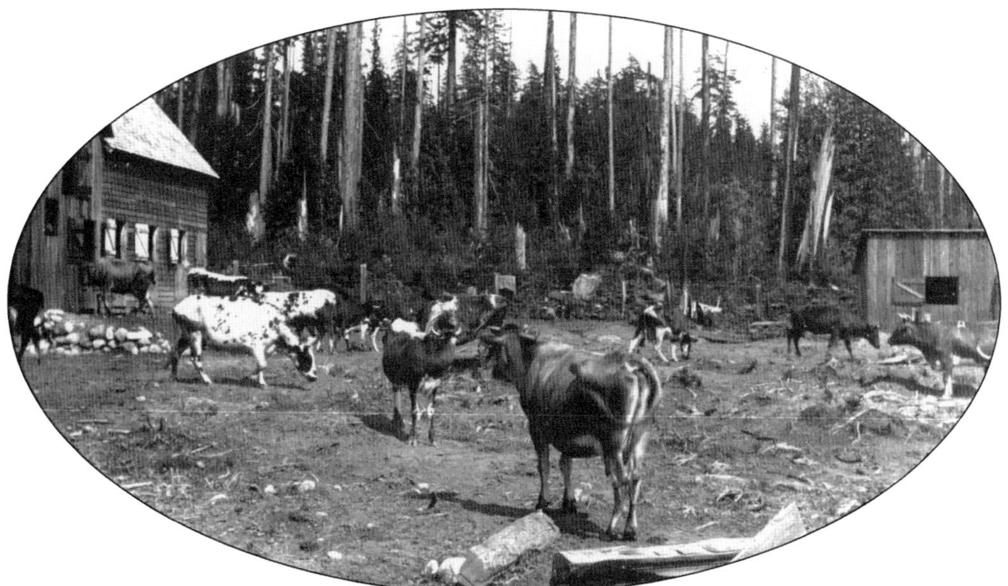

This milking herd, which belonged to William L. Keene, supplied milk to the early settlers. The barn can be seen on the left in this photograph, taken around 1906. The Keene property was located at 1500 St. Georges Avenue, parallel to Lonsdale Avenue, one block to the east.

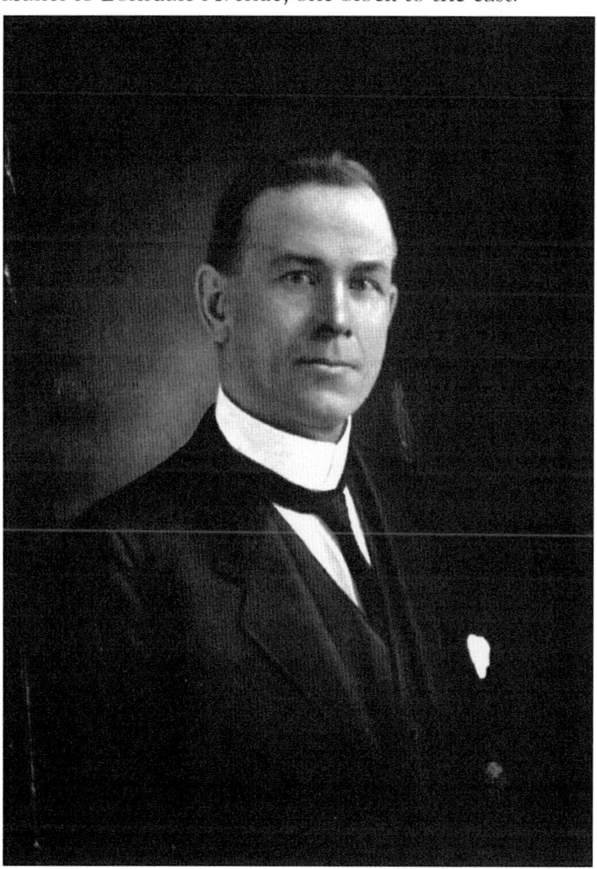

Thomas Kennedy was born in New Brunswick and moved to North Vancouver in 1894. Following his arrival in North Vancouver, Kennedy went into the lumbering and contracting business and built many of the early roads throughout the area and the first ferry float at the foot of Lonsdale. He was also an early chief of the North Vancouver volunteer fire brigade and served on the city council from 1913 to 1915. While on council he was responsible for setting aside a lake northwest of Upper Lynn Valley as a potential water supply, now named Kennedy Lake.

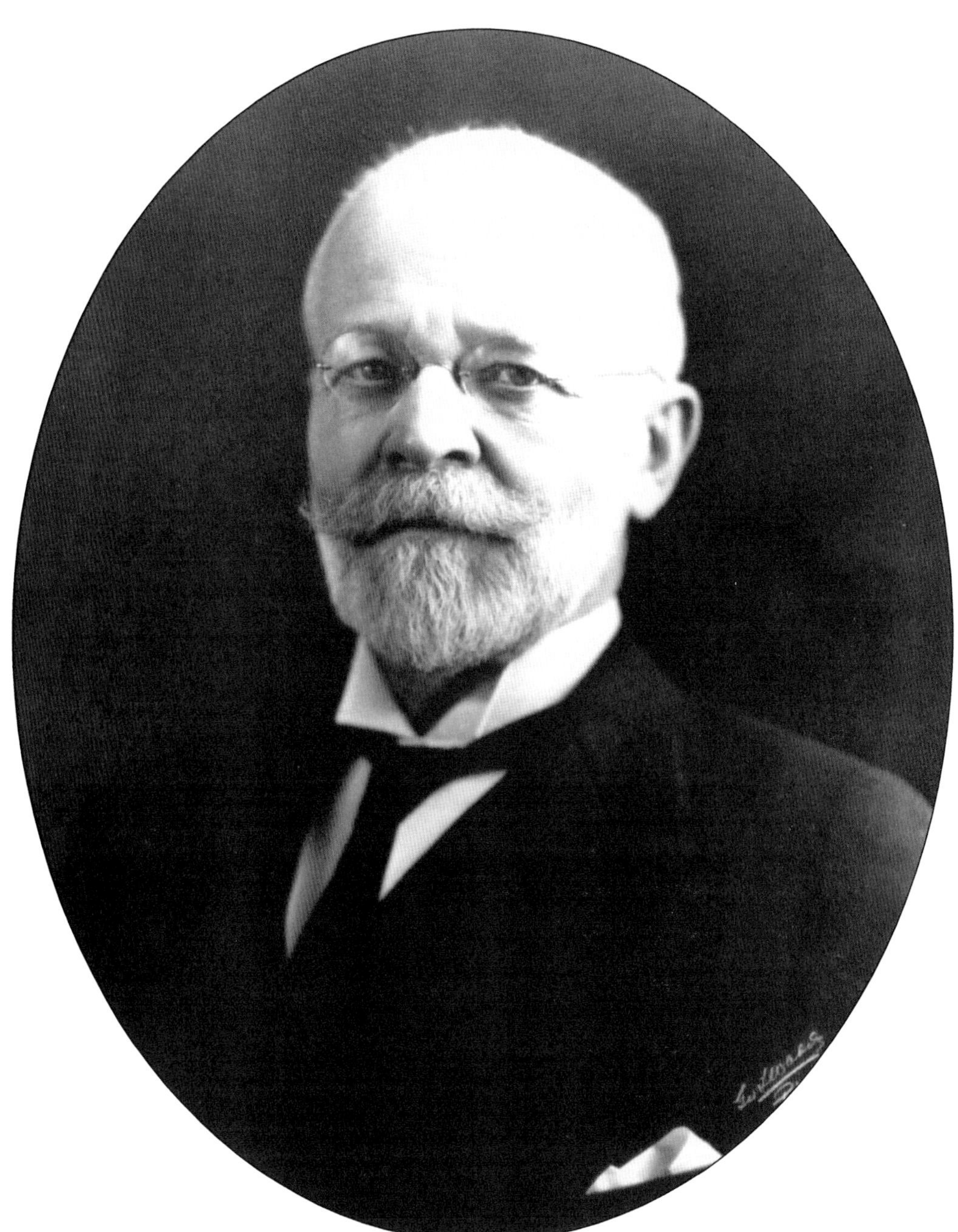

With the advent of the Depression in 1929, the City and District entered difficult financial times. Debentures that had been issued earlier to raise money for local improvements had fixed repayment schedules. When property tax revenues declined because many property owners defaulted on their payments, the municipalities had difficulty repaying their lenders. With the District bankrupt, Charles Tisdall was appointed as commissioner to run the District of North Vancouver on December 16, 1932. In 1933, he also took over as commissioner of the City. Commissioners were appointed by the Province and were responsible for the overall conduct of civic affairs, with the emphasis on running a stripped-down infrastructure incurring minimal expense.

George Vance, who with A. V. Markle became active in real estate in North Vancouver in 1909, had offices at Eighth Street and Lonsdale Avenue. He later served on the city council, and was mayor from 1917 to 1921. While on council he chaired the Lands and Lanes Committee. He was later commissioner for the City and District of North Vancouver from 1936 until his death in 1944.

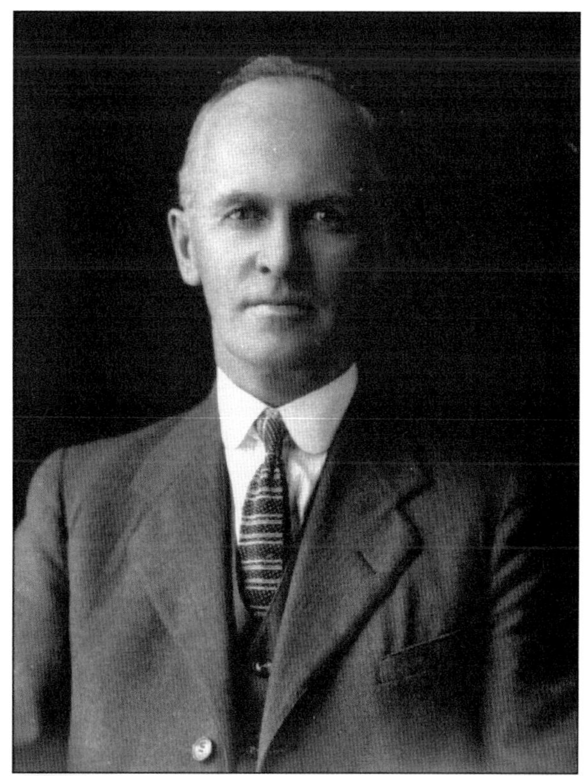

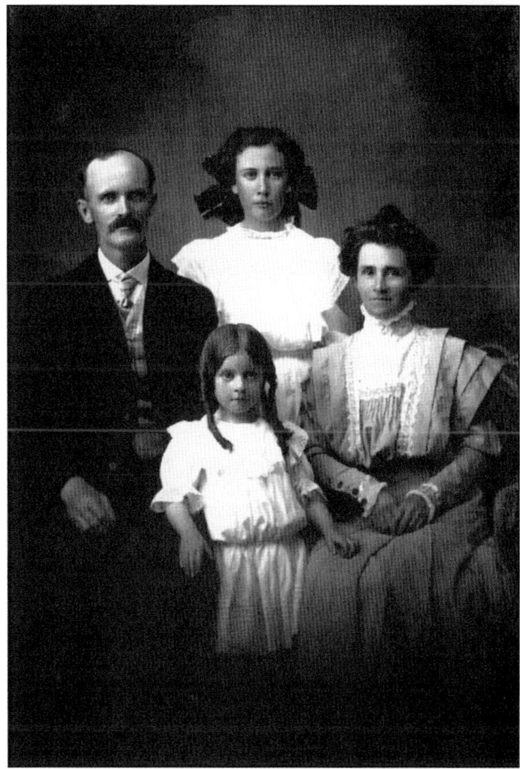

This photograph, taken around 1910, shows George and Catherine Vance with daughters Leila (centre back) and Thelma. George Vance oversaw improvement efforts regarding the finances for both North Vancouver municipalities during his service as commissioner.

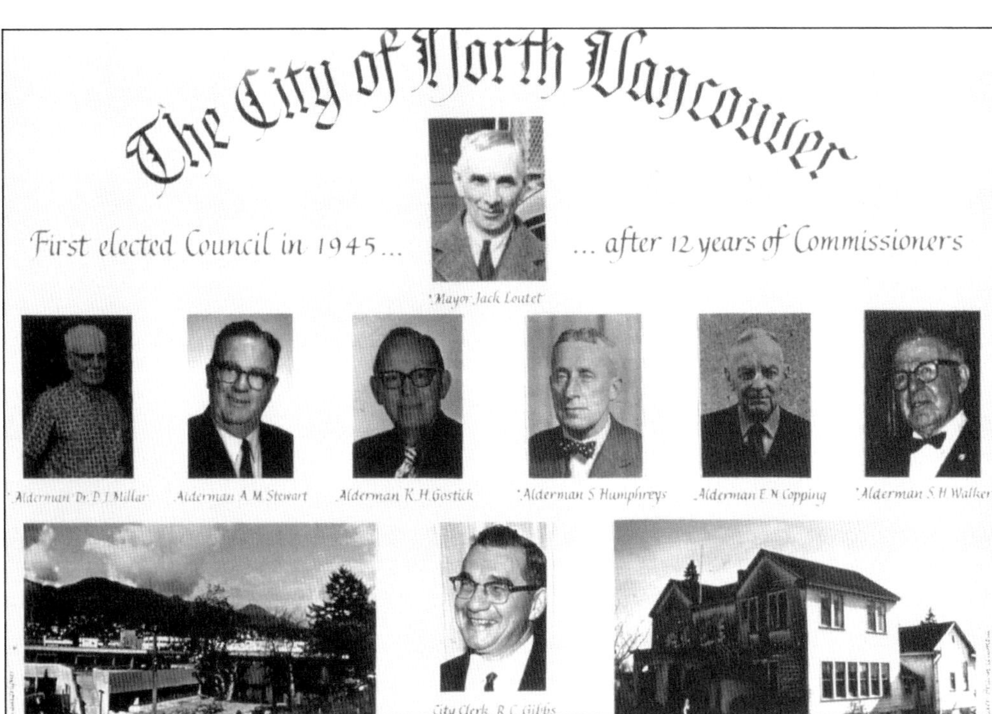

In 1945, residents of the City of North Vancouver selected their first elected council after 12 years of commissioners. Council members were (top) Mayor Jack Loutet, (centre, from left to right) D. J. Millar. A. M. Stewart, K. H. Gostick, S. Humphreys, E. N. Copping, and S. H. Walker. City clerk was R. C. Gibbs (bottom).

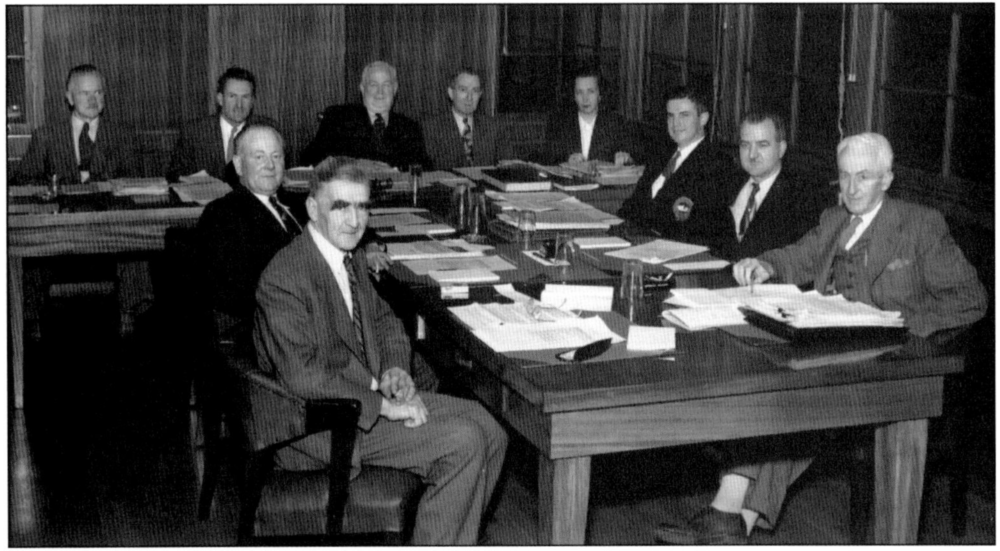

It took the District longer than the City to emerge from bankruptcy. The first new District of North Vancouver Council is shown in this 1950 photograph after commissionship. From left to right, at the outer edge of the table, are E. Valentine, Superintendent of Works; R. Howard, Solicitor; Reeve M. E. "Sam" Sowden; F. G. Saunders, Municipal Clerk; B. Westmoreland, stenographer; Councillors D. Grant Currie, M. Reid, C. E. Scanlan. In the left foreground are Councillors G. Sargent and W. Griffin.

Two

INFRASTRUCTURE

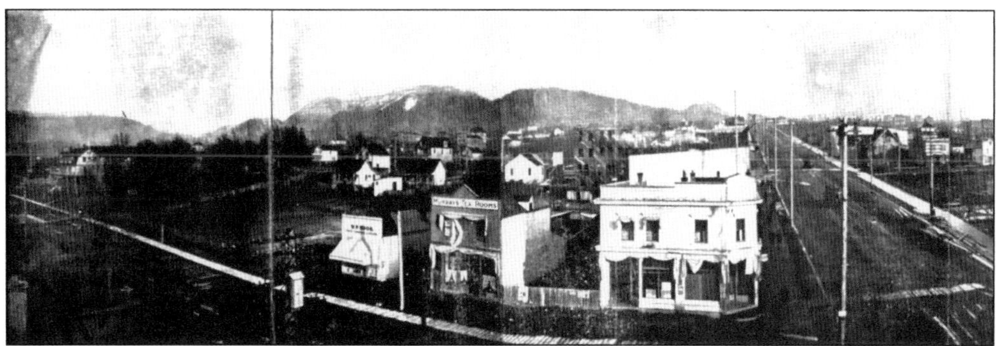

This photograph, taken around 1907, presents a panorama view of Lower Lonsdale looking north from West Esplanade. The Hotel North Vancouver is seen at the far left, with Hogg Confectioners, Murrays Tea Rooms, and McMillan's Grocery toward the centre. Streetcars operate on Lonsdale Avenue. The North Vancouver City Hall and Palace Hotel are seen up the street on the east side of Lonsdale.

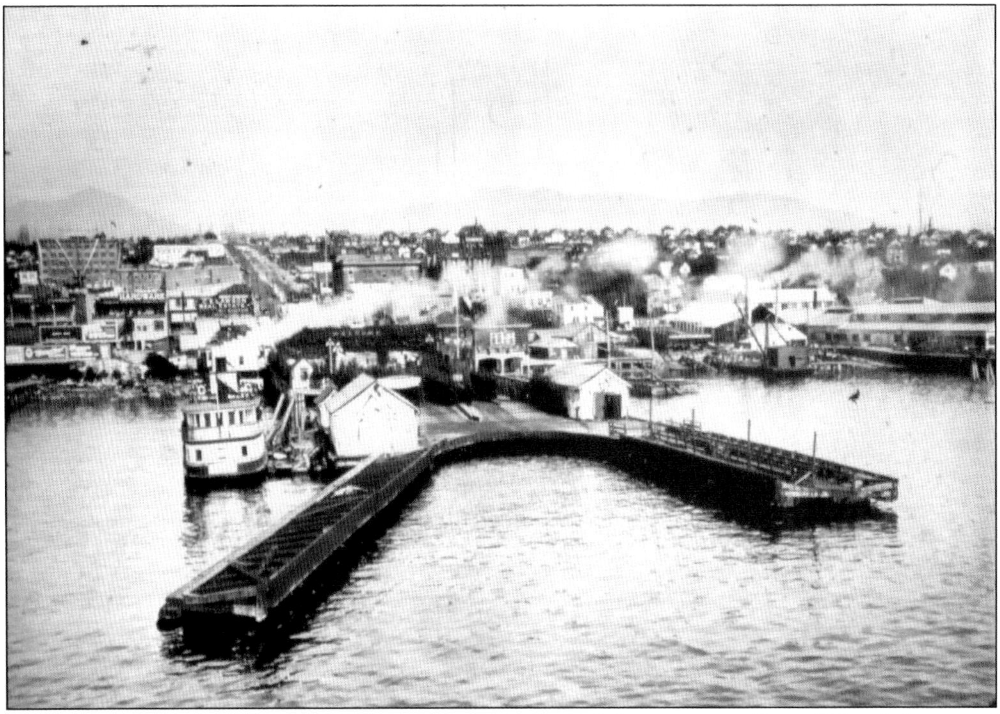

This photograph, taken in September 1912, shows the North Vancouver Ferry Wharf, decorated for a visit of the Duke of Connaught. North Vancouver ferry No. 1 is at the left.

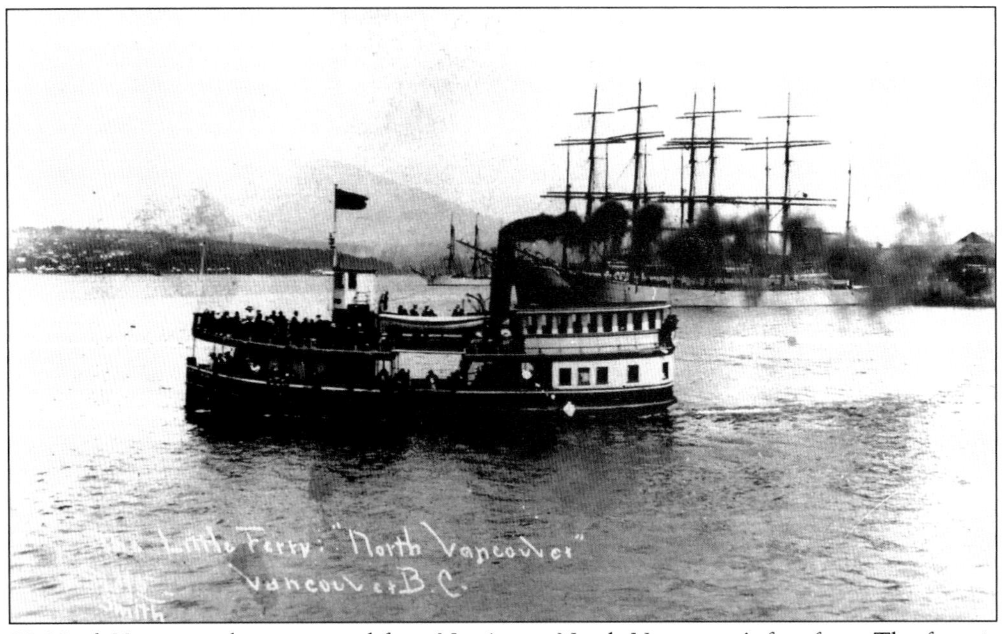

SS *North Vancouver*, later renamed ferry No. 1, was North Vancouver's first ferry. The ferry is seen in this photograph, taken around 1900, leaving a couple of sailing vessels and the south shore of the Burrard Inlet behind while heading toward North Vancouver. Ferry service was crucial for North Vancouver in the early days, as there was no bridge connection across Burrard Inlet until 1925.

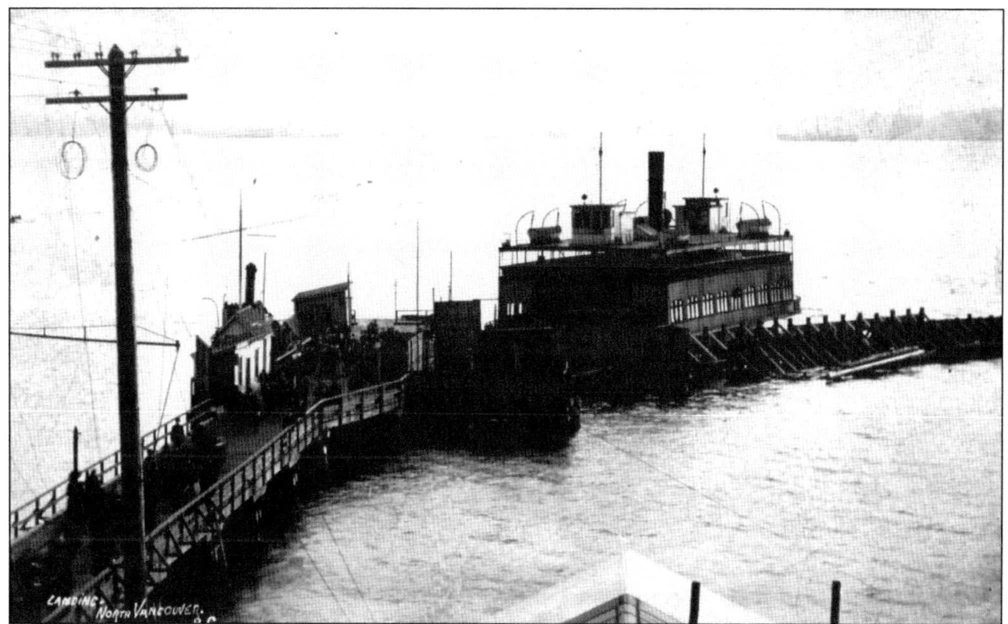

North Vancouver ferry *St. George*, named initially after Alfred St. George Hamersley and later renamed ferry No. 2, is shown at the ferry landing at the foot of Lonsdale Avenue. Passengers can be seen boarding and disembarking the ferry in this 1906 photograph. Goods, as well as residents, visitors, and workers, were all transported by ferry. Ferry No. 2 was in operation from 1905 to 1936 and carried approximately 30 million passengers and 2 million vehicles in that period.

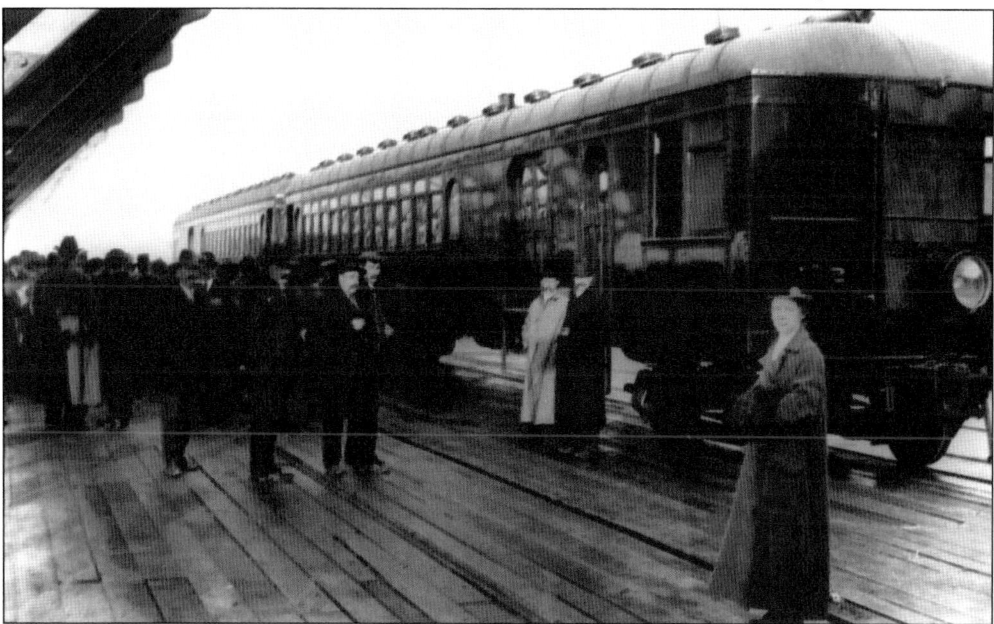

In 1913, the western world was in an economic depression and North Vancouver needed some good news. J. P. Fell paved the way by selling a half-mile of foreshore to the Pacific Great Eastern Railway (PGE). On January 1, 1914, the inaugural run of the railway from North Vancouver to Dundarave took place. The PGE station was at the foot of Lonsdale Avenue. In 1928, PGE's North Shore run was closed.

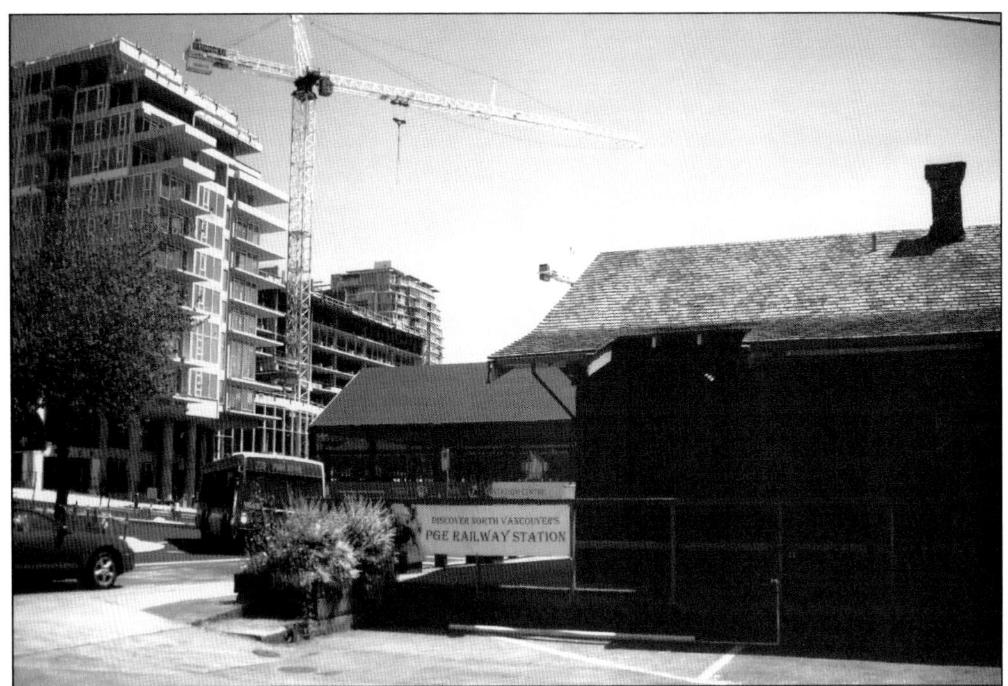

Today the PGE station is a facility of the North Vancouver Museum & Archives Commission and sits at the foot of Lonsdale Avenue, as shown in this May 31, 2009, photograph. Behind the station is one of Burrard Dry Dock's buildings, the Coopersmith Shop, still standing and waiting to be integrated into a new waterfront development, as well as a new hotel, under construction, to the left.

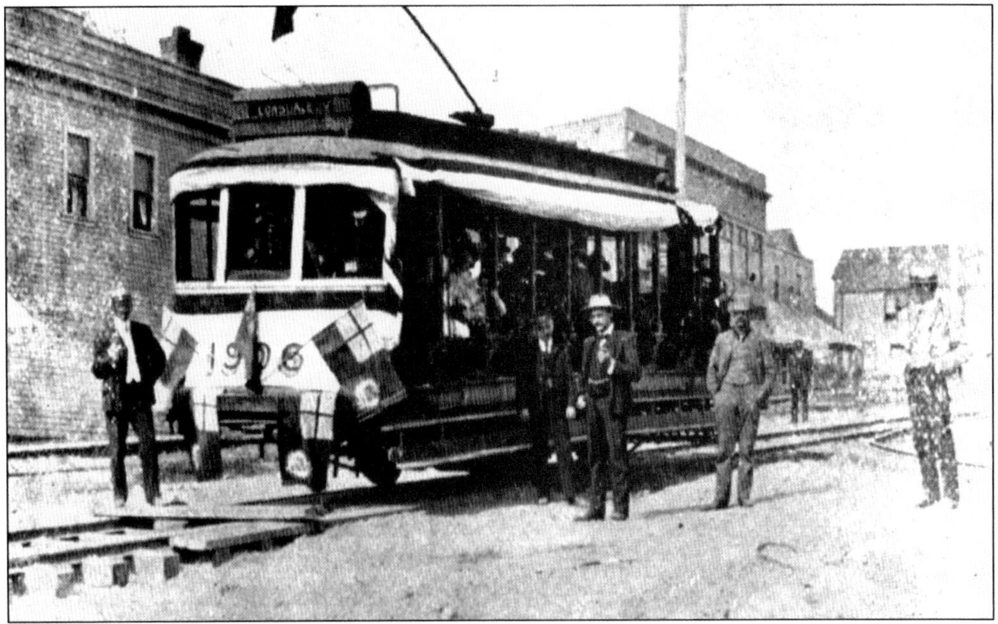

North Vancouver's first streetcar, decorated with flags, is pictured on Lonsdale Avenue just north of Esplanade in 1906. As seen in this photograph, this streetcar had an open side. The Syndicate Block and other buildings on the west side of the street are in the background.

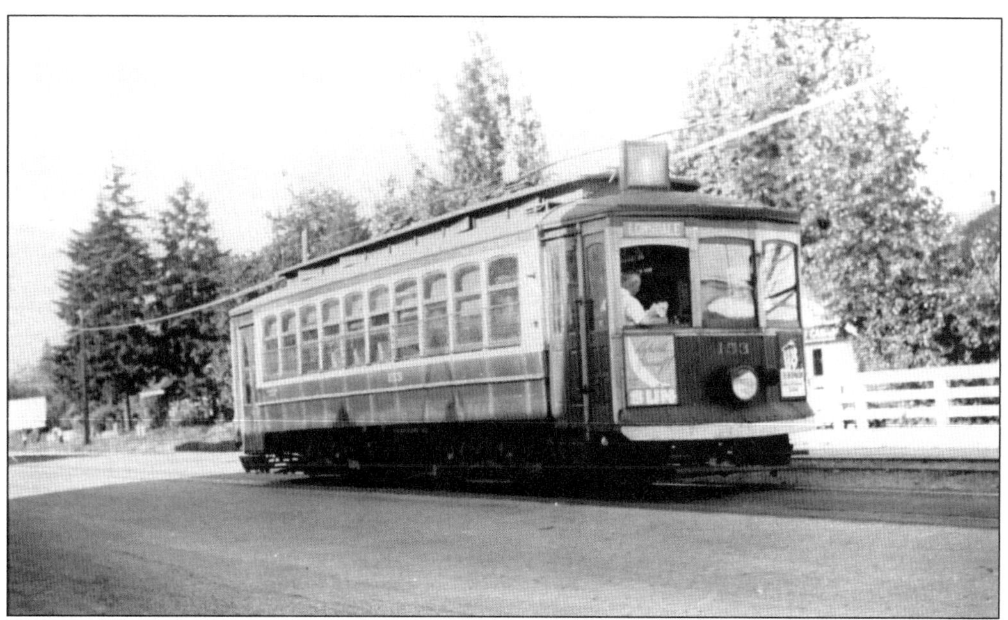

Lonsdale streetcar No. 153 is seen on a passing track at Sixteenth Street in a photograph taken between 1942 and 1947. The bus would emerge as a more affordable, more flexible public transit alternative to reach the new suburbs. Eventually it would replace streetcars such as No. 153, shown next to a bus with drivers chatting at the foot of Lonsdale Avenue.

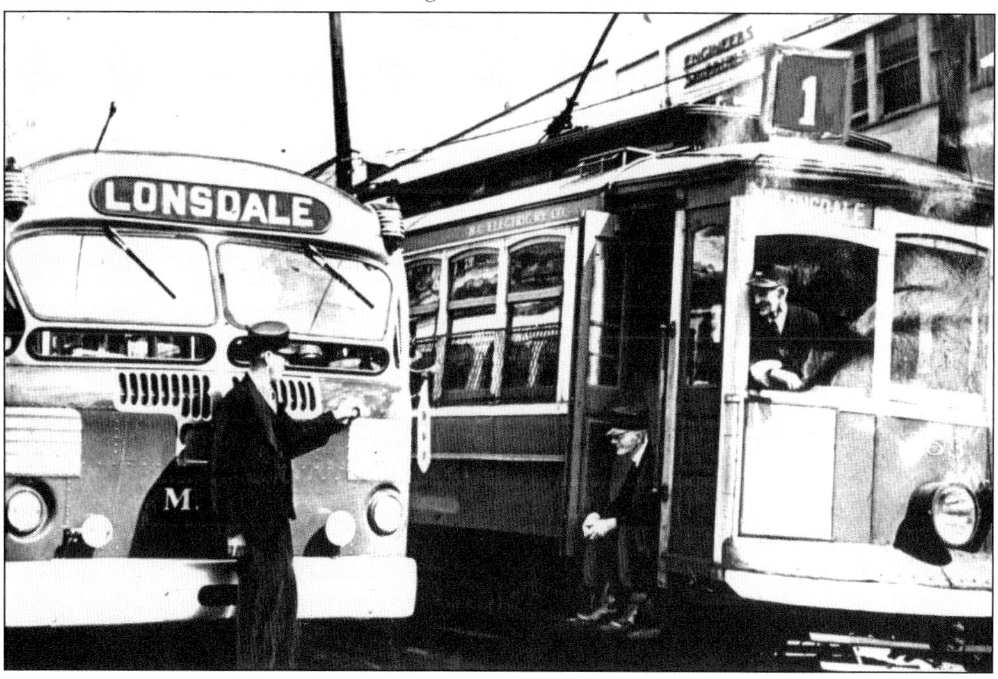

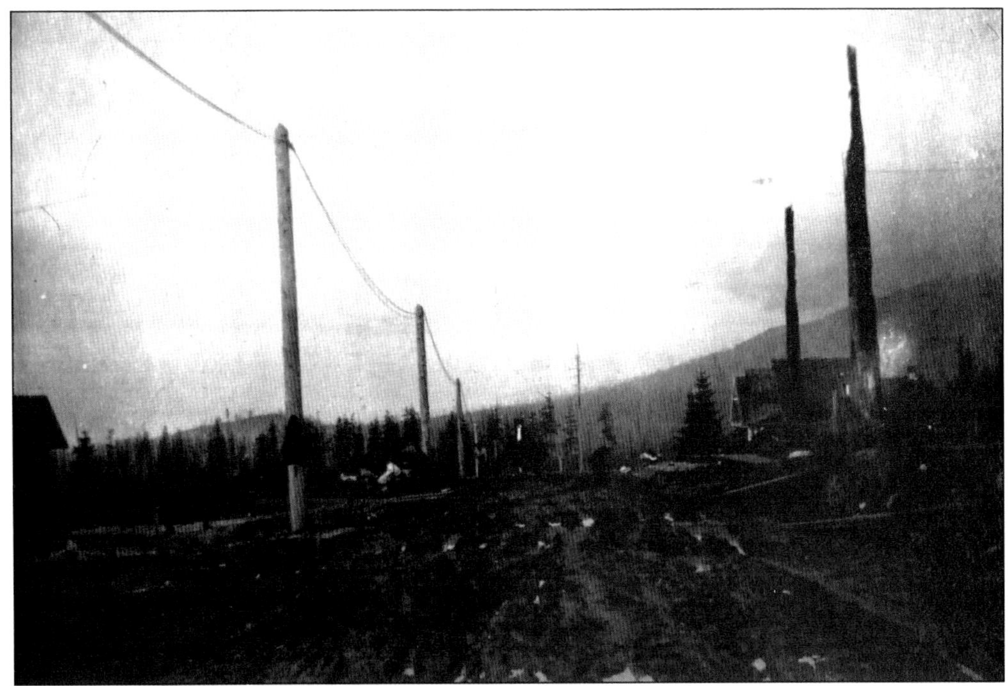

The installation of the Lonsdale streetcar, which was extended to Windsor Road and Lonsdale Avenue on December 9, 1912, opened up the top of Lonsdale to residential development. This photograph, taken on April 3, 1914, shows then District councillor and later reeve Jack Loutet's house at 177 East Carisbrooke Road, three blocks north of Windsor Road, looking west toward Lonsdale Avenue.

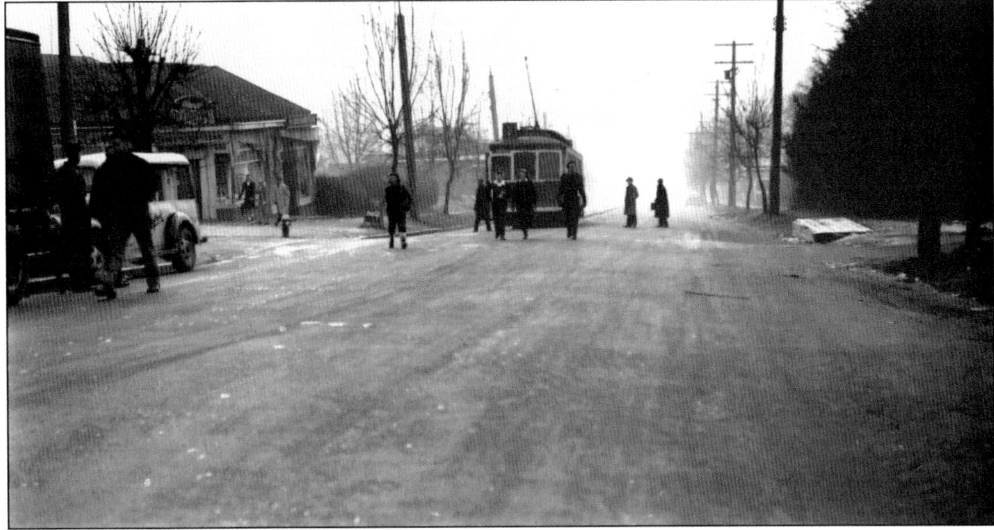

A streetcar waits at the Windsor Road terminus on Lonsdale Avenue in the 1940s. The streetcar system allowed working people to buy homes on cheaper lots and commute to work. The building on the left is North Lonsdale Pharmacy. Carisbrooke Park was near the terminus, offering a picnic destination in the early days of the streetcar's operations. The streetcar also provided access to Grouse Mountain, a popular hiking and skiing destination, accessible through trails from the top of Lonsdale Avenue.

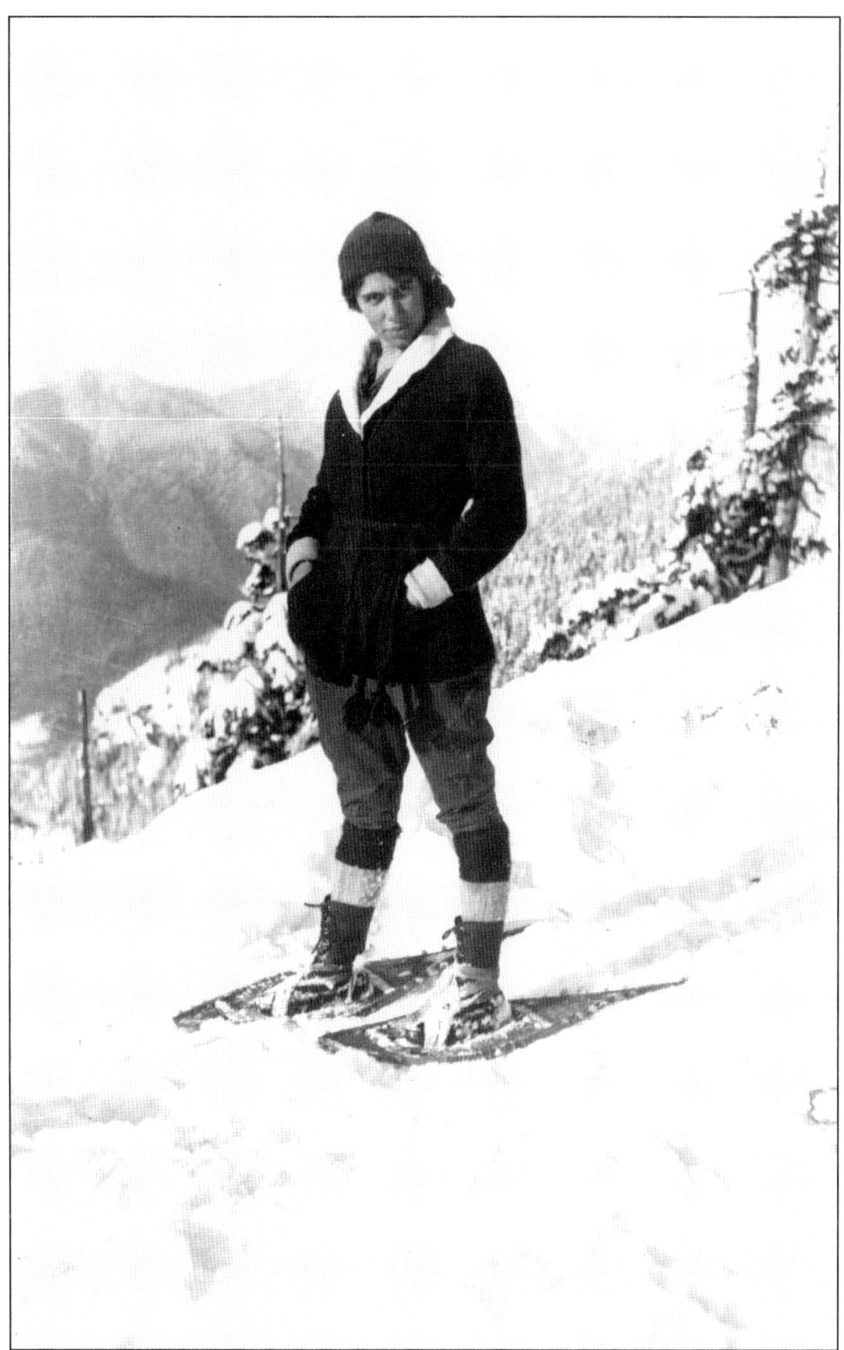

This photograph shows mountaineer Phyllis Munday on snowshoes on the Grouse Mountain plateau in 1924. The book *Off the Beaten Track: Women Adventures in Western Canada*, by Cyndi Smith, relates that women wore bloomers for hiking and climbing. In order to accommodate this within the context of yesteryear's traditions, Phyllis would go up to the Windsor terminus of the streetcar with a skirt on and then would hide the skirt under a log near a hiking trail. On the way back from a hike she would pick the skirt up and ride the streetcar back home.

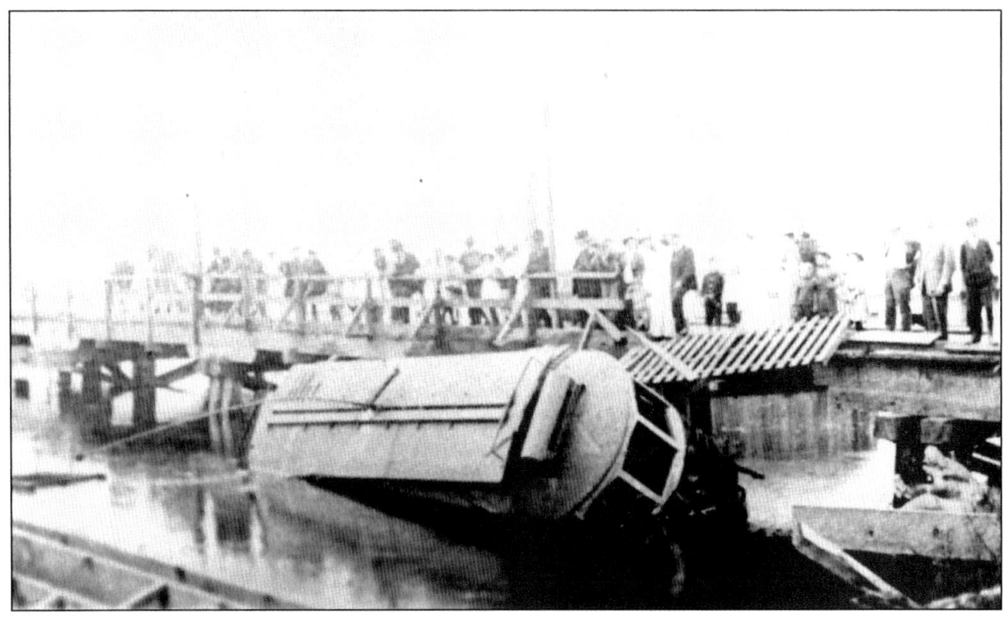
The steep areas of Lower Lonsdale Avenue at times caused the streetcars to slip off their tracks. On August 12, 1909, streetcar No. 42 went into the water at the foot of Lonsdale. A crowd of people observes the damaged pier and the streetcar below it.

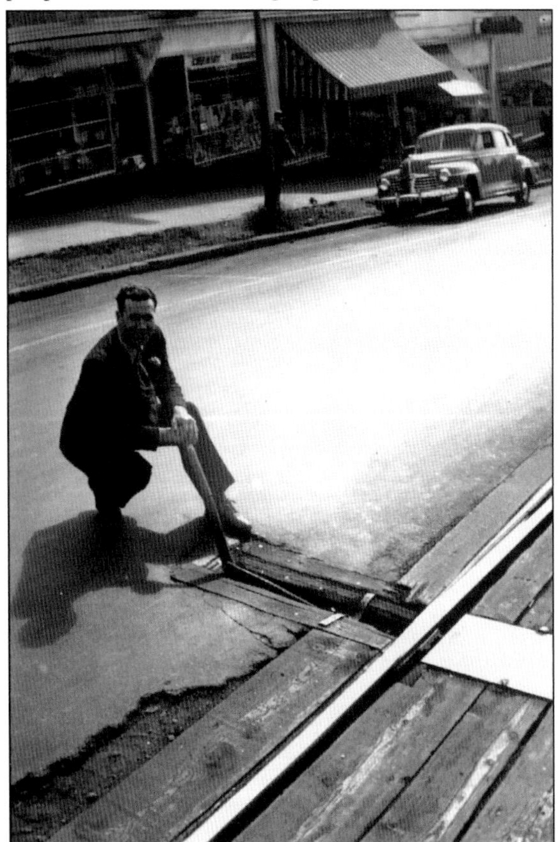
In 1947, conductor H. Bullock closes a manual derail southbound, in the 200 block of Lonsdale Avenue. The purpose of the derail was to prevent runaway streetcars from ending up in Burrard Inlet.

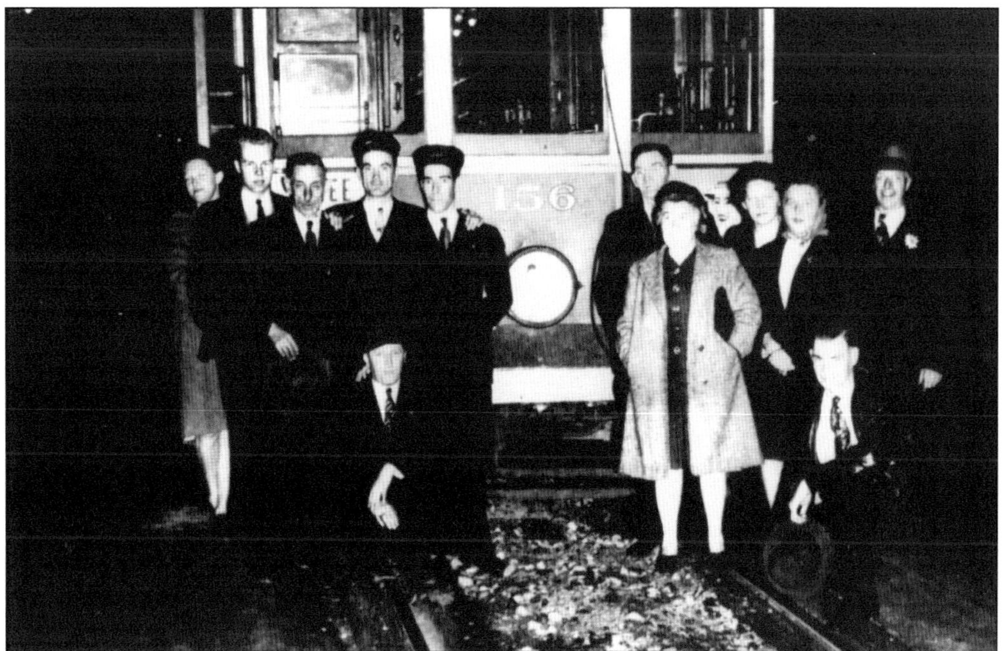

Saying goodbye to the streetcar marked the end of an era for some residents and frequent commuters. People in this photograph are standing in front of Lonsdale streetcar No. 156 at Windsor Road on its last trip at 12:55 a.m. on September 25, 1946, and are identified from left to right as an unidentified woman, Bill Harris, Johnny Swallow, Ed Long, Ted Long, Harold Stackhouse, Bert James, Mrs. Shannon, Ted Robson, Patricia Plant, Audrey Plant, Catherine Plant, Bert Giffen, and Bert Hughes.

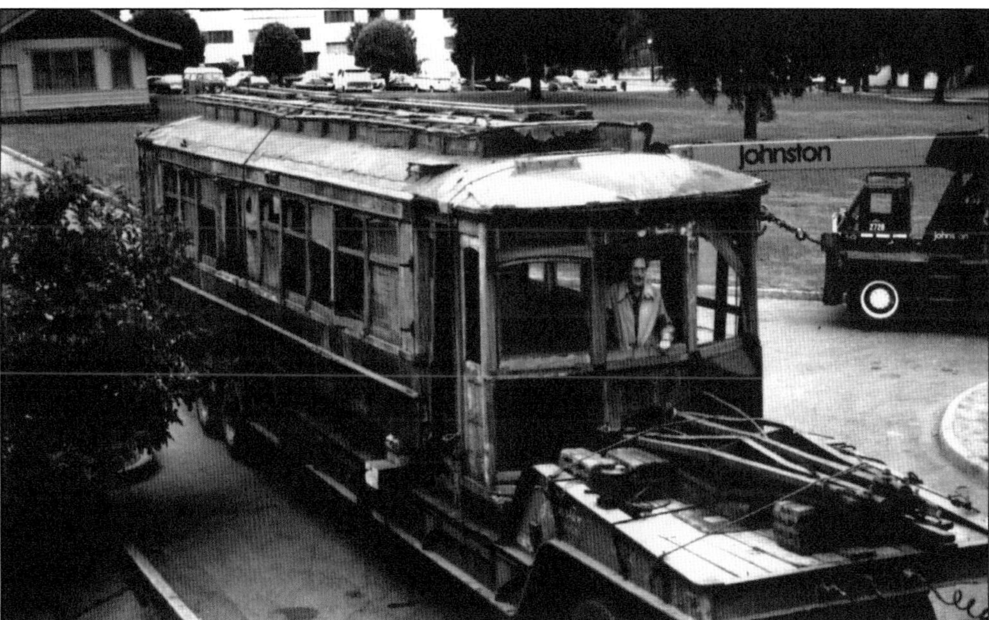

Years later in 1986, Bill Baker, North Shore Museum director, would secure and bring a dilapidated Lonsdale streetcar No. 153 into Mahon Park for preservation and restoration. No. 153 had been used as a chicken coop in the Fraser Valley.

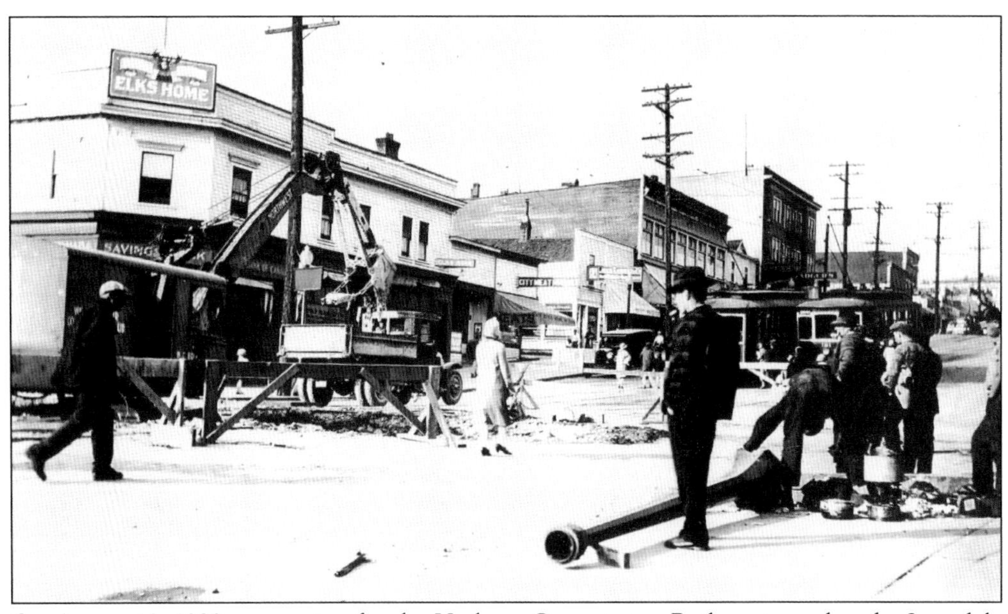

On August 18, 1928, excavation for the Harbour Commission Railway tunnel under Lonsdale Avenue and Esplanade was underway. Streetcars and businesses on the west side of Lonsdale can be seen in the background.

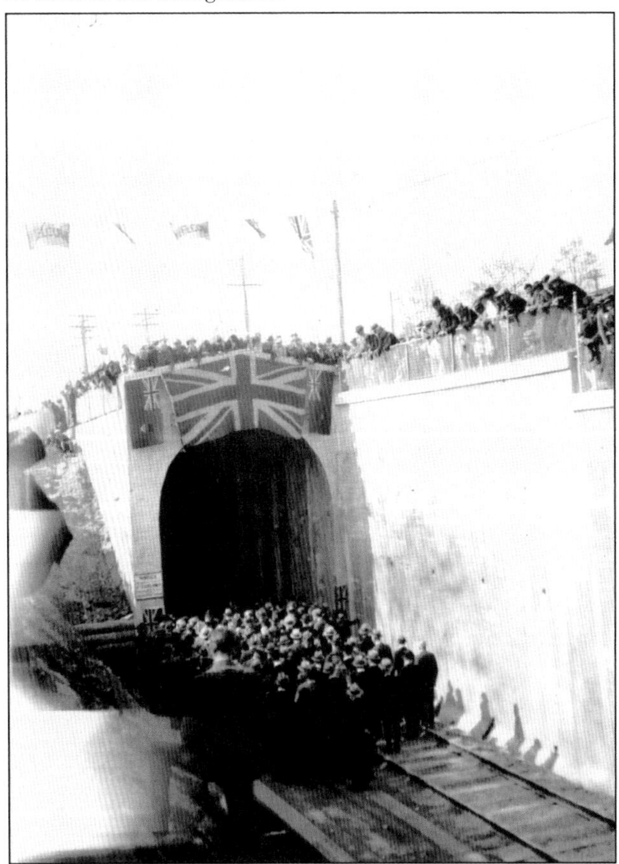

On April 24, 1929, the official opening of the Harbour Commission Railway tunnel attracted the Governor General of Canada Viscount Willingdon and Lady Marie Willingdon.

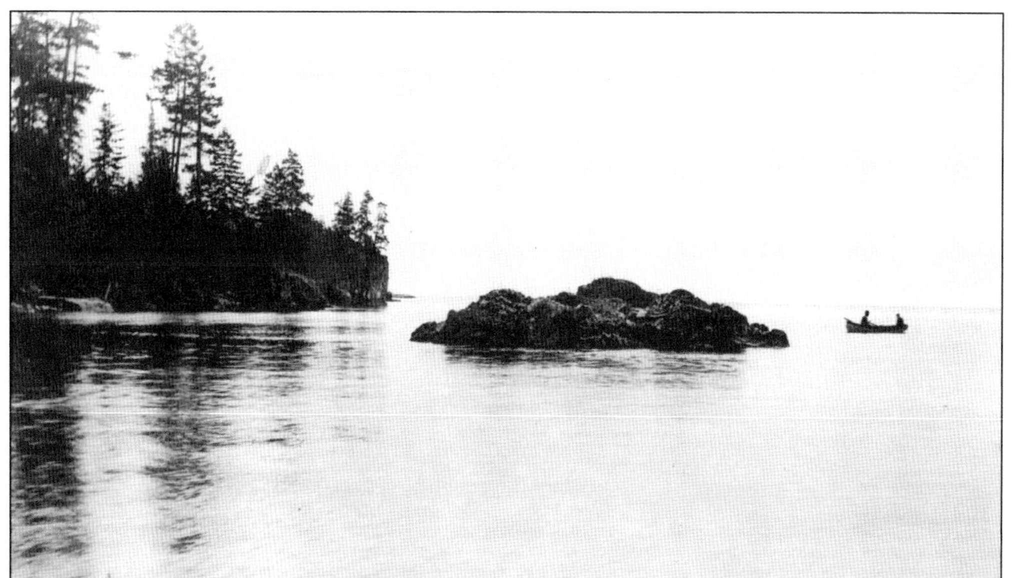

Keith Road extended to the western reaches of the North Shore, once part of the District of North Vancouver and now the District of West Vancouver. This 1911 photograph shows Eagle Harbour where the road terminated. Much of the early settlement in this and surrounding areas was made possible by the construction of Keith Road, which, although subject to numerous washouts, linked distant communities to the Lonsdale core.

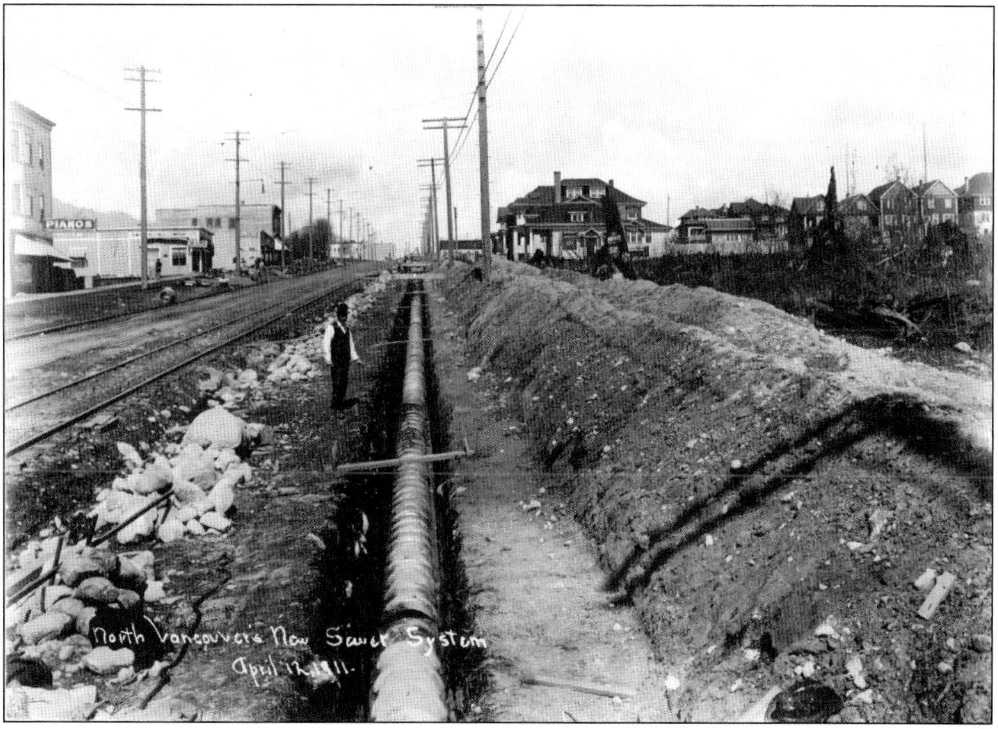

This photograph shows the construction of a new sewer system on April 12, 1911. The 400 block of Lonsdale Avenue can be seen with the Irwin & Billings store as well as a piano retail store on the left. Electric lights can be seen suspended from the poles.

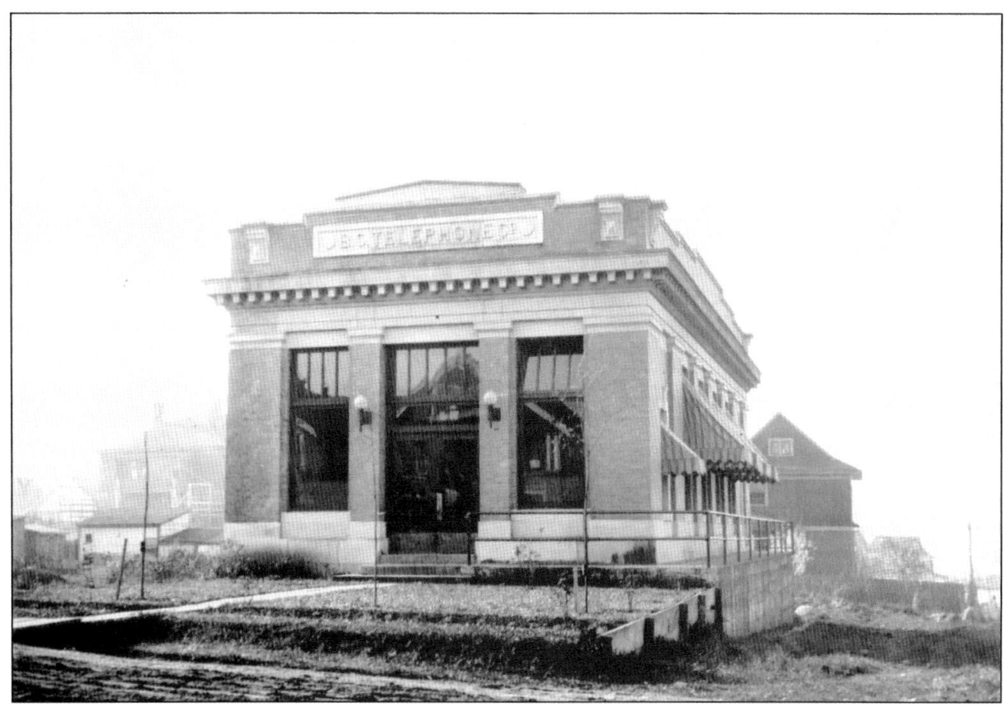

The BC Telephone Company asked permission to canvas for subscribers in 1905 and started offering services a year later. In 1911, the company built this North Vancouver central office and exchange at 143 East Eleventh Street. In the photograph below, operators are at the switchboard in the central telephone office around 1915. Standing at the left is Ann Thompson. Her headset is preserved in the North Vancouver Museum's collection.

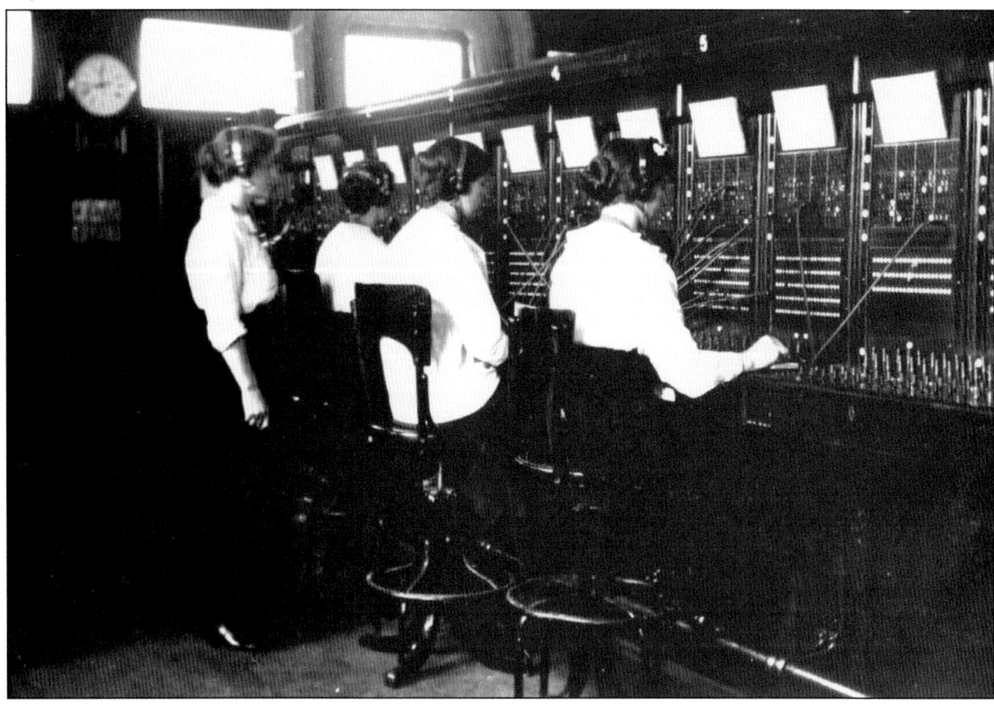

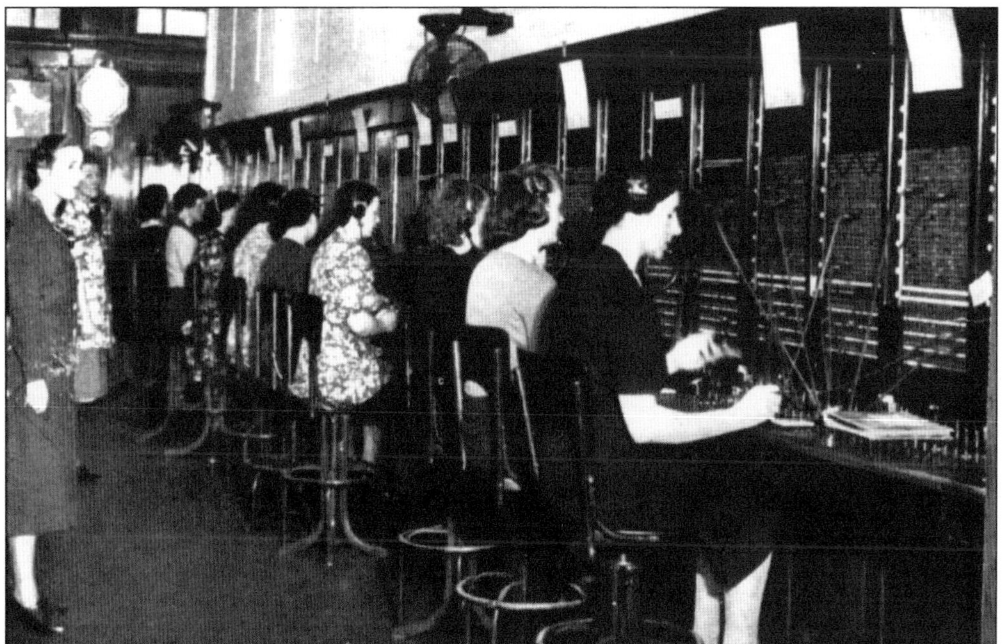

By 1939, the BC Telephone Company's North Vancouver exchange was considerably larger. From right to left, the women are identified as A. M. Howard, Gladys Powell, Kay Gillis, Evelyn Phillips, Lily Ward, Mary Holmes, Mary Empey, Lucy Redford, and Mildred Summerville.

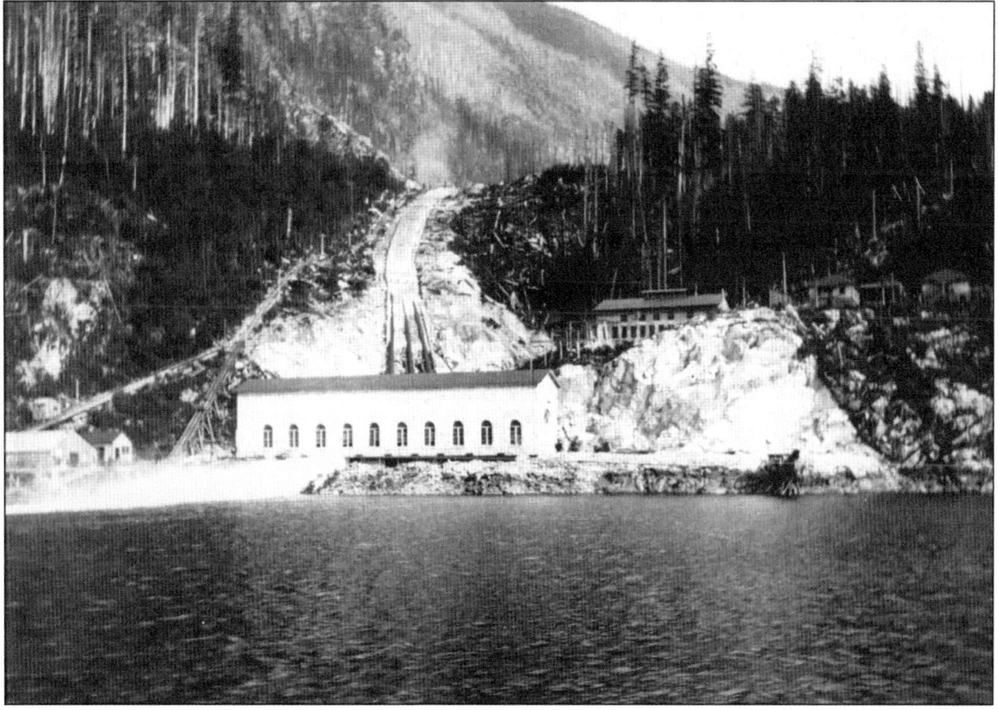

This photograph, taken around 1905, shows the hydro-electric generating plant and pipeline on Indian Arm. It produced electricity for North Vancouver and other centres after construction of the tunnel between Coquitlam and Buntzen Lakes and the dam at Buntzen Lake.

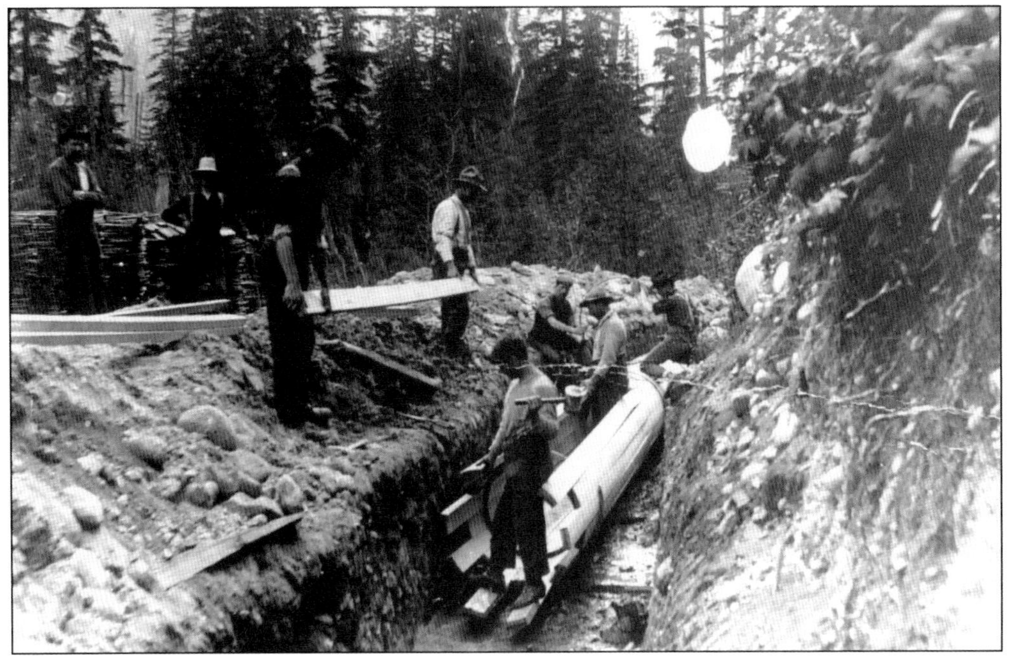

In 1905, five and a half miles of pipe from Lynn Creek to the foot of Lonsdale Avenue was turned over to the municipality. Approximately 15 hydrants had been installed and 100 homes were connected. However, demand for water kept increasing and more intakes were constructed in North Vancouver. In this photograph, men construct the Seymour River pipeline, which was completed in October 1908.

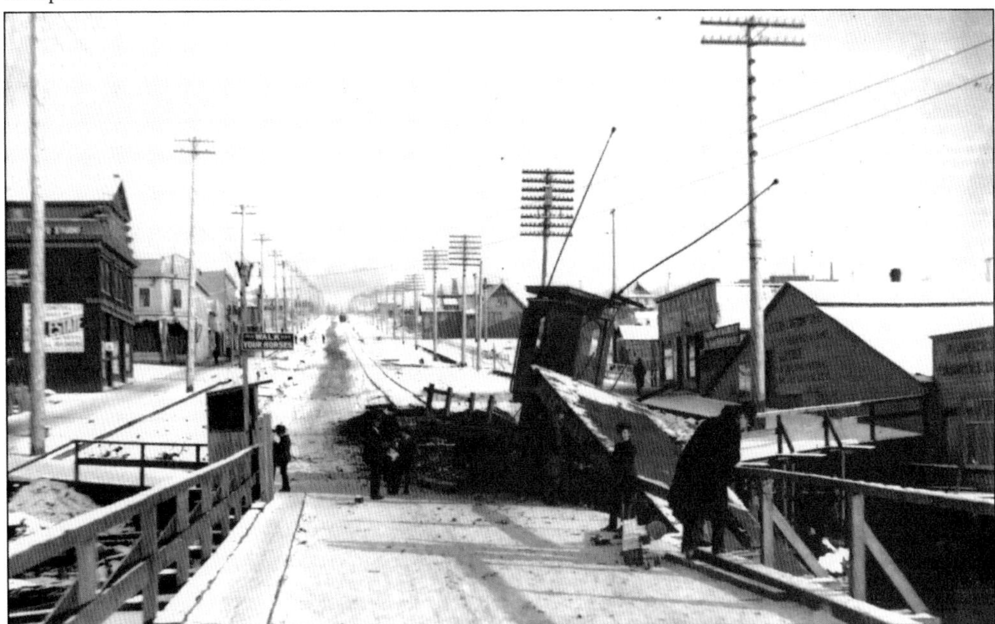

The BC Electric Railway Company was responsible for major infrastructure projects, such as installing North Vancouver's first lighting systems in 1906. However, such projects were not without accidents. In this photograph, taken in 1907, a flatcar delivering equipment to Diplock and Wright Sawmill slips and sends a passenger car into Burrard Inlet.

Three

BUSINESS ACTIVITY

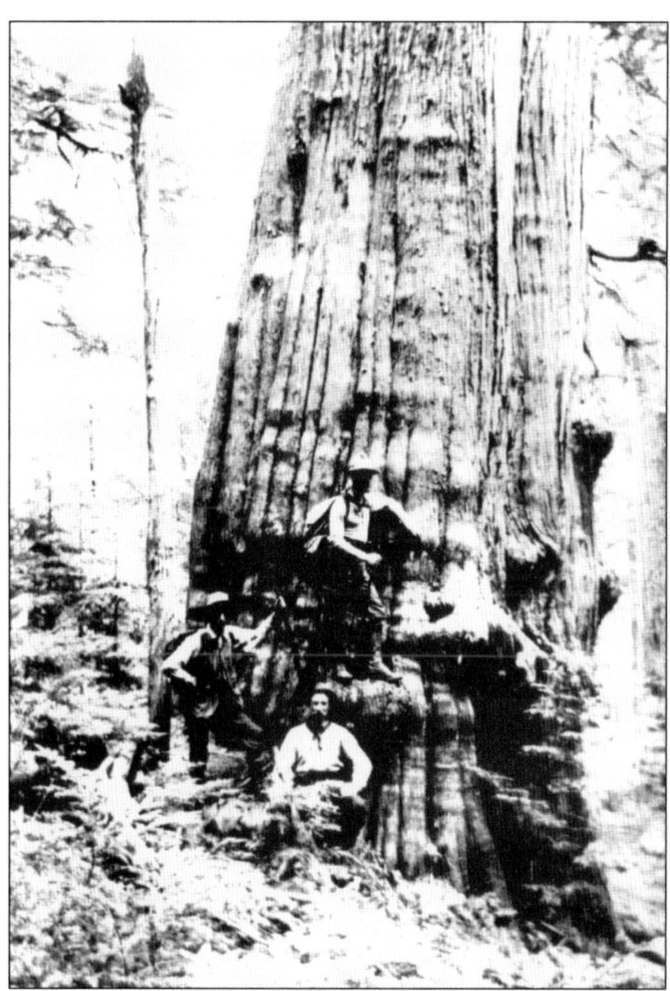

This c. 1910 photograph taken at Bishop Creek, just north of the District of North Vancouver boundary, is a reminder of the towering giants that once blanketed the slopes of North Vancouver. Tall, straight-grained Douglas firs sustained North Vancouver's first industry—logging—and were a major reason that the community became a desired destination for industries and early settlements.

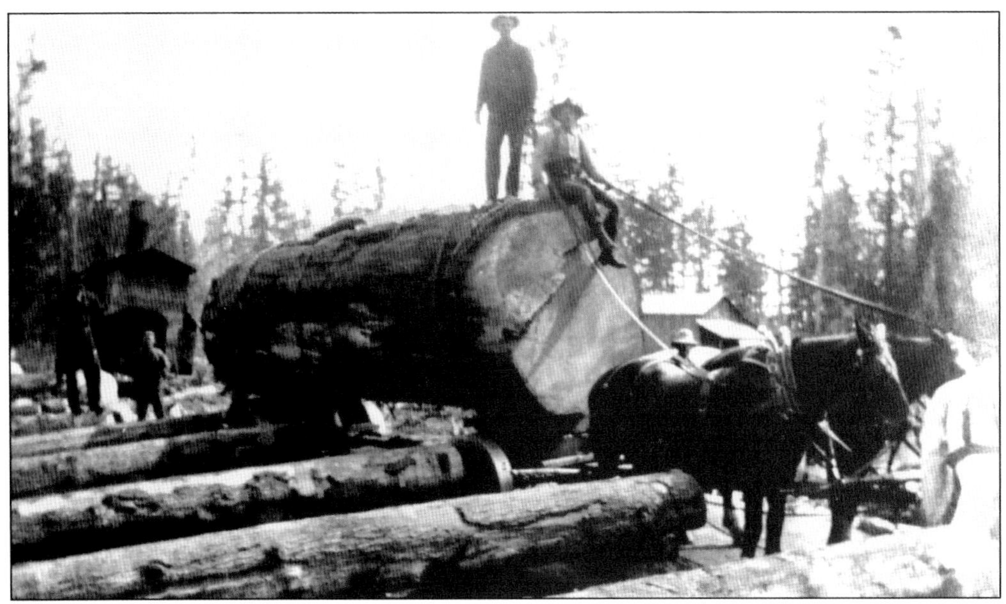

This photograph, taken around 1906, shows a single large log being transported to the Seymour Lumber Company sawmill. A donkey engine, frequently used to pull logs, can be seen to the left of the log.

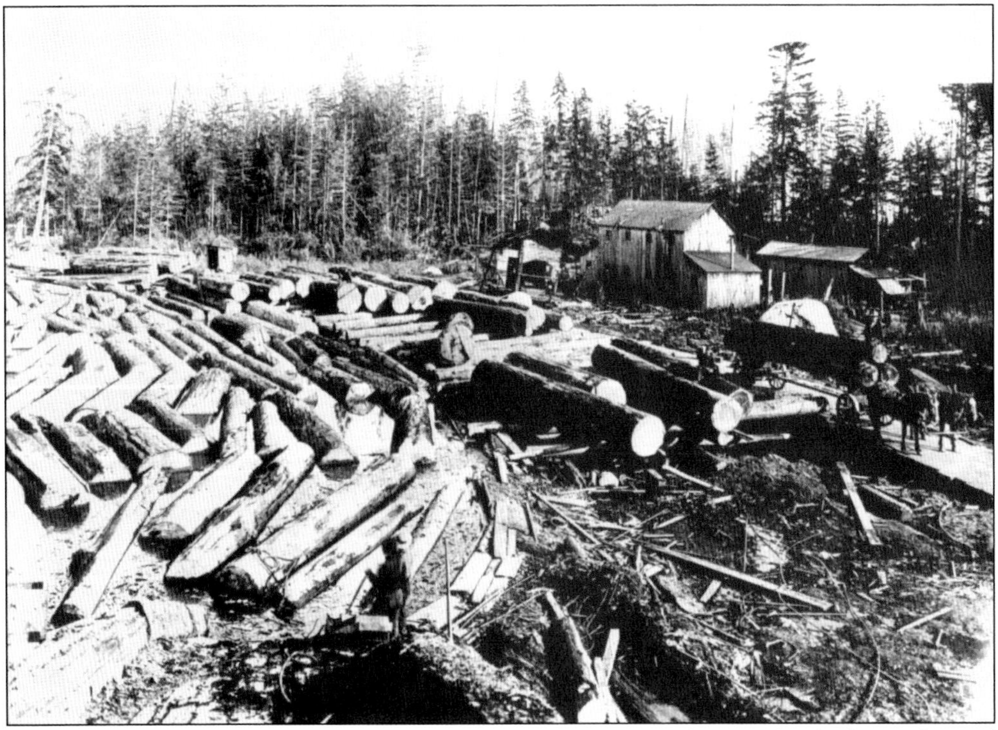

The logs were dropped off in the Seymour Lumber Company's log pond, which was located alongside a workers' housing unit on East Seventeenth Street at Sutherland Avenue, about six blocks east of Lonsdale Avenue.

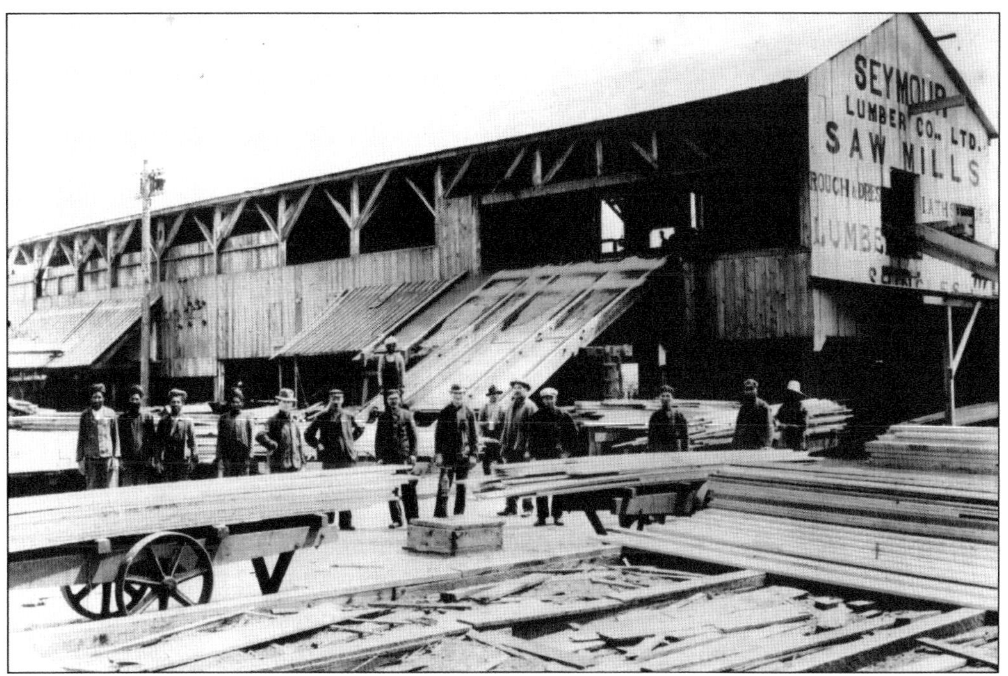

This photograph, from about 1906, shows the multicultural mix in the Seymour Lumber Company's workforce in those early years, as evidenced by the presence of East Indian, Chinese, and Caucasian workers.

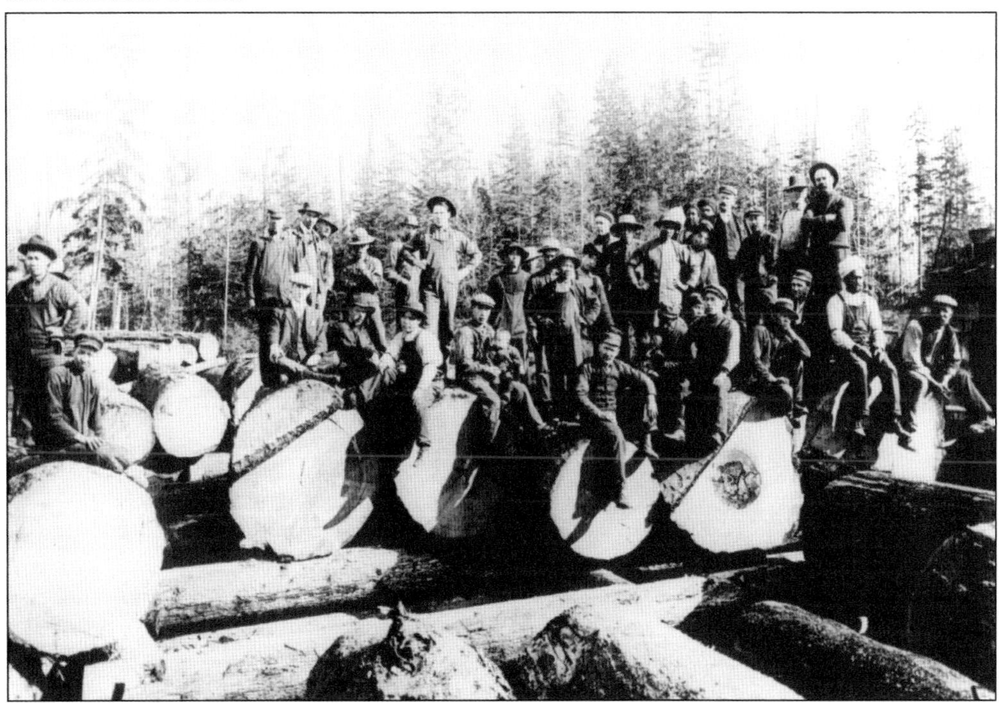

Seymour Lumber Company workers of various ethnic backgrounds, most dressed in overalls and two of them holding young children, pose for this photograph atop a pile of huge logs around 1906.

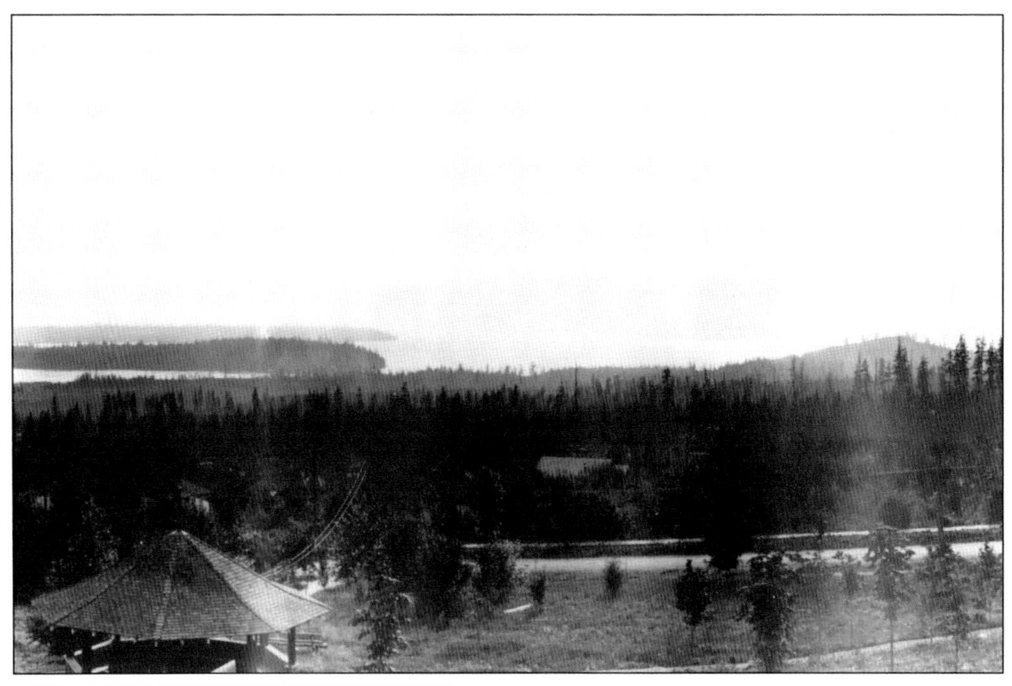

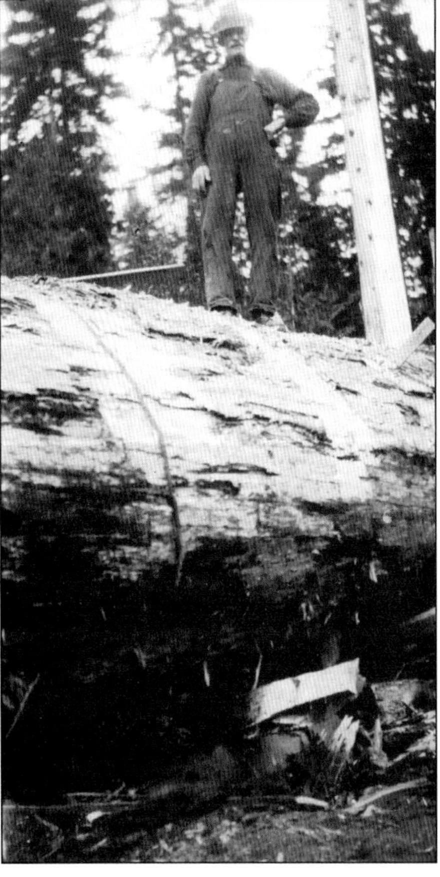

This panoramic view looks southwest in 1914 from Carisbrooke Park in Upper Lonsdale. The vista shows that even though logging had started years previously, much of North Vancouver's Lonsdale neighbourhood and surrounding areas were still heavily forested. The second picture was taken about a year later on John or Bill Cowan's property at Lonsdale Avenue and Queens Road, four blocks below Carisbrooke Park. The height of the man standing on the tree is unknown, but clearly he is shorter than the diameter of the tree.

On November 10, 1905, the *Express* newspaper touted the establishment of a branch of the Bank of British North America as a sign that North Vancouver was a city full of promise. The Upper Lonsdale branch of the Bank of British North America, located at 1335 Lonsdale Avenue, opened in January 1911. This photograph shows an unidentified young man standing in front of the bank.

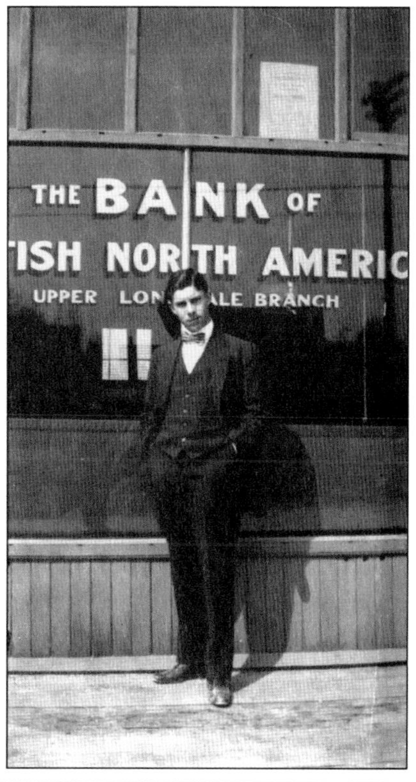

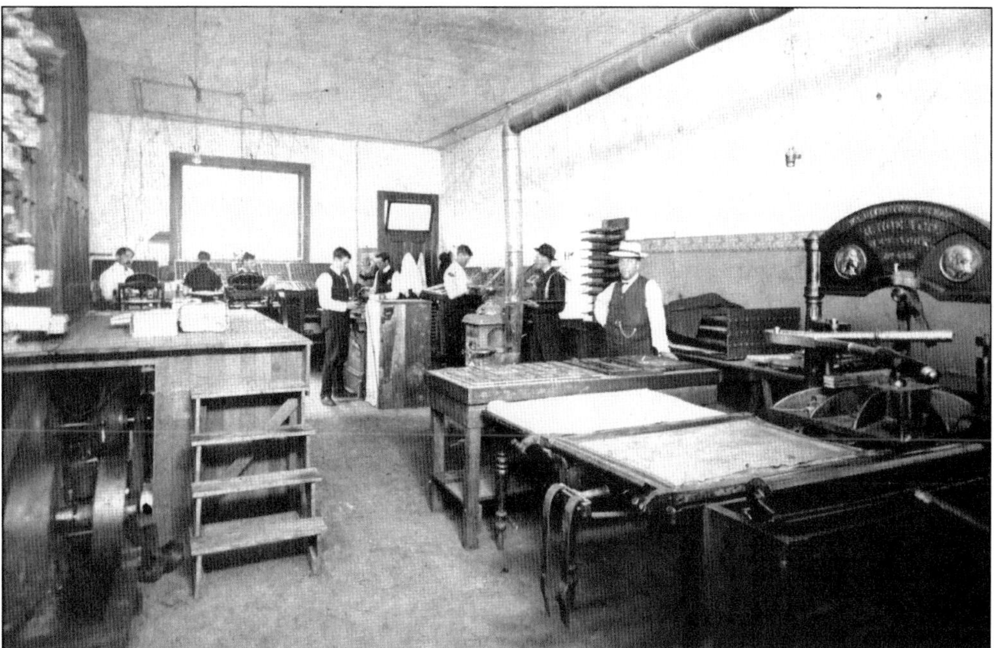

The *Express* was North Vancouver's first newspaper. This interior view of the Express office, taken on June 27, 1906, shows staff with printing equipment. The office was on West Esplanade at Lonsdale Avenue. Today the name Express lives on in the newsletter published by the Friends of the North Vancouver Museum & Archives Society.

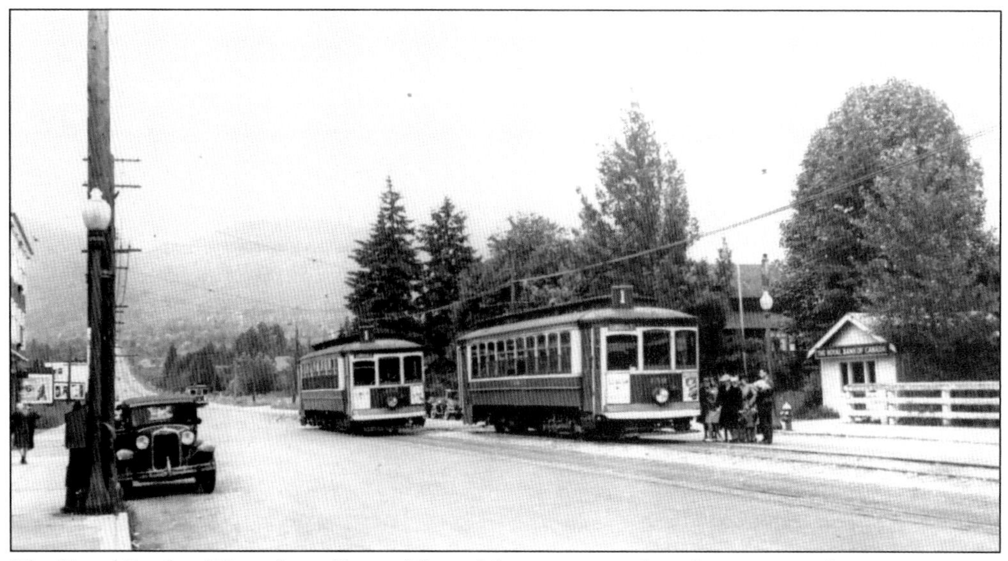

The Royal Bank of Canada in Central Lonsdale was situated in this converted garage, seen on the right, for about 10 months in 1946. Men, women, and children stand ready to board streetcar No. 159 in front of the bank.

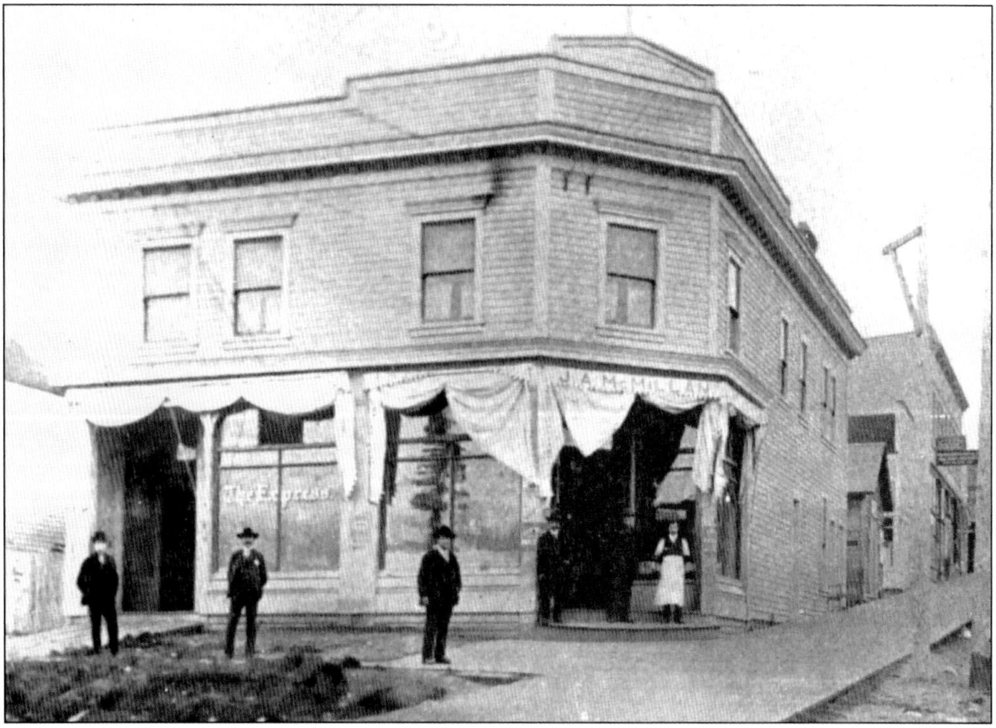

The first business block in North Vancouver, known as the Syndicate Block, was erected in 1903 by the Western Corporation, Limited. It was situated on the northwest corner of Lonsdale Avenue and West Esplanade; it housed the Express newspaper office (left) and J. A. McMillan Grocers on the corner.

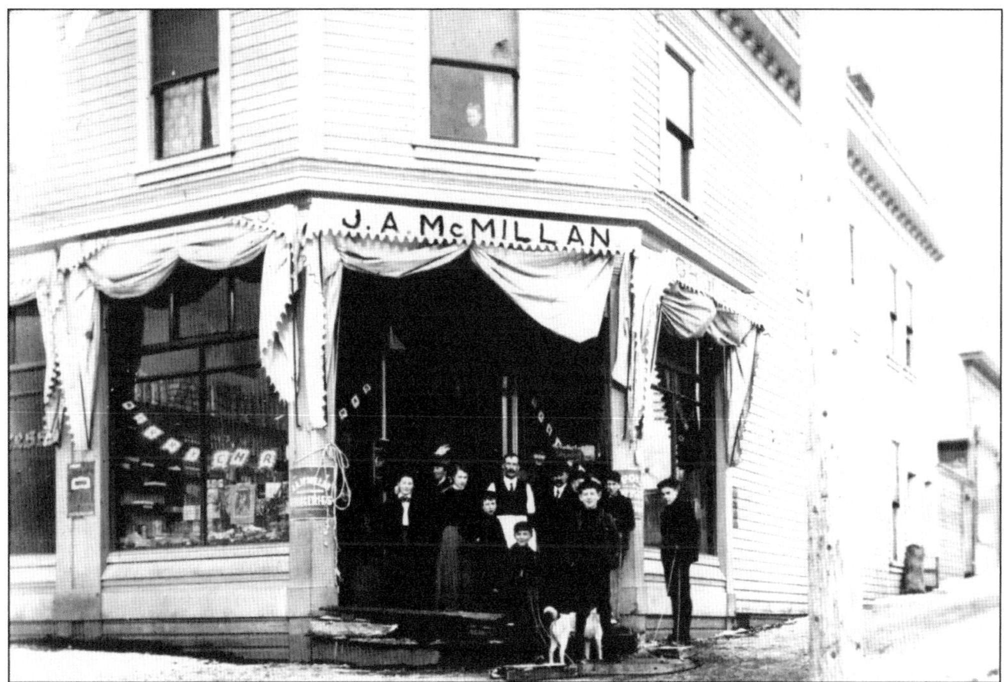

John Archibald McMillan Grocers, at the northwest corner of Lonsdale Avenue and Esplanade, was one of the earlier businesses in North Vancouver and quite possibly North Vancouver's first store, as shown here in the winter of 1905. This photograph was taken around Christmas as evident by the Merry Christmas signs and decorations inside the window on the left. The boy watching from the window on the second floor is John's son Lea McMillan.

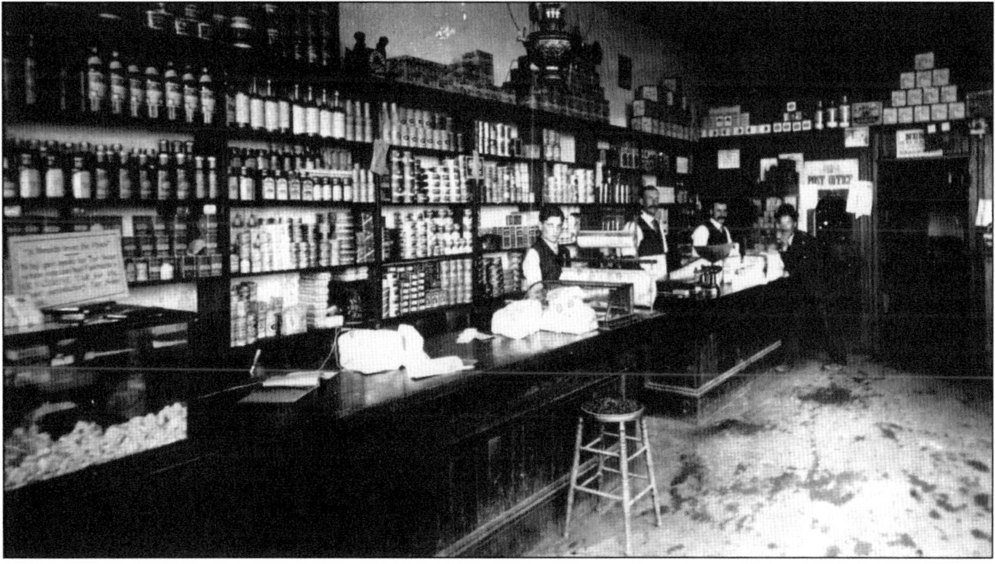

This photograph shows the interior of McMillan's Grocery with John Archibald McMillan behind the counter (third from left). Others in the picture are (from left to right) Robert Wheeler, junior clerk; Mr. Louden, senior clerk; and Jesse Williams to the right of McMillan. One can observe the old-style balance scales and a hanging kerosene lamp. The post office, which was relocated to this store after Moodyville's sawmill closed down, can be seen behind Williams.

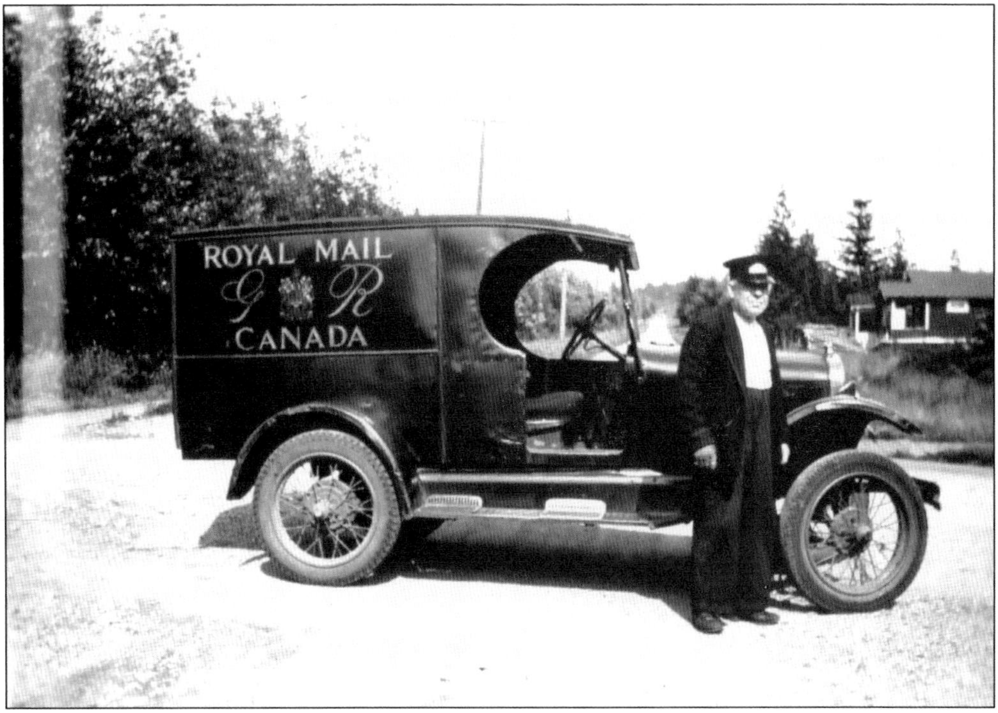

Around 1922, postmaster John Burniston stands next to his Royal Mail truck at West Twenty-second Street and Mahon Avenue, two blocks west of Lonsdale Avenue.

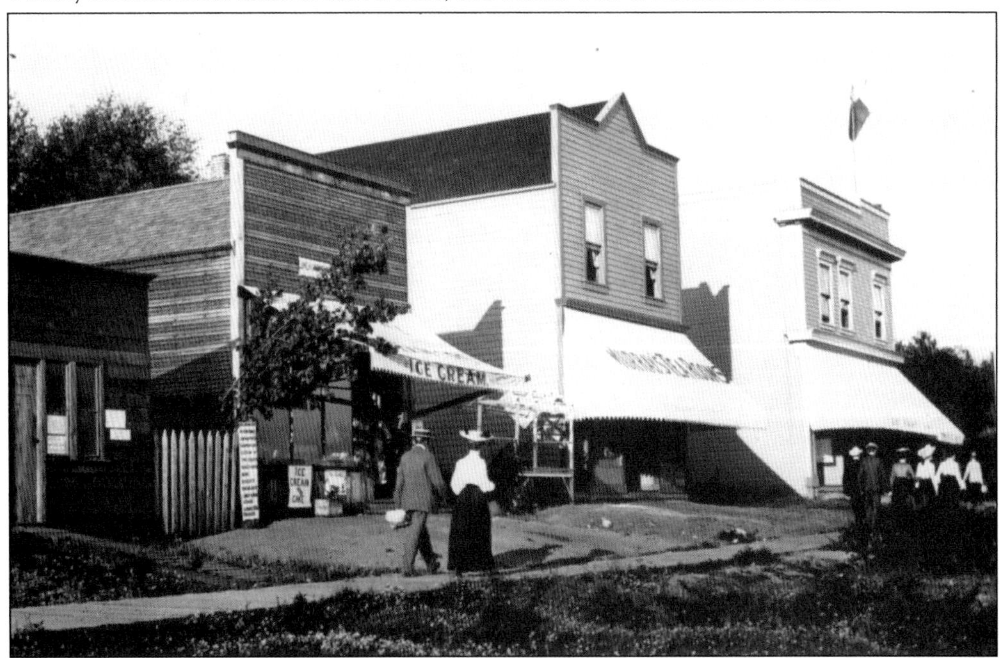

A confectionery next to Murray's Tea Room in the 100 block of West Esplanade advertises ice cream and cake in this charming photograph. Men and women, perhaps having come from the Hotel North Vancouver just to the west, can be seen taking an evening stroll on the boarded sidewalk, which also passed by McMillan's Grocers on the corner at Lonsdale Avenue.

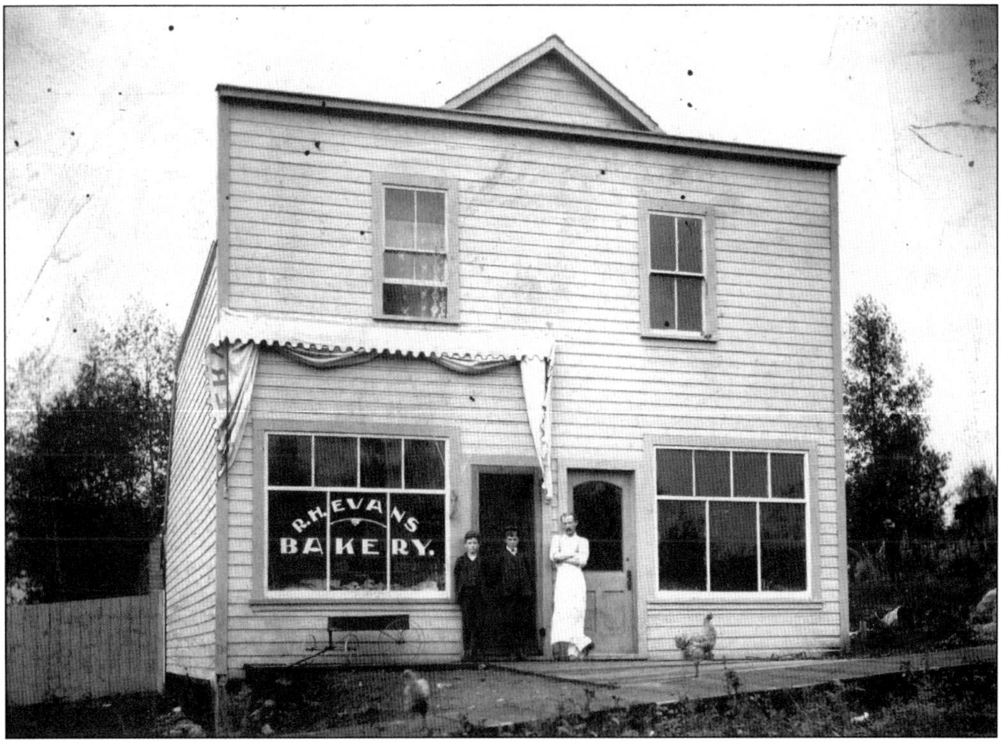

This 1905 photograph shows R. H. Evans Bakery in a building called the Wright Block on the west side of Lonsdale Avenue between Esplanade and First Street. In less than a year, other buildings were constructed on either side of the Wright Block, mainly to house real estate businesses taking advantage of a booming real estate market.

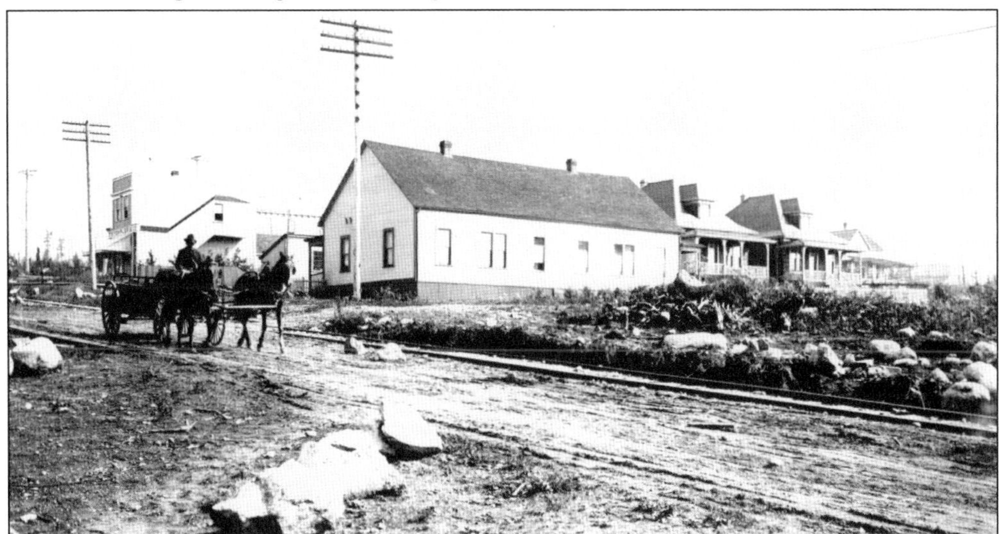

Councillor William Morden built the hall located at centre on the northeast corner of Keith Road and an unpaved Lonsdale Avenue, around 1907. Early basketball on the North Shore was practiced here, attracting players from Vancouver. The first high school in North Vancouver was temporarily located upstairs in the Morden Block at left, at Eighth and Lonsdale Avenue, in 1911.

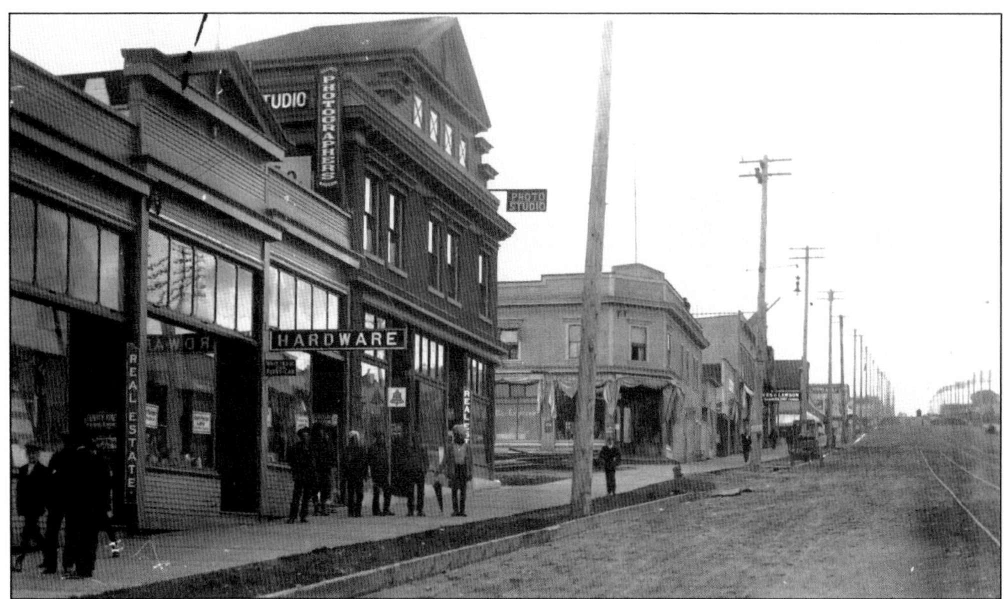

North Vancouver's early years were documented by photographers Albert Elliott and Fred Baglow, whose studio was located atop the Junction Block at the southwest corner of Lonsdale Avenue and West Esplanade. This 1908 photograph by Albert Elliott shows a group of men from India standing on the sidewalk below their studio.

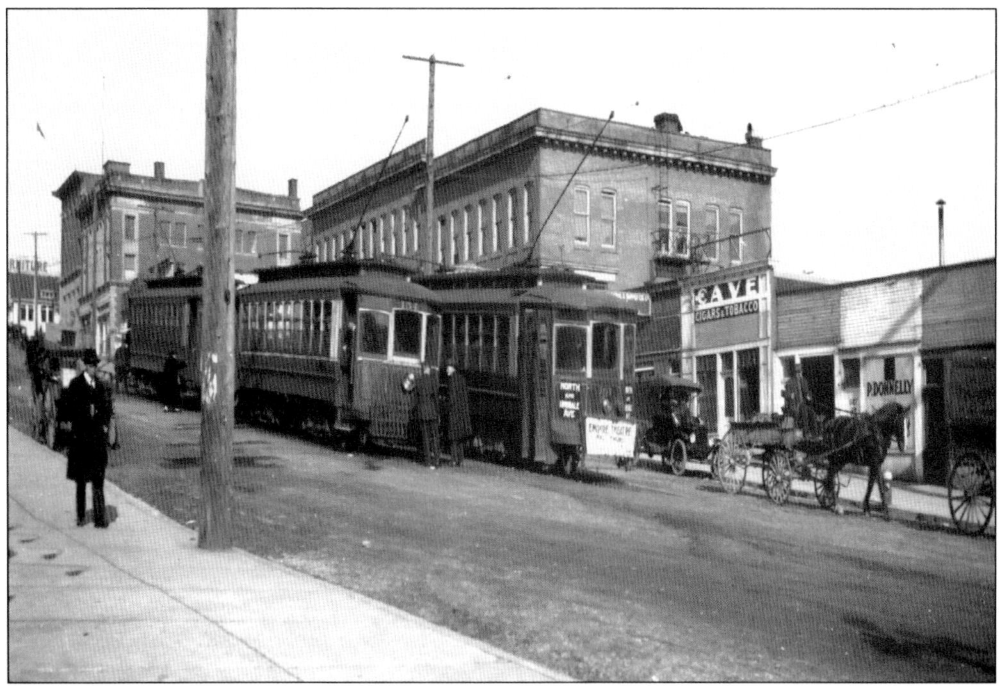

This photograph, taken after 1915, shows how people walked or rode the streetcar, a horse-drawn wagon, or an automobile to get to their desired destination in those days. Streetcars No. 154 (Lynn Valley) and No. 161 (Lonsdale) are present. The buildings on the east side of Lonsdale are (from left to right) the Bank of Hamilton, Aberdeen Block, Wallace Shipyards office, and the Cave confectionery.

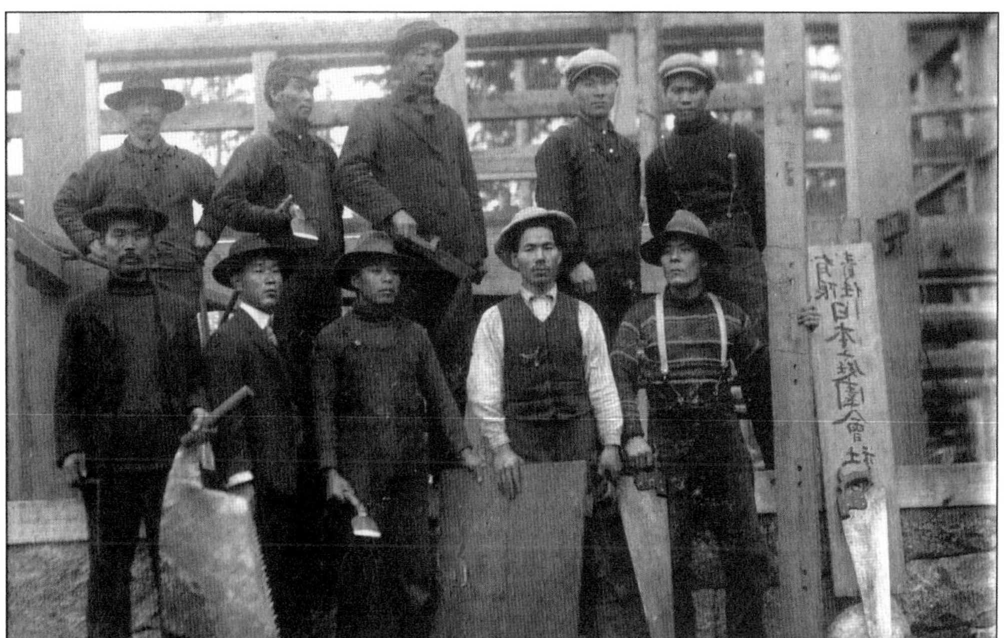

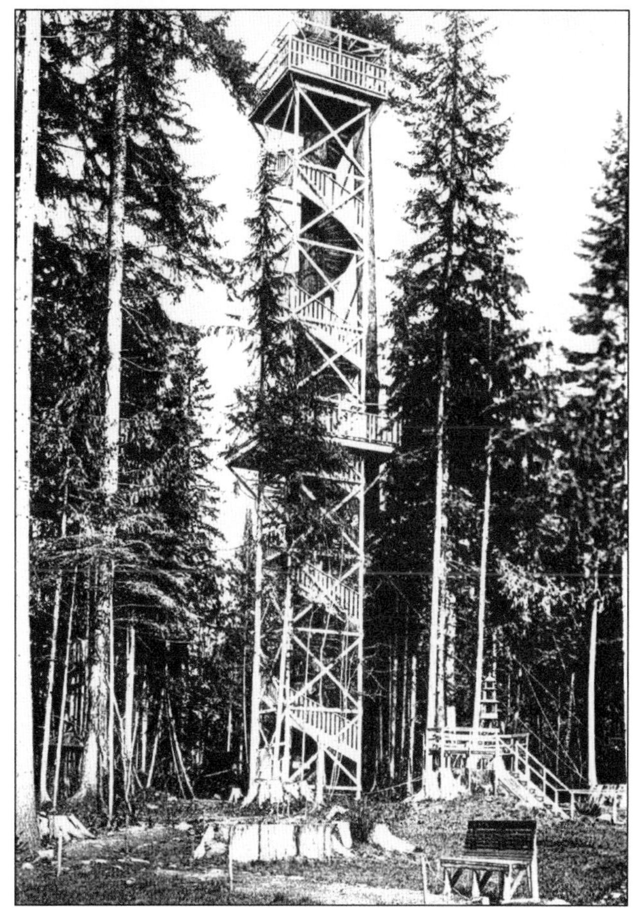

In 1910 the Japanese Tea Gardens opened near today's St. Georges and Twenty-first streets. Workers are shown in the photograph near a calligraphy sign that says Yugen Sekinen Japanese Garden Limited Liability Company. The Japanese Gardens contained a tower, quite likely the first observation tower on the North Shore, offering unobstructed tree-top views of the North Shore, Burrard Inlet, and beyond.

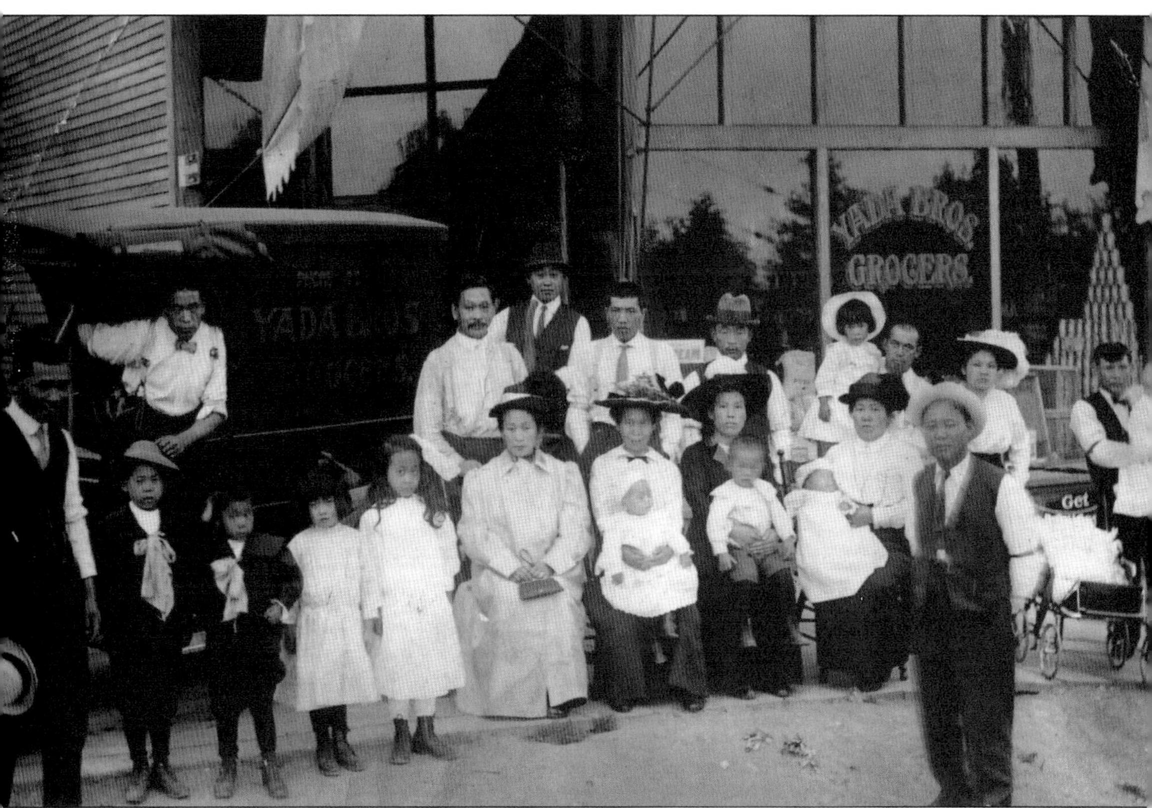

The Yada family and relatives are shown in this photograph taken around 1915 in front of their grocery store. The family operated the Yada Brothers Grocers on 701 East Fourth Street. Japanese Canadians were among North Vancouver's early settlers and owned businesses and land on the North Shore prior to World War II. In 1942 the Canadian government uprooted and relocated all Japanese Canadians in North Vancouver and other coastal areas, seizing their properties and belongings, including land and cars, for "protective measures."

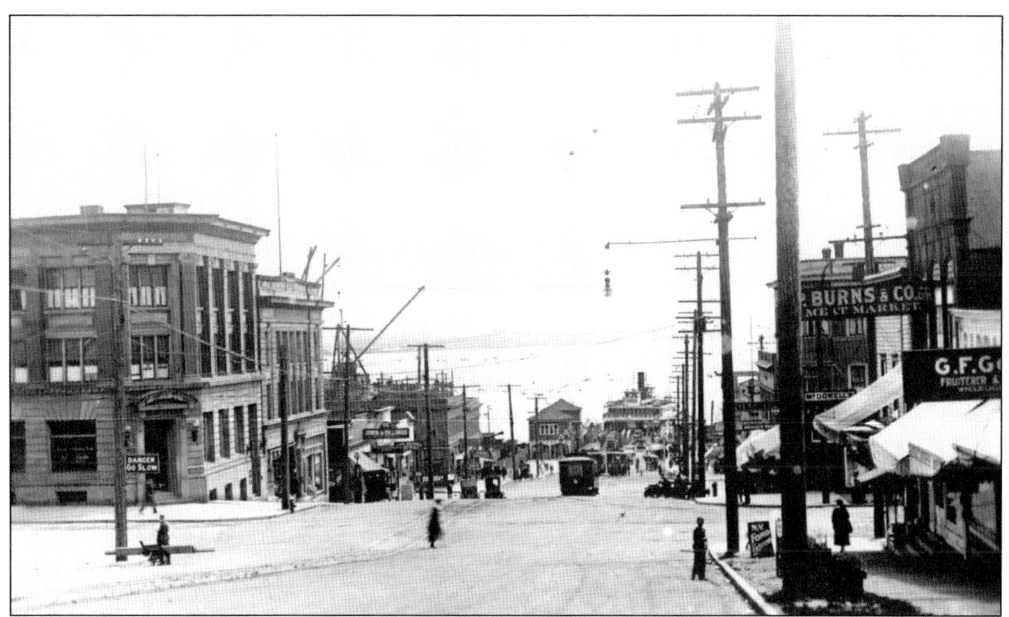

This 1919 photograph shows the Bank of Hamilton building and the Aberdeen Block on the left, looking southward on Lonsdale Avenue. The Bank of Hamilton building, built in 1910, stood out as a brick structure at a time when most structures were made from wood. North Vancouver ferry No. 3 can be seen at the ferry landing in the distance. Notice that automobiles were still driving on the left-hand side of the road in 1919, changing over in 1922. The building symbolizes an era confident of future prosperity. To the right of the bank is the Paine & McMillan Hardware Store. Co-owner John Paine is standing at left in the interior of the store in the photograph below.

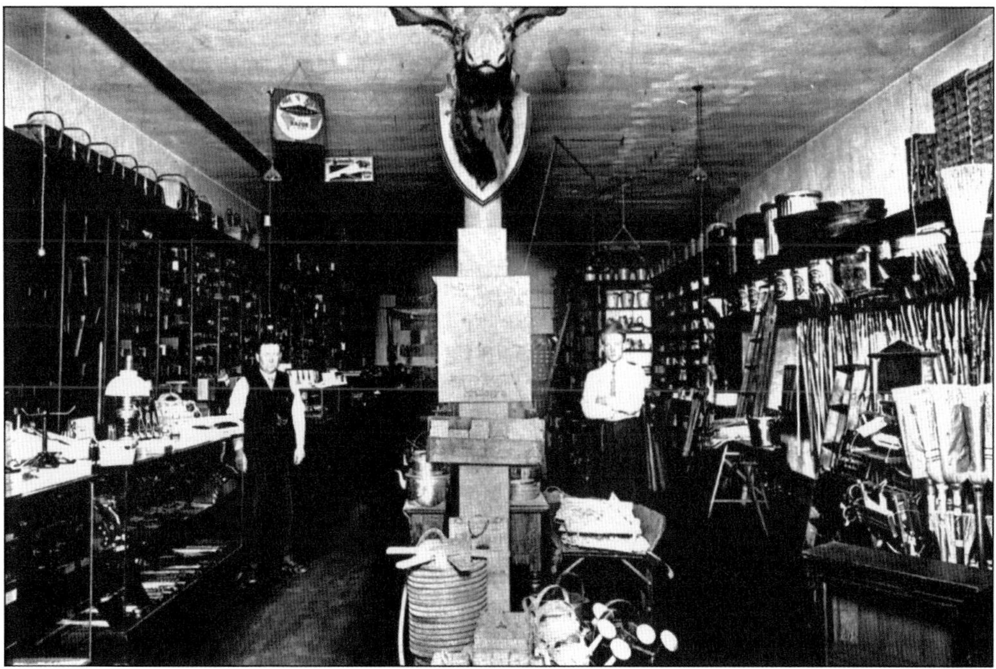

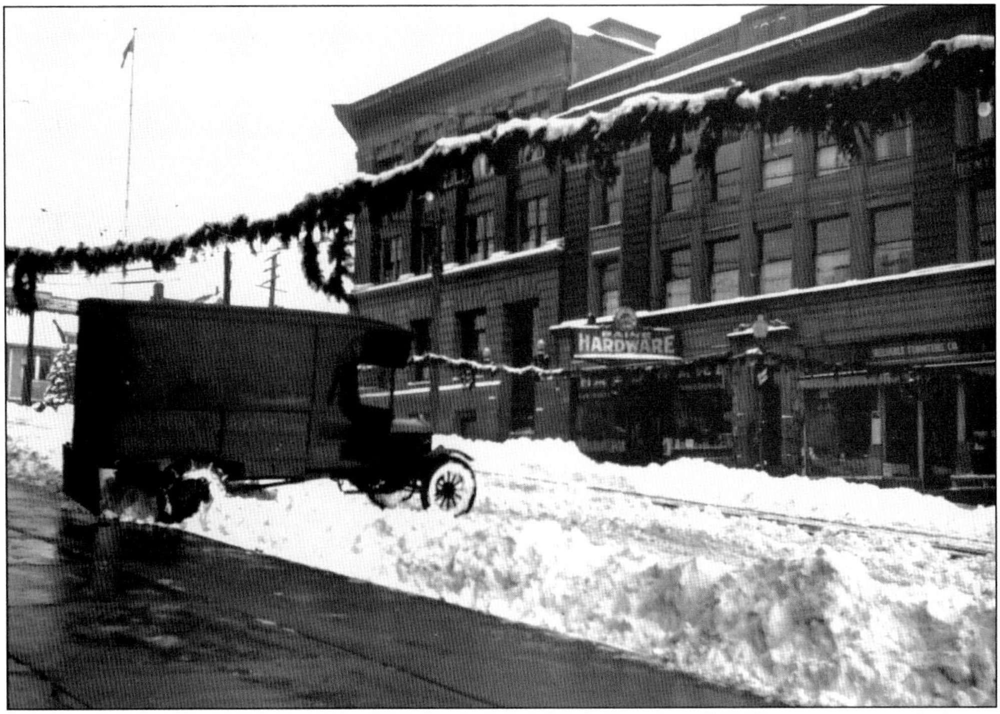

This December 12, 1927, photograph shows a Western Grocer's truck, advertising "Drink Great Western Tea You'll like it" on its side, in the snow in front of the Aberdeen Block. Seen in the background are (from left to right) the Canadian Bank of Commerce, Paine Hardware, and Reliable Furniture Company. The streetcar tracks have been snow ploughed, and snow-topped Christmas greenery decorates the street.

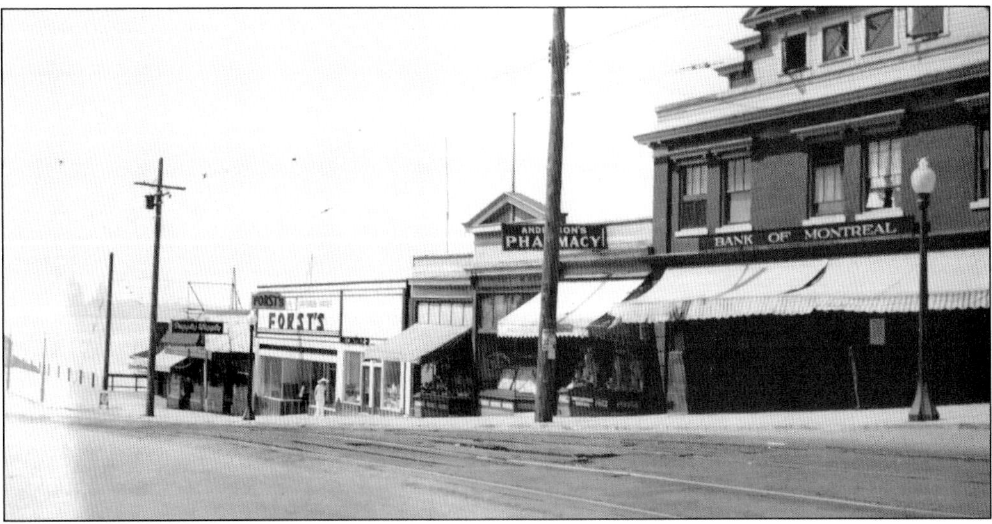

This picture, taken in the late 1930s, shows how seemingly close to the water's edge the Junction Block on the west side of Lonsdale Avenue was in years past. Forst's sold appliances, furniture, radios, and pianos on the same block. The business directories of the same period contain advertisements for Forst's stores in Vancouver (three locations), New Westminster, and this store at 66 Lonsdale Avenue.

Alfred Wallace, pictured here with his wife Eliza, founded Wallace Shipyards in Vancouver in 1894 and in North Vancouver in 1906. Alfred (Andy) Wallace started a shipbuilding and ship repair business on False Creek in Vancouver, specializing in the construction of small fishing boats. In 1905 the Wallace Shipyards Company was incorporated, and in 1906 a new shipyard was established in North Vancouver, located at the corner of Lonsdale Avenue and Esplanade, with the yard extending eastward along the waterfront. During and after World War I, the Wallace yard produced cargo vessels for the Imperial Munitions Board and the Canadian Government Merchant Marine. A scarcity of shipbuilding work during the interwar period contrasted with the shipbuilding output demanded by World War II, which led to a major expansion of the plant, shipbuilding operations, and workforce, including women workers.

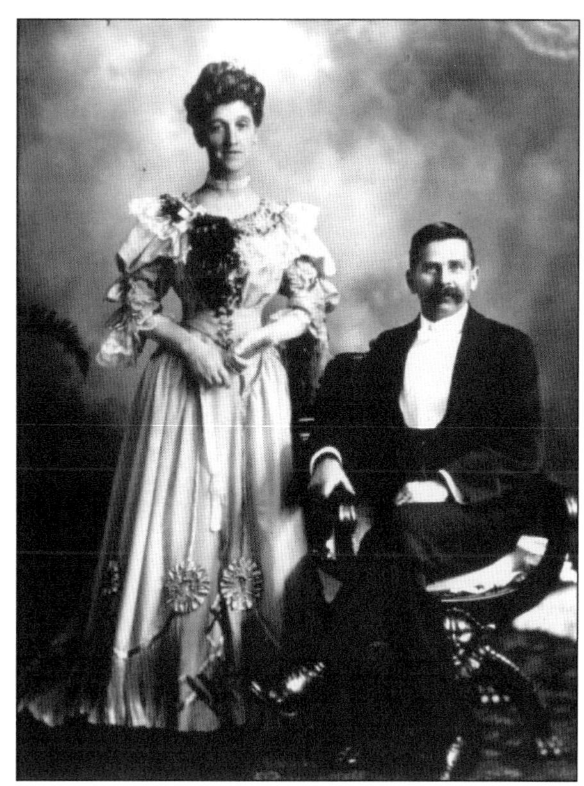

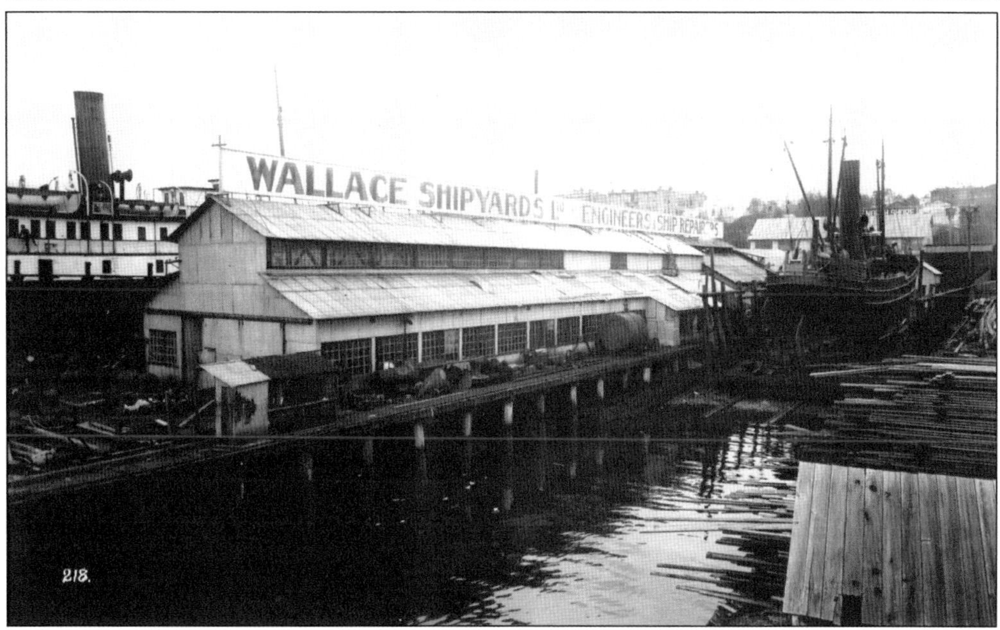

Wallace Shipyards is seen here in April 1916. The vessel *Ballena* is on the extreme left and the vessel at the right is possibly the *New England*. In its early years, Wallace Shipyards' core business was coastal vessel repairs. Two marine railways were built to haul out vessels that weighed up to 2000 tons. When World War I started, Wallace also received contracts to make explosive shells.

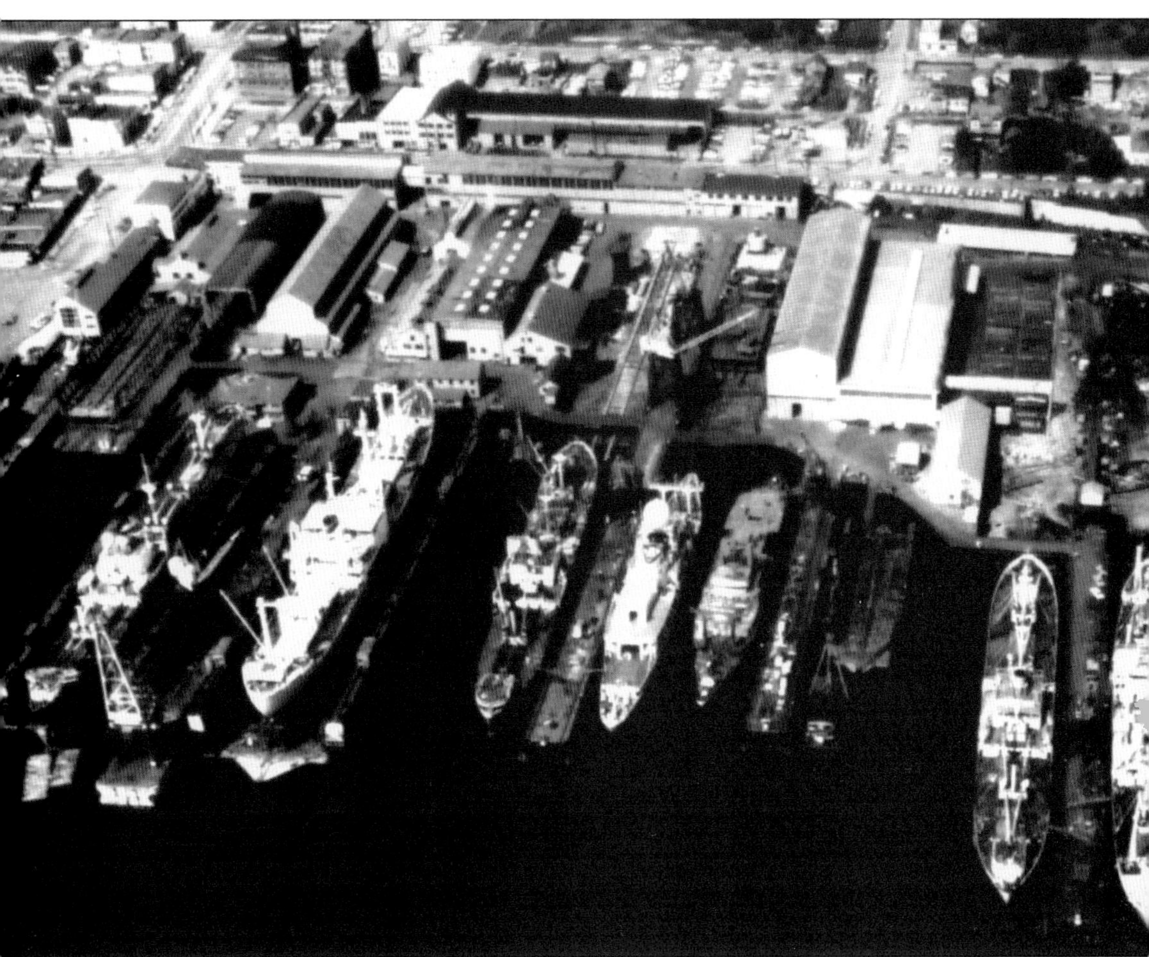

This *c.* 1947 picture shows an aerial view of Burrard Dry Dock grounds. With the outbreak of World War II, large contracts were awarded and a substantial expansion resulted; this was unique among communities in British Columbia and meant building of wartime housing and a substantial increase in North Vancouver's workforce population. The wartime houses had no basements to make their anticipated removals easier.

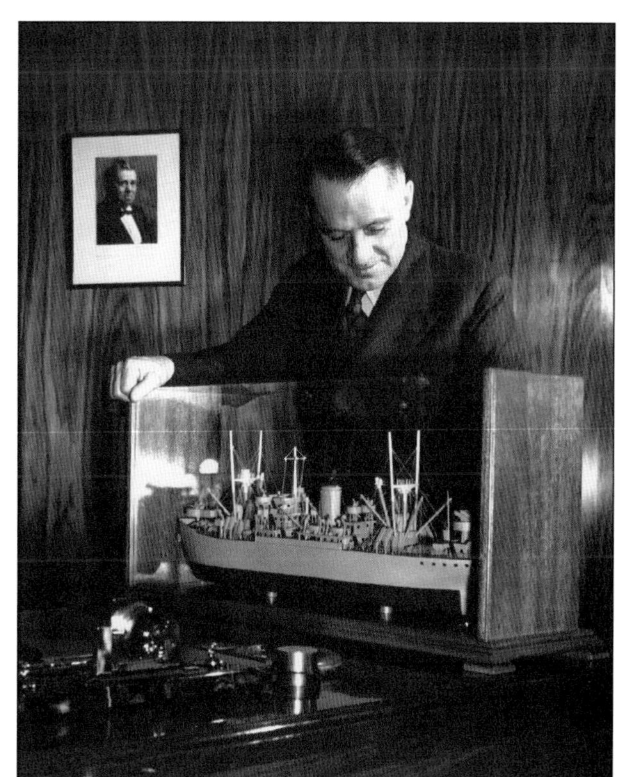

By 1943 when these photographs were taken, Clarence Wallace, seen with model of a 10,000-ton maintenance ship, had been president of Burrard Dry Dock since 1929. A picture of his father Alfred (Andy) is on the wall behind him. The Victory ship *Fort Wallace* was launched the same year.

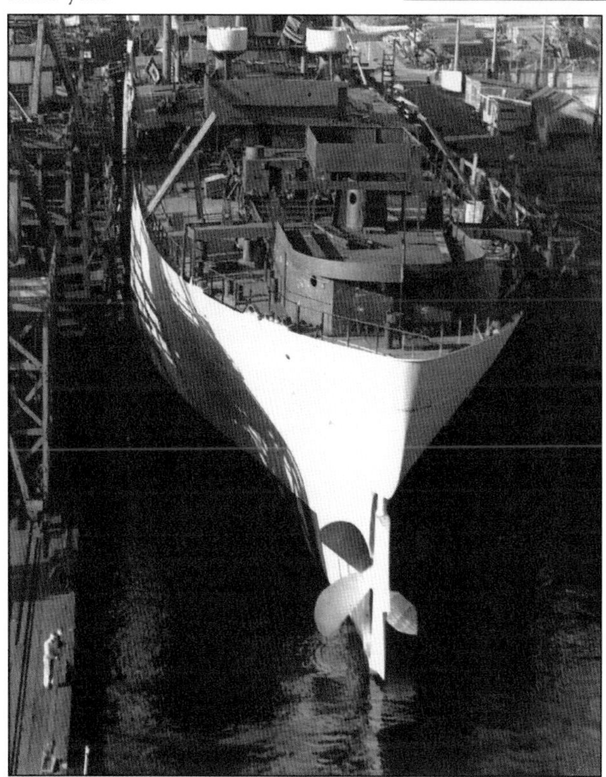

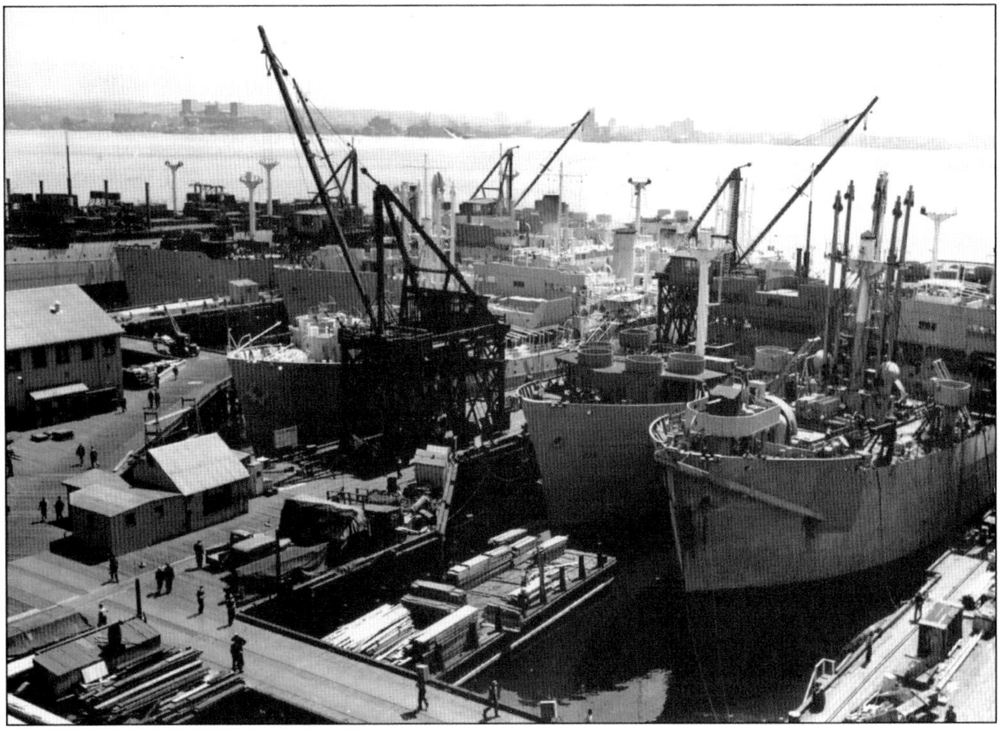

Three Victory ships, HMS *Girdle Ness*, HMS *Dodman Point*, and HMS *Fife Ness* are seen under construction at Burrard Dry Dock in 1945. All Victory ships built at the Burrard Dry Dock were made to the same design, with minor modifications, as the U.S. Liberty ships.

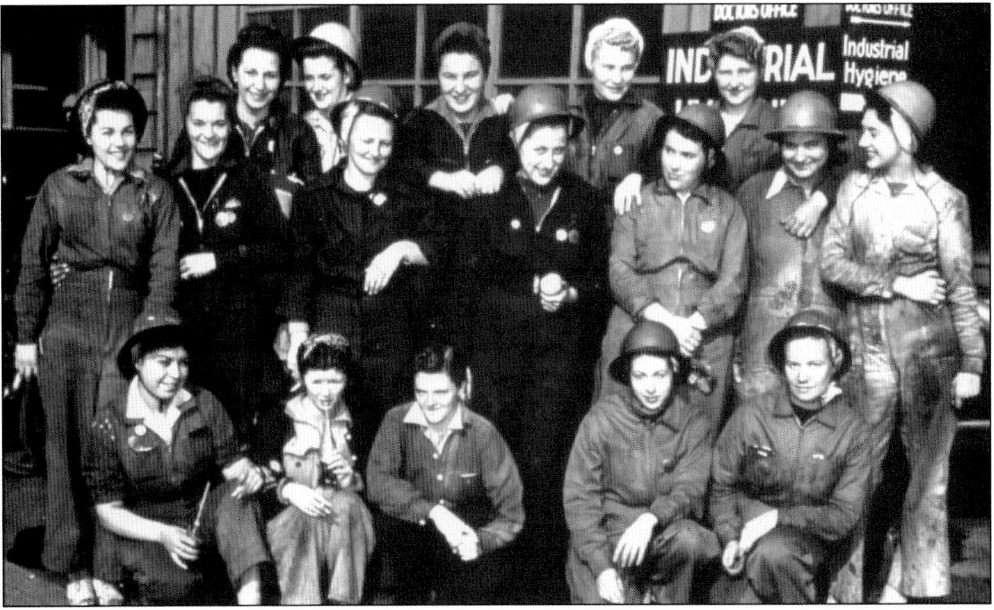

These women shipyard workers, around 1944, at Burrard Dry Dock include Evelyn Pearce (later McDonald) first row, third from left; Lillian Matheson Rance, third row, second from left; Gertie Todd, third row, second from right; and Anne Delphine Horvath (later West), second row, second from right.

Women in this c. 1945 photograph are (from left to right) Maria Bouvier, Norma Courtray, and Laurette Bonneville. Behind them, across east Esplanade from Burrard Dry Dock, is the Syndicate Block. At the height of its activity during World War II, the Burrard Dry Dock and associated subsidiaries employed as many as 14,000 men and women.

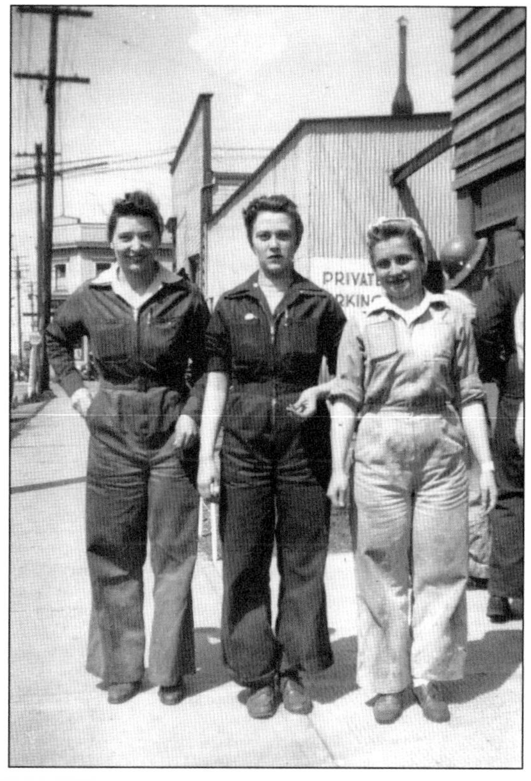

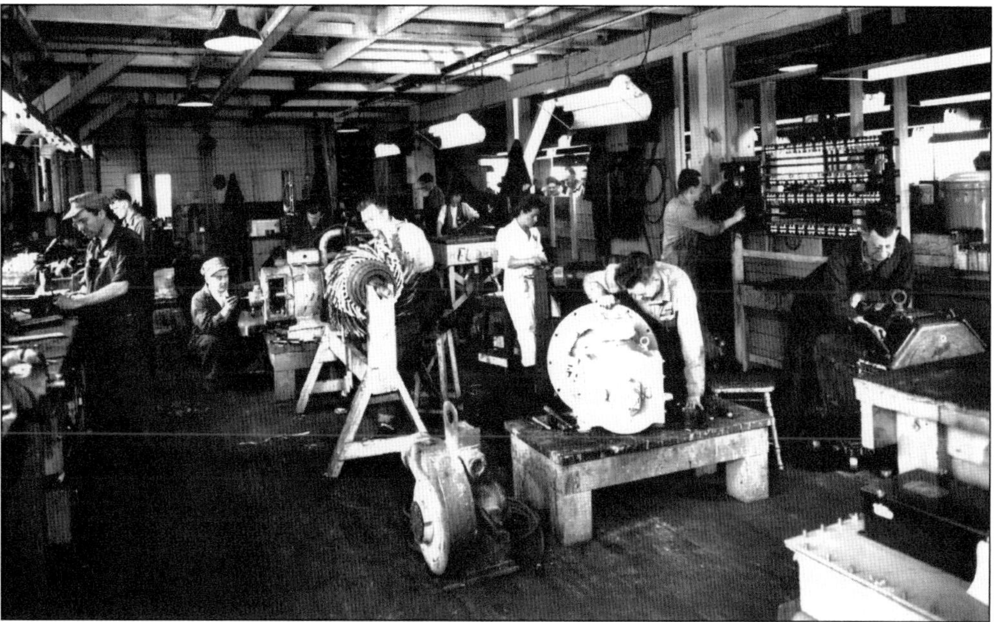

In June 1945 armature winding and motor repairs were done in this electric shop at Burrard Dry Dock by (from left to right) Dave Coward, Ralph Pithart, Henry Brewar, George Mason, Percy Ruffle, Alex Russell, Ellen Hutson, Dave Hanson, and John Wallace reseating brushes on commutator. Gus Hassell is the man winding the big armature for a winch motor, while Tommy Laurie inspects a ventilator motor.

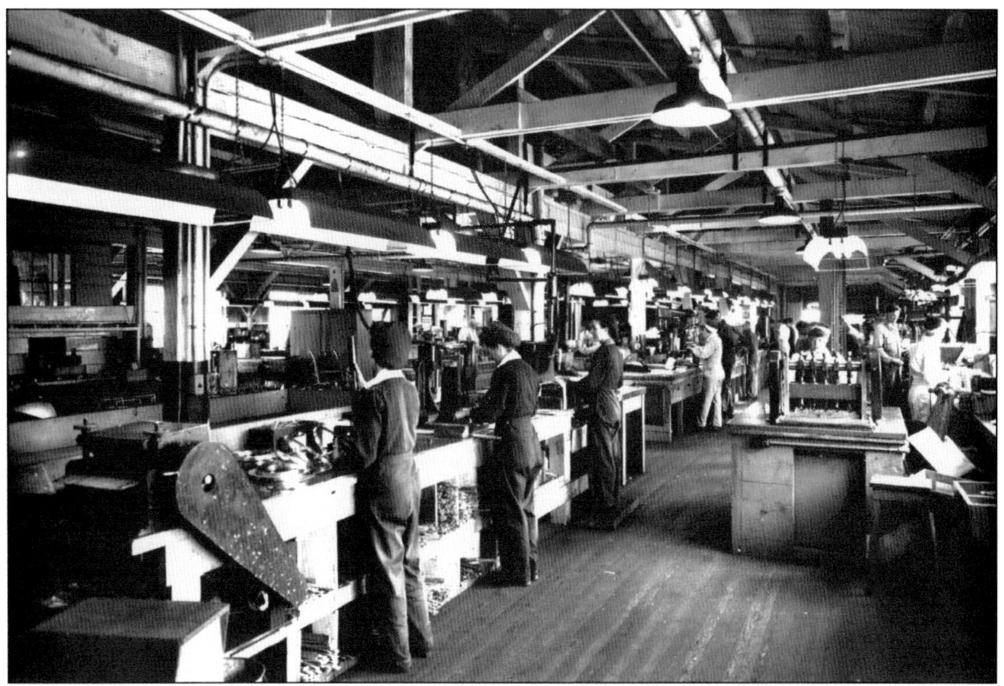

In July 1945 the Electrical Shop is seen staffed by women, with (from left to right) Val Attwood, Peggy Milstead, and Sue Ferguson making straps for electric cable while Gladys Conway, further down, is drilling fixtures. To the right, Jonas Wallin and Betty Trythall are busy at switchboard work while Jean McKay punches straps on the punch machine.

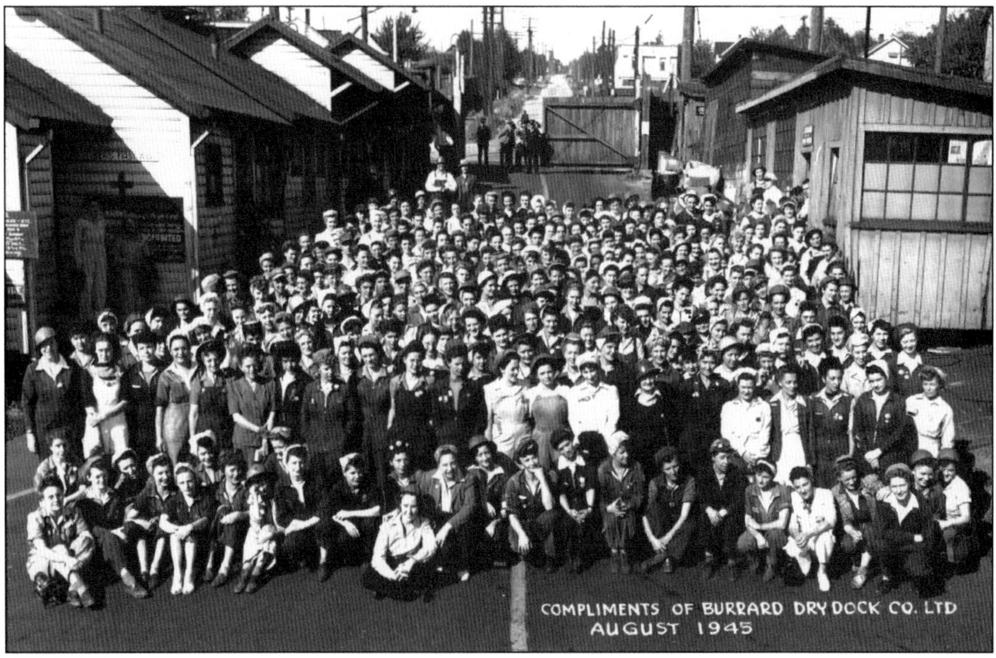

Female employees of Burrard Dry Dock are seen here in a photograph from August 1945. Women on the North Shore generally embraced the opportunity to work at the shipyards, something that had not been possible in earlier years.

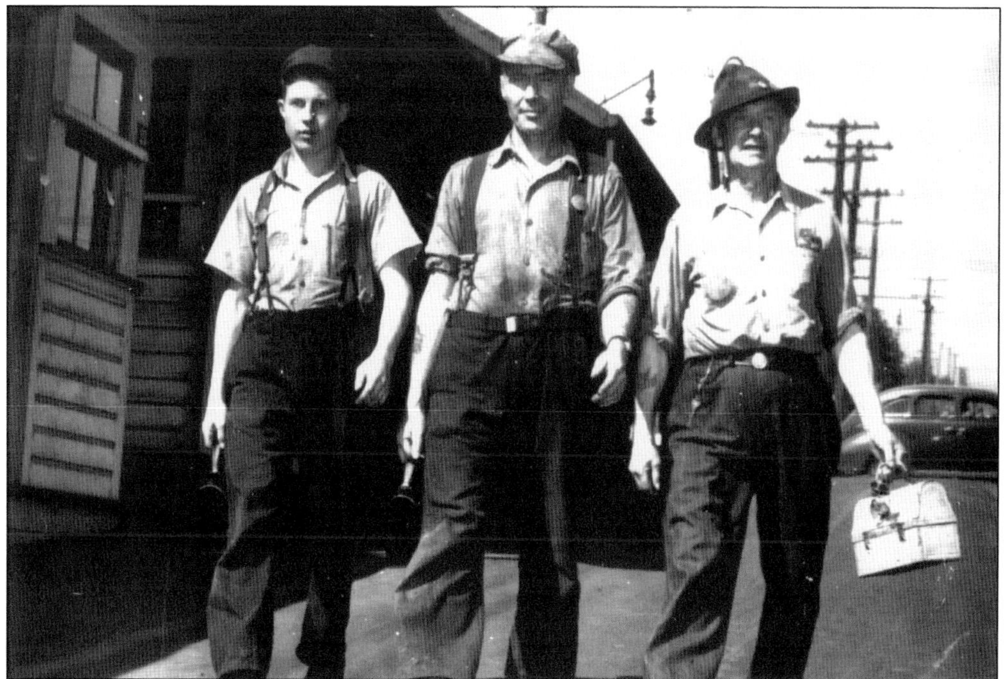

Burrard Dry Dock offered employment to men across different age groups. Three generations of Millers are seen here going to work at Burrard Dry Dock during World War II. They are (from left to right) George (fitter's helper), Harry Jr. (fitter's helper), and Harry Sr. (caulker). The photograph was taken in August 1944, just inside the shipyard entrance at the foot of St. Georges Street.

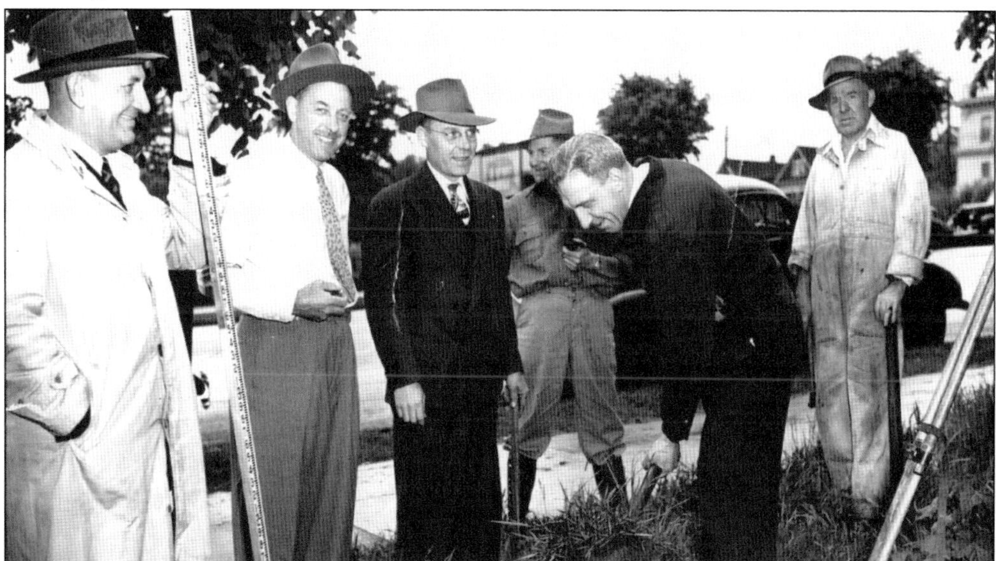

The North Vancouver Chamber of Commerce began in 1906 as the North Vancouver Board of Trade. In 1948, 320 Lonsdale Avenue became the location for the first Board of Trade office. Present in this sod-turning event are (from left to right) Capt. John Cates, G. Jardine, Jack Suttis, and Murdo Frazer. The Board of Trade changed its name to North Vancouver Chamber of Commerce in 1961.

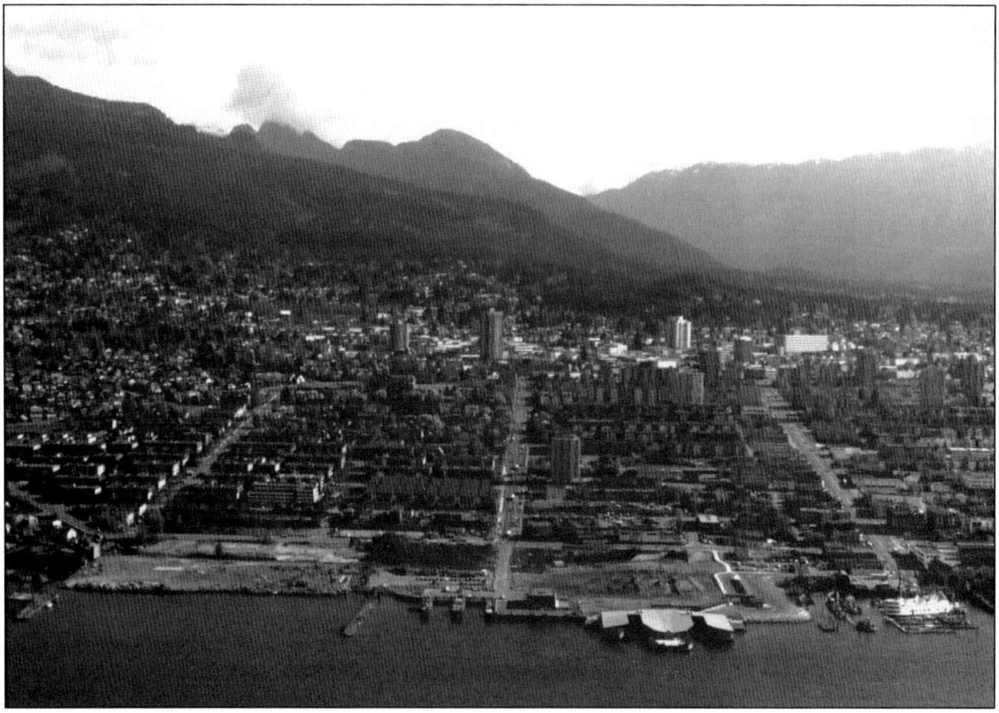

Upon ferry No. 4's last trip across the Burrard Inlet in August 1958, Lower Lonsdale lost its income-generating traffic and remained mostly vacant for a generation. This aerial photograph, taken around 1977, shows the beginnings of the rise of Lower Lonsdale with the provisioning of the Seabus. Ferry No. 5 was now the Seven Seas restaurant at the foot of Lonsdale Avenue. Construction of the Insurance Corporation of British Columbia (ICBC) headquarters in 1981, pictured here, followed by the opening of Lonsdale Quay Hotel and Market, in 1986, next to the Seabus, provided a needed boost to the Lower Lonsdale economy.

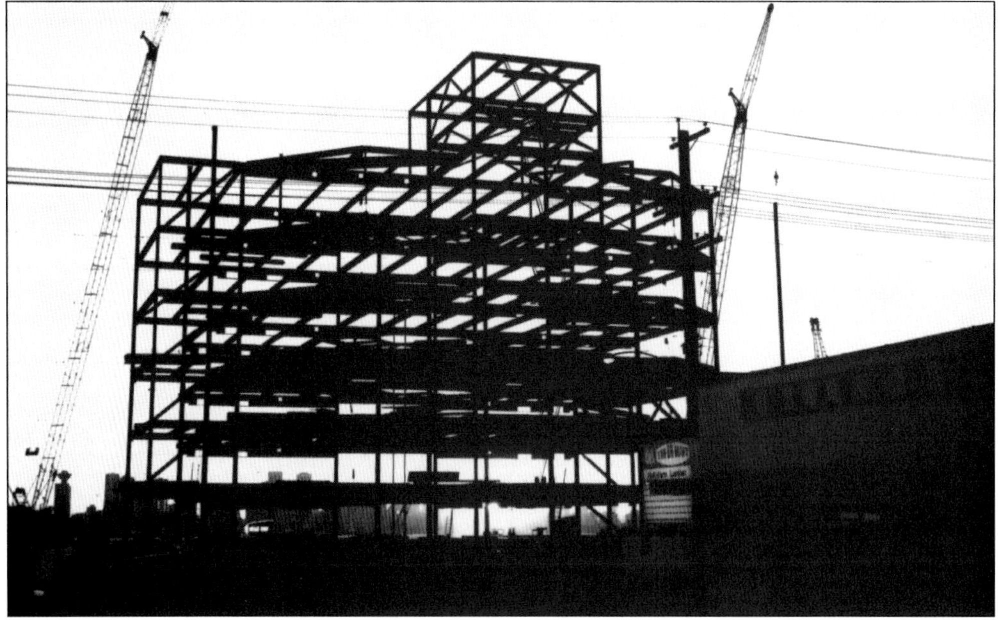

Four

PARKS

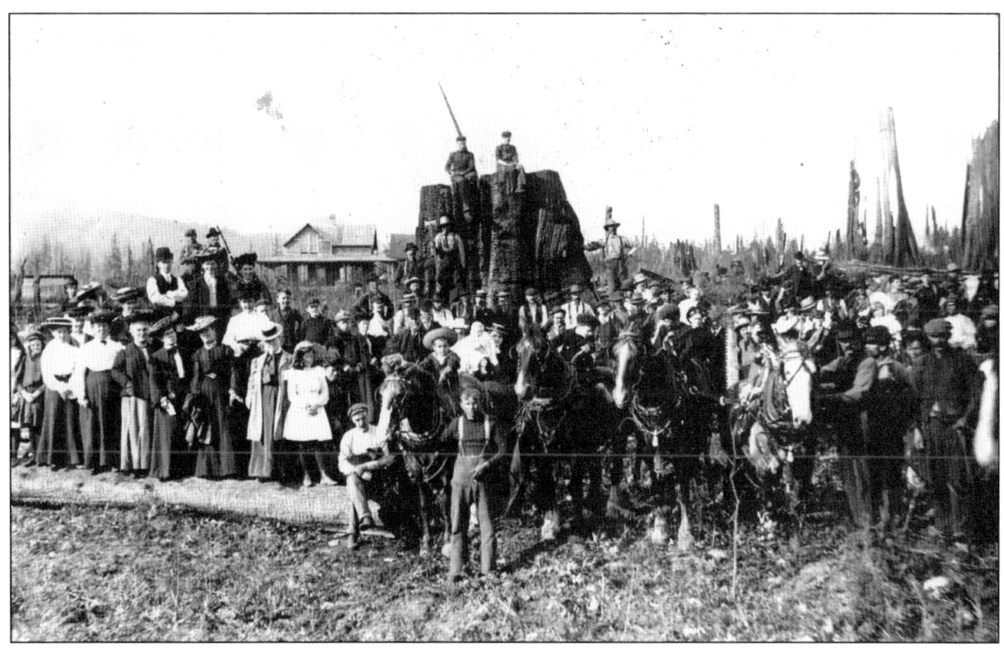

In 1905 the North Vancouver Land and Improvement Company wrote to the municipal council stating that it would donate half of Victoria Park provided that the balance was also donated by the other landowner, who was none other than Alfred St. George Hamersley, who agreed to donate the other half. A volunteer clearance bee was held to prepare the land for park use. Horses were brought in to help with the work. The Diplock brothers sit on the large stump.

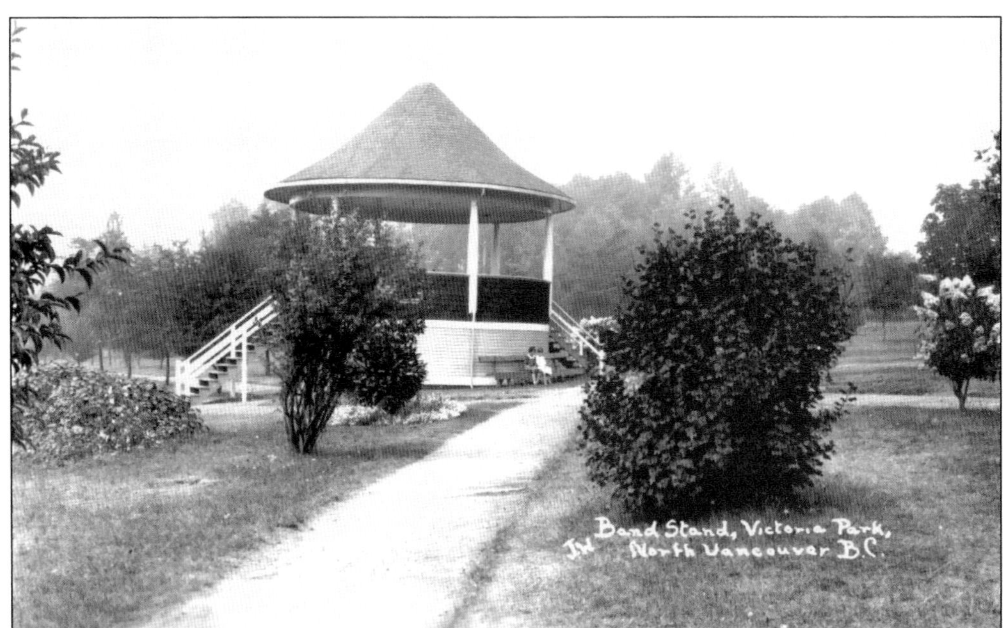

By the 1920s Victoria Park had matured into a green and welcoming area, complete with bandstand. Today Victoria Park, as shown in the May 31, 2009, photograph below, forms a key component of the "green necklace" of City parks and greenways with well-maintained greenery and trees. Back in the early part of the 20th century, a "quadrangle of boulevards" was being advertised by real estate businesses and these boulevards or parks survive as Ottawa Gardens, Victoria Park, Grand Boulevard, and Mahon Park.

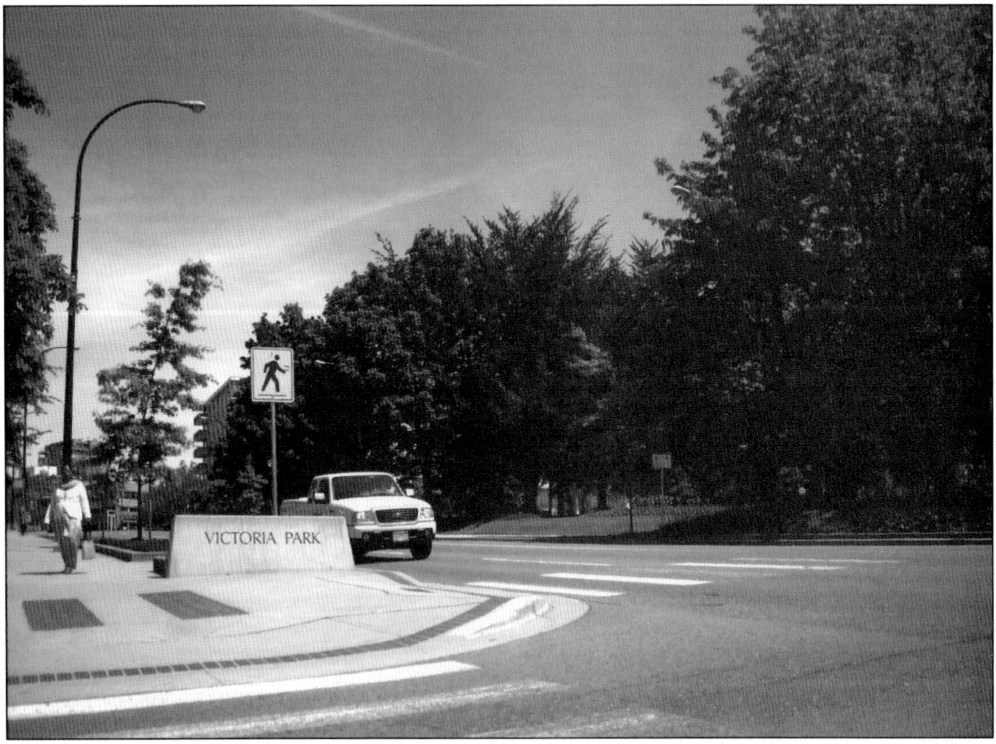

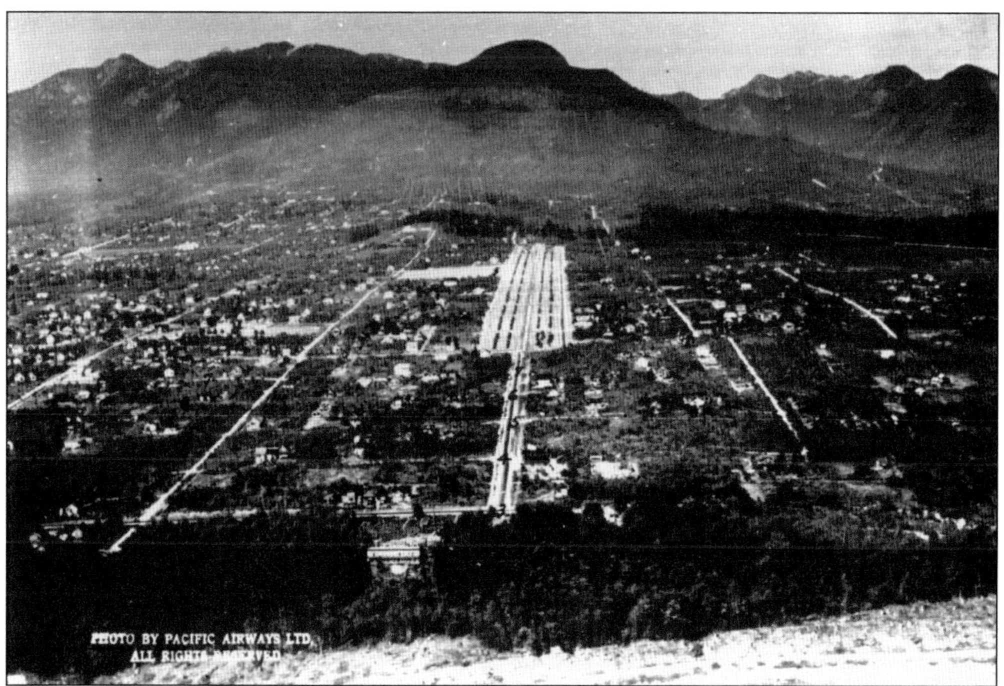

The clearing of Grand Boulevard began in 1906. The developer was North Vancouver Land and Improvement Company. The Boulevard was said to be to North Vancouver "what the Champs Elysees is to Paris." Grand Boulevard boasted a length of nearly one mile and was approximately 346 feet wide. Land promoters believed Grand Boulevard was to be Burrard Inlet's leading residential area, attracting the wealthy and the influential. (Courtesy of Pacific Air.)

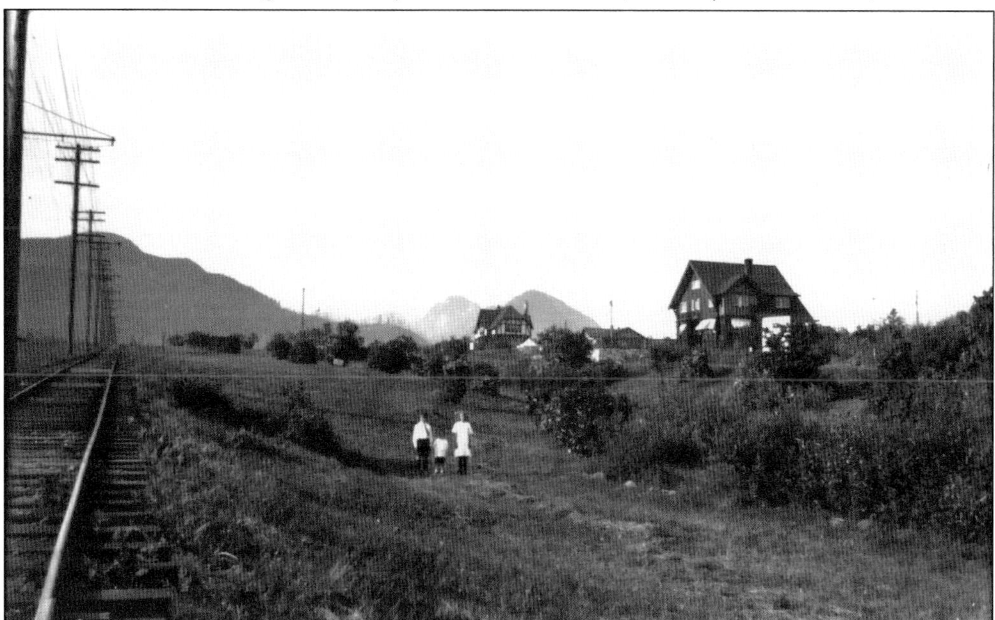

The Grand Boulevard view looking north from East Keith Road around 1915 shows three unidentified children near three houses against the backdrop of the North Shore mountains. Streetcar tracks for the Lynn Valley line can be seen on the left.

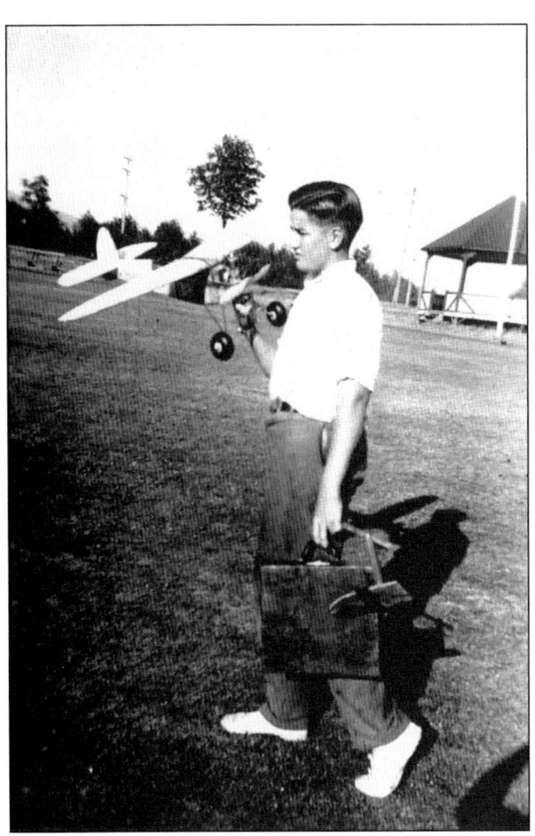

Mike Calloway poses in Grand Boulevard Park, a perfect place to fly his line control model plane. The park bandstand can be seen behind him in this 1941 photograph.

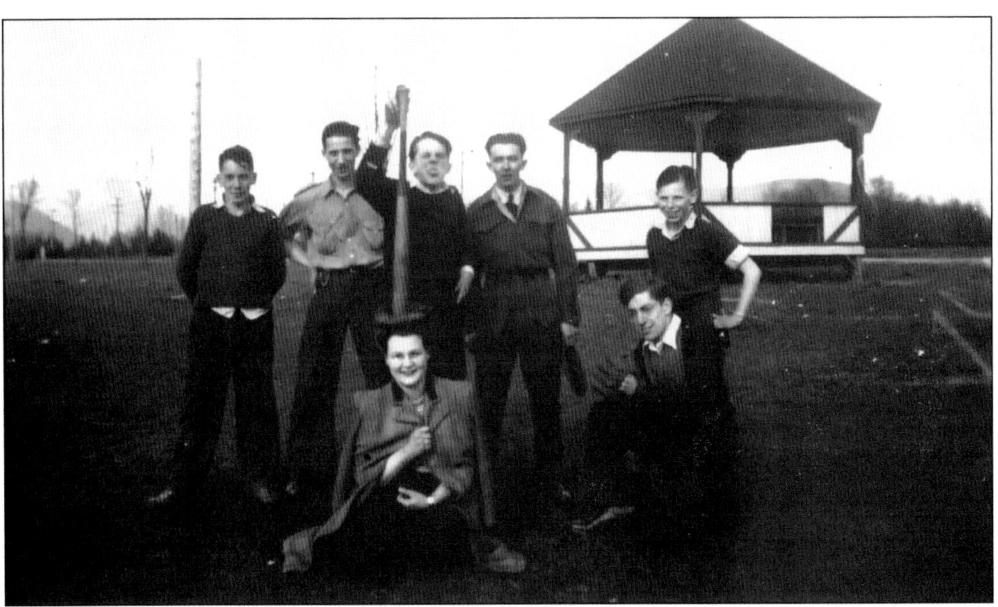

Members of a scrub baseball team have an enjoyable time posing for this photograph, taken around 1945, in Boulevard Park, north of Thirteenth Street. They are, from left to right, (sitting) Lillian Billesberger and Ken Dawson; (standing) unidentified, Paul Gaudreault, Maurice Jones, and two unidentified boys. The bandstand can be seen in background.

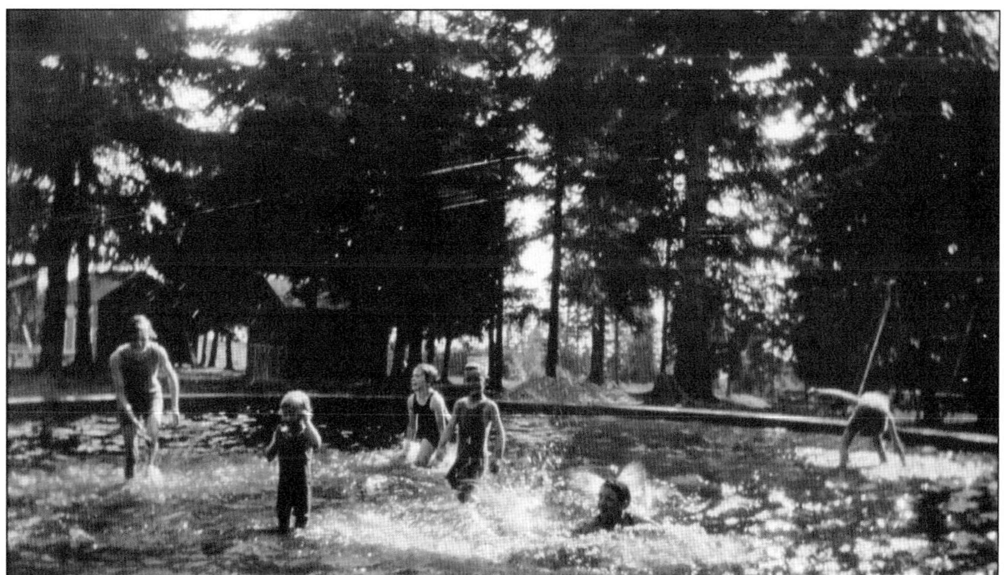

Around 1905, Lonsdale neighbourhood's premier park, Mahon Park, also acquired from North Vancouver's Land and Improvement Company, was developed. Later an open wading pool was constructed. In these pictures, taken in the 1920s, children and friends are splashing around in the pool and slide.

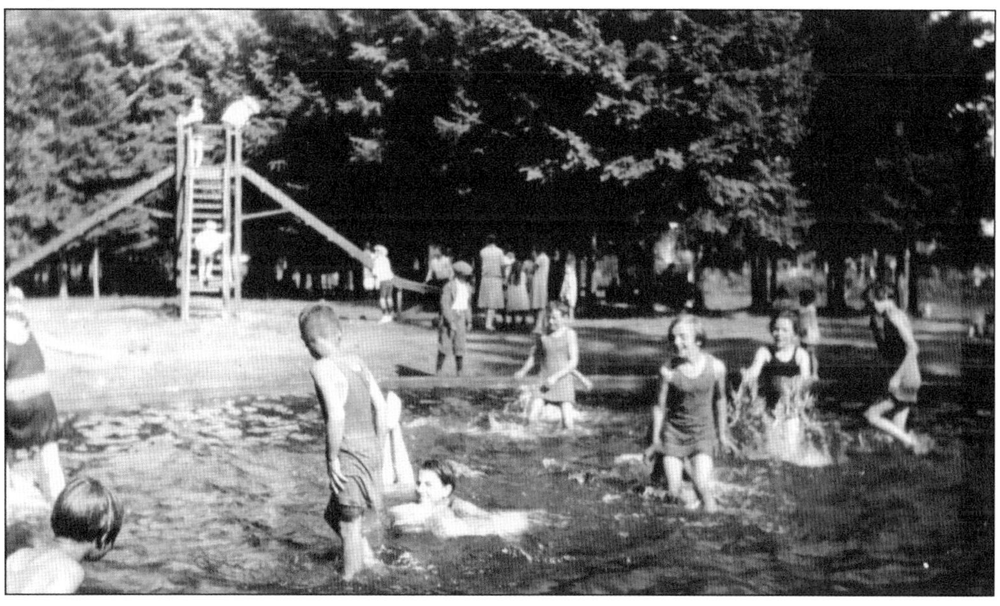

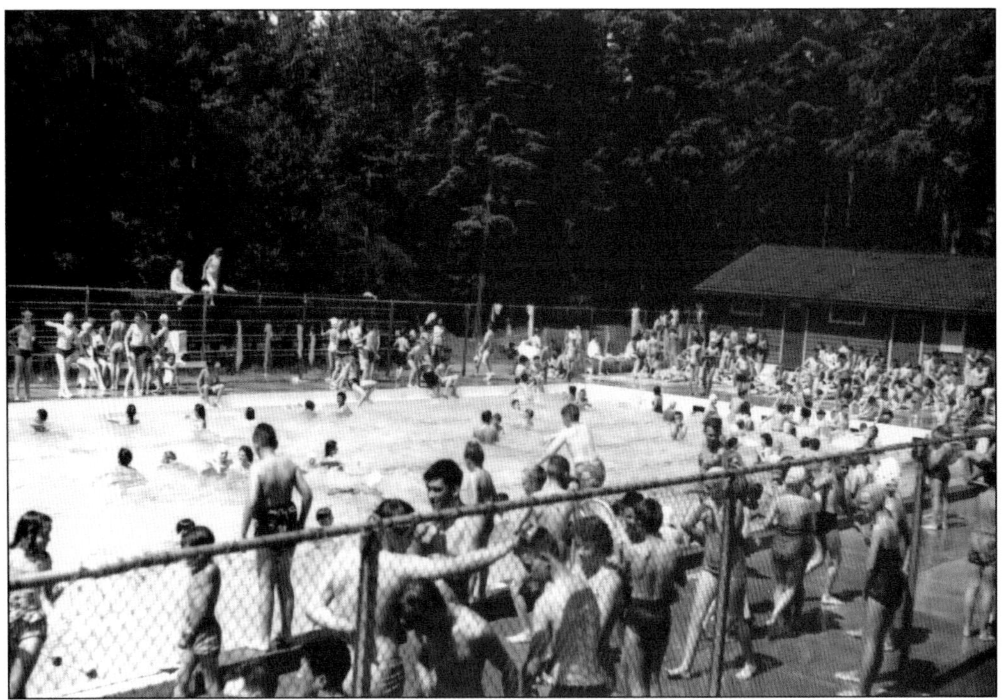

A large crowd of people is cooling off in Mahon Park Pool in 1960. The pool does not exist today and has been converted to horseshoe pitching pits. However, kids often enjoy a modern water park on hot summer days.

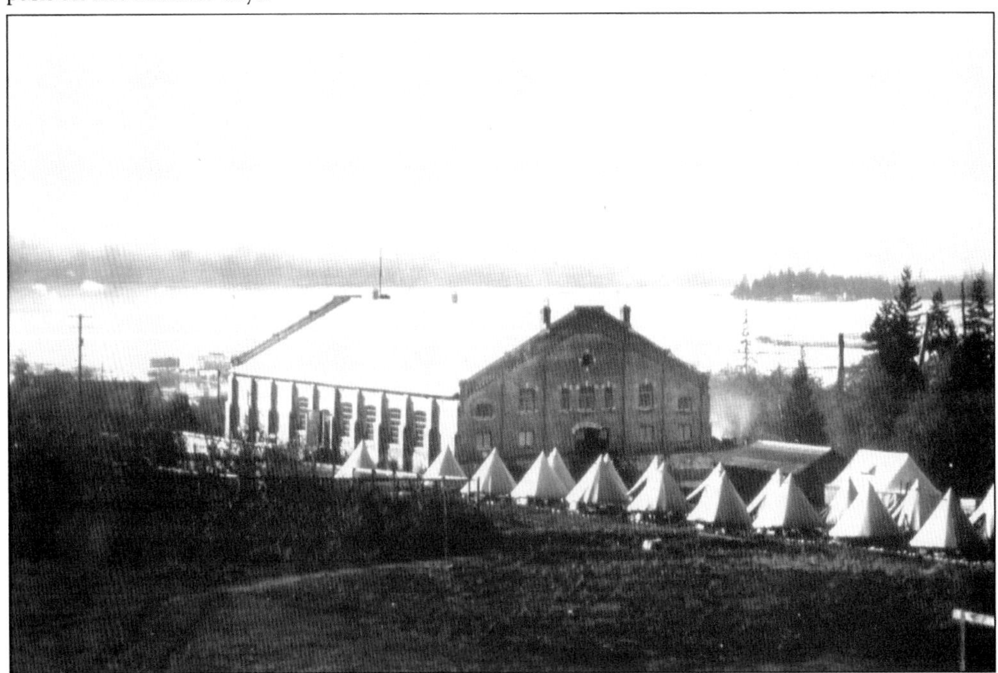

This photograph, taken during World War I between 1916 and 1918, shows the drill hall and tents at the headquarters of the 6th Field Company in Mahon Park. Vancouver can be seen in the background across Burrard Inlet. The view is from Mahon Park's grandstand.

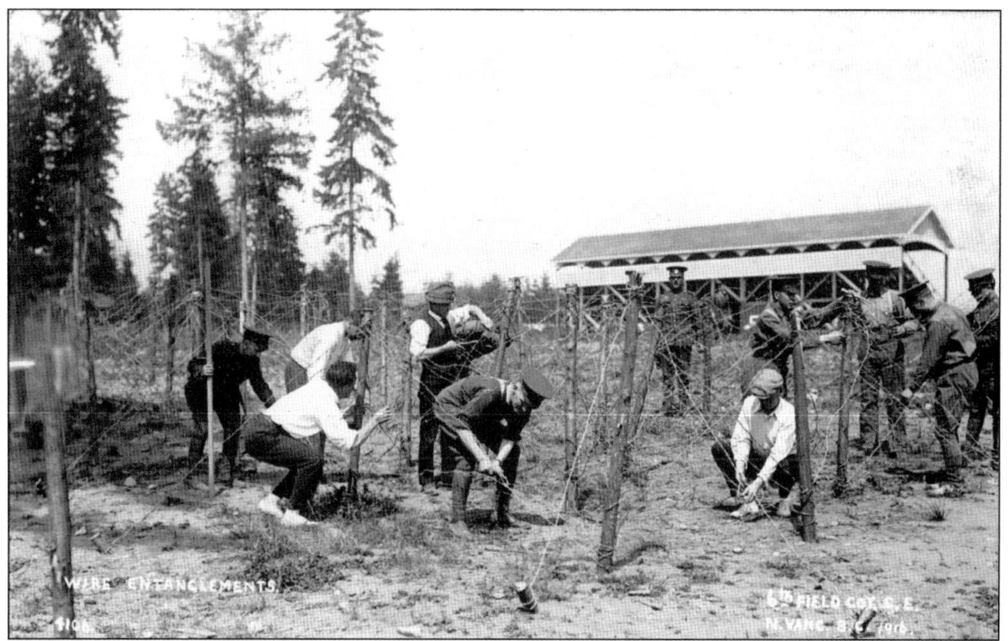

With Mahon Park Grandstand in the background, men from the 6th Field Company arrange wire entanglements in 1916. The 6th Field Engineer Squadron, Canadian Engineers, then known as the 6th Field Company, was formed on February 1, 1911. Based in North Vancouver, the first enrolment was in 1912. In 1947, the unit was renamed the 6th Field Squadron, Royal Canadian Engineers. Between 1955 and 1975 the Squadron was part of the militia. Since 1975, the unit has been known as the 6th Field Engineer Squadron. In peacetime, the unit maintained a state of readiness to assist civilian authorities, usually during floods and other natural disasters.

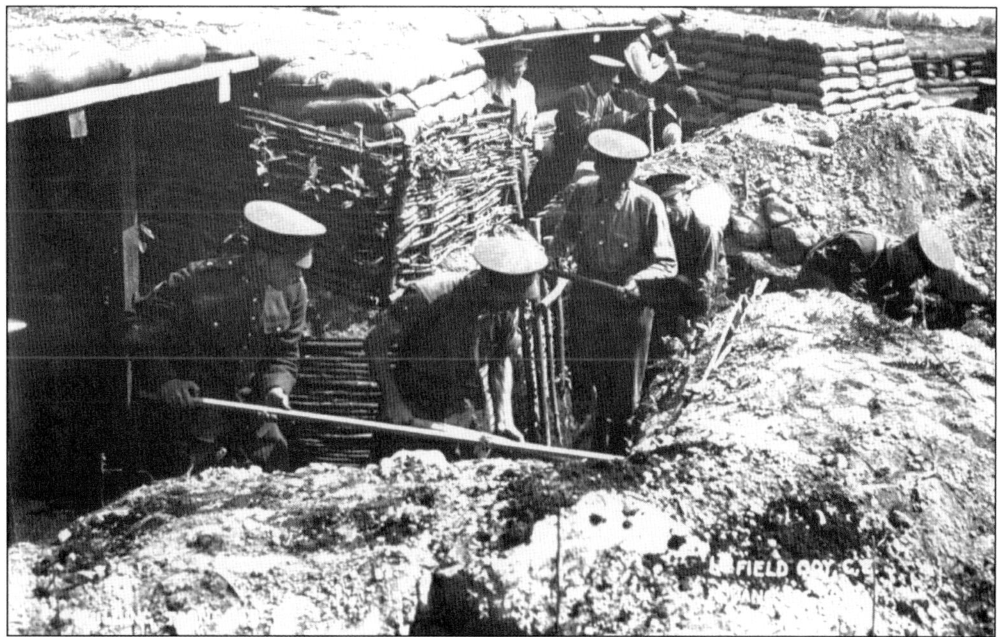

The 6th Field Company served in Europe during both world wars. In this photograph, engineers are building and examining mock trenches in Mahon Park in 1916.

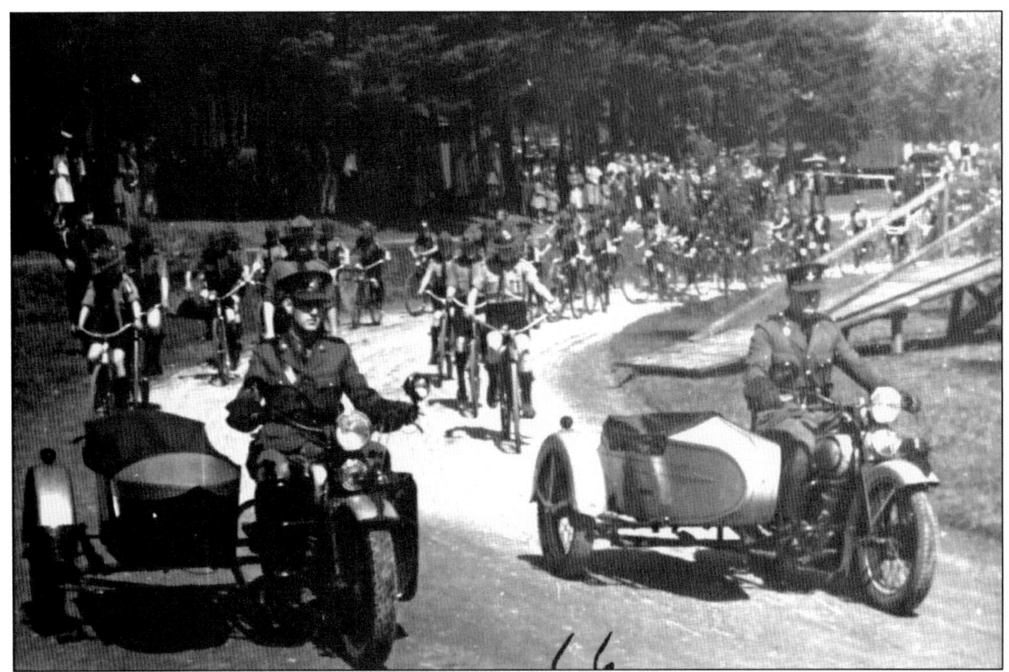

Motorcycles with sidecars are followed by Boy Scouts on bicycles in this North Vancouver Air Raid Precautions (ARP) Parade in Mahon Park on May 18, 1941. The ARP was created in response to the perceived threat of a Japanese coastal air attack during World War II and consisted of volunteers. Also, No. 3 Company, Canadian Women's Training Corps (CWTC) members with telephones are seen at ARP headquarters in the park during a demonstration on the same day.

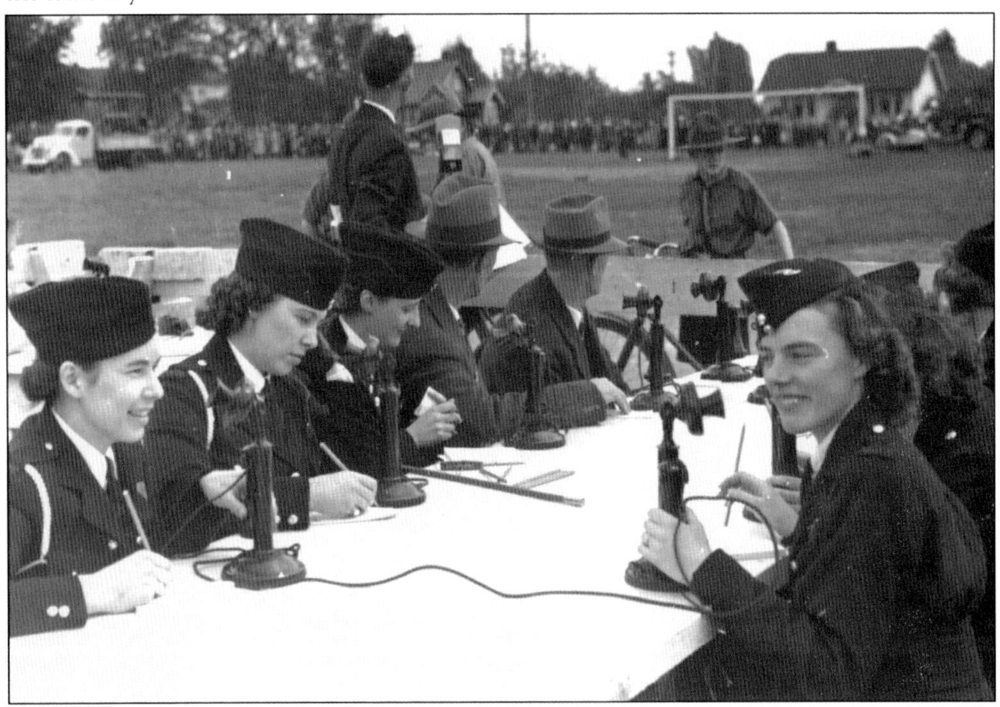

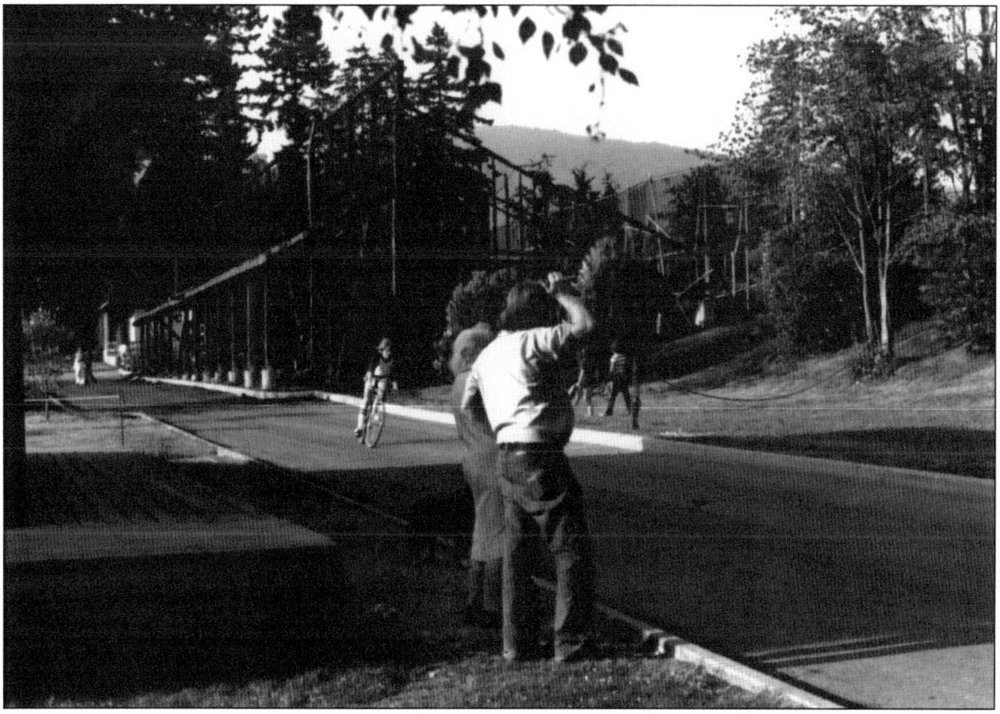

The grandstand remains can be barely seen after a fire in the 1970s. The first home of the North Shore Museum situated in the PGE station stands on the left.

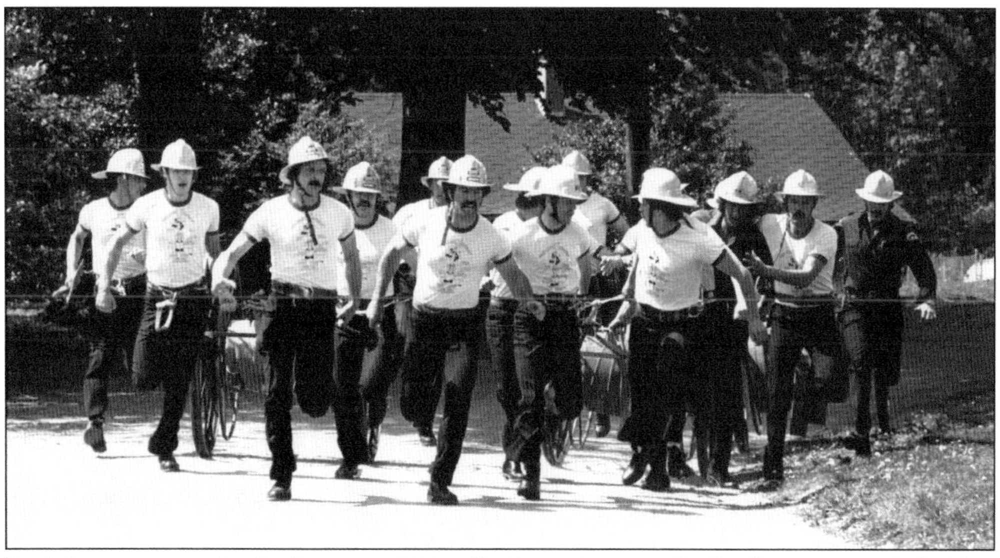

Firefighters compete in the first annual Hose Reel race between the fire departments of the City of North Vancouver, District of North Vancouver, and West Vancouver, held on May 15, 1982, in Mahon Park.

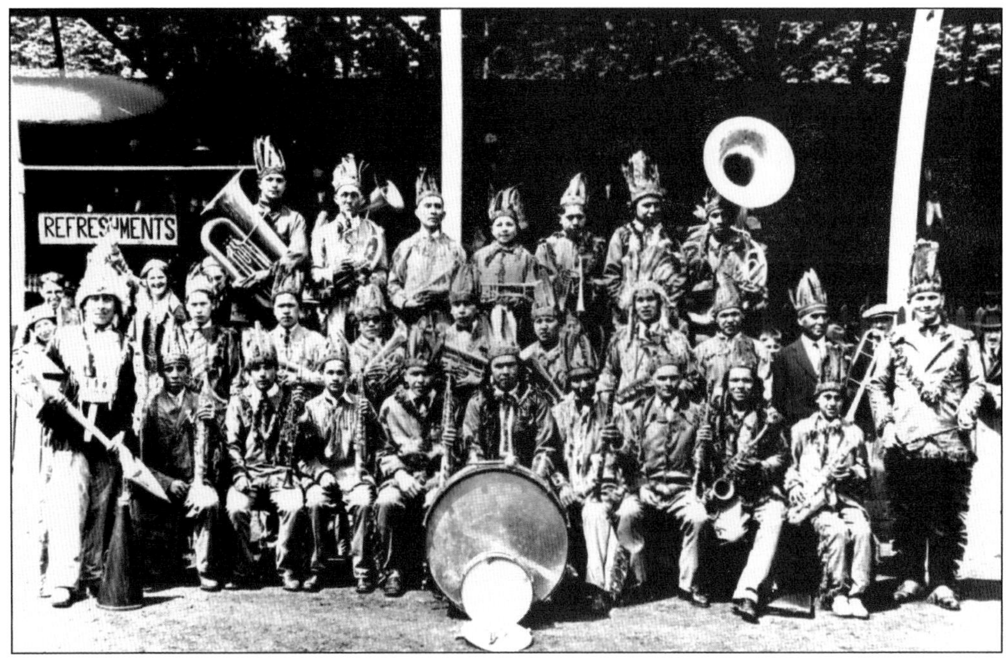

Squamish Indian Band Orchestra members had their photograph taken at the time of a performance in 1928 at Mahon Park. They are identified as, from left to right, (first row) Chief Joe Mathias, Earl Newman, Joe Johnson, Tim Moody, Bobby Baker, Stan Joseph, Gus Band, Fred Johnson, Charlie Newman, Ralph Band, and Andy Paull; (second row) George Joe, Herman Lewis, Ralph Lewis, Speedy Guss, Stephen George, Chief Moses Joseph, Dominic Baker, and Daniel Paull; (third row) Simon Baker, Tommy Johnson, Henry Jack, Manney Paull, Joe Martin, Duck Mack, and Joe Harry. Along with men who were or would become political representatives (Chief Mathias, Simon Baker, Tim Moody, Moses Joseph) are the young men who became part of the workforce in the lumber, industry, waterfront, and fisheries.

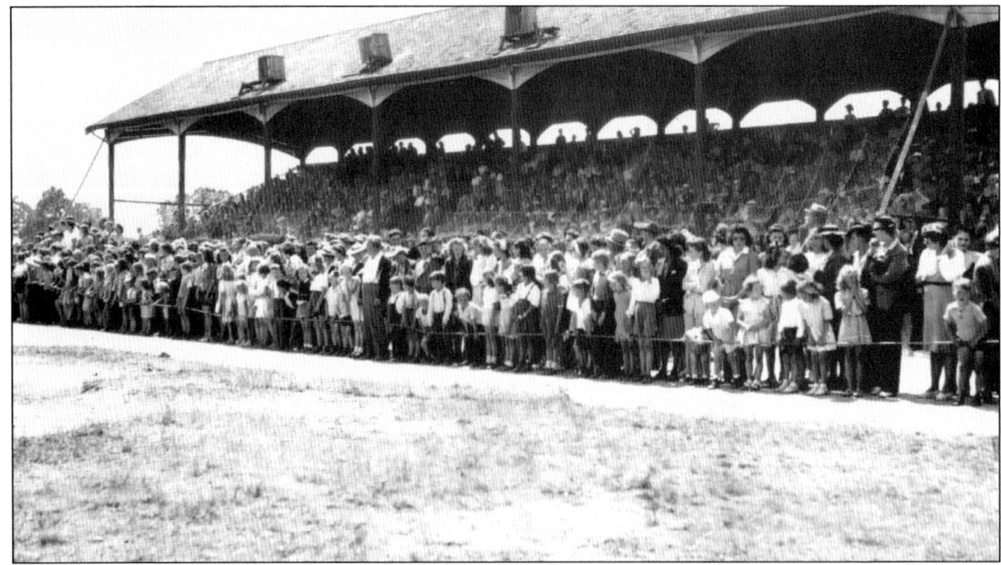

Throughout the 1920s, 1930s, and 1940s, many of North Vancouver's celebrations were held in Mahon Park. In this picture, a large crowd is watching the Kinsmen Carnival.

Five

CIVIC AND CULTURAL INSTITUTIONS

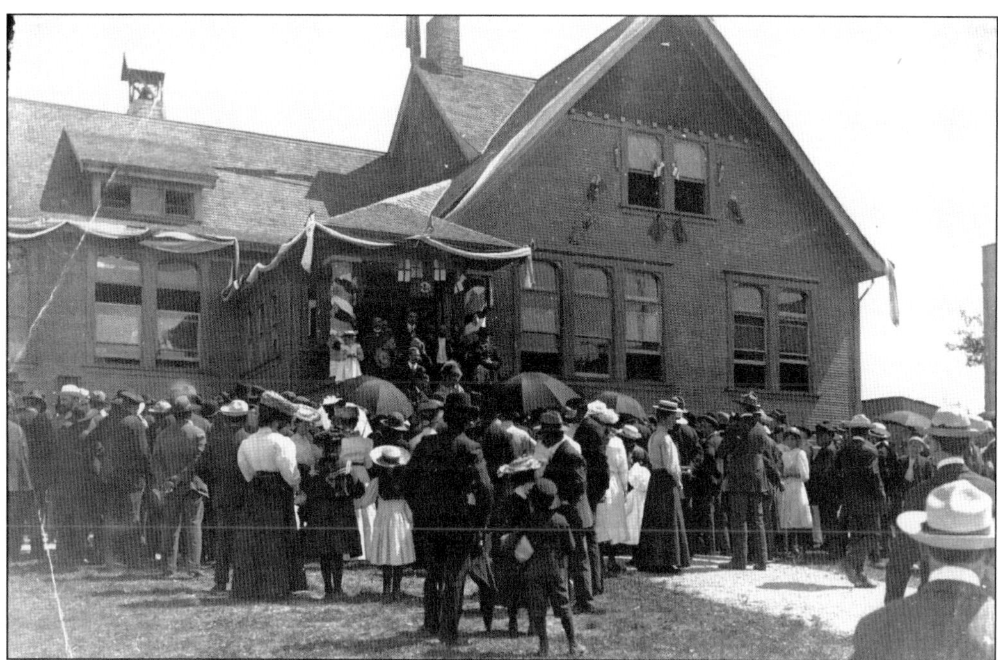

Men, women, and children gather in front of the District municipal hall, later the first city hall, at First Street and Lonsdale Avenue (around 1906). Since incorporation of the District municipality in 1891, the council meetings had been held in Vancouver. In 1903, the municipality built this hall at the northeast corner of Lonsdale and First; it became the city hall in 1907. Chief Joe Capilano of the Squamish Nation can be seen wearing a fur hat on the steps. At about the same time this photograph was taken, Chief Capilano, travelled to meet King Edward VII in Buckingham Palace.

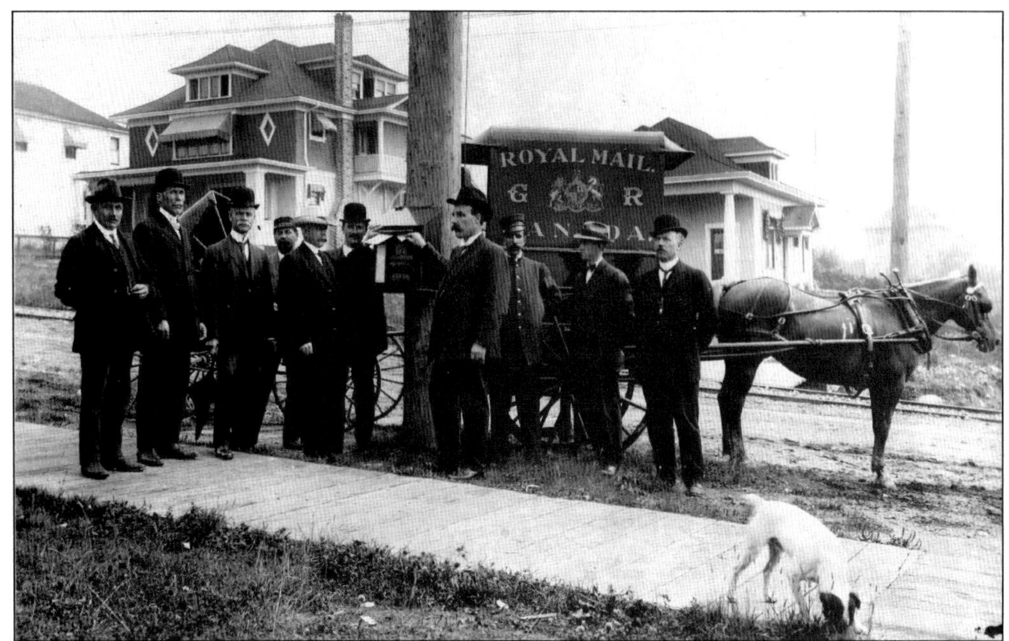

Dignitaries and the royal mail wagon assembled outside Irwin & Billings first office on Lonsdale Avenue and Fifth Street for this 1910 photograph to mark the first letter mailed in a street letterbox in North Vancouver. Identified people (from left to right) are Mr. Keene, Alderman George Macrae, post office inspector Greenfield, George Sugden of Lynn Valley, City mayor W. H. May, Post Master J. A. McMillan, Alderman W. J. Irwin, driver of the mail wagon, Walter Green of the Express newspaper, and Alderman William McNeish. The house at 518 Lonsdale Avenue is in the background.

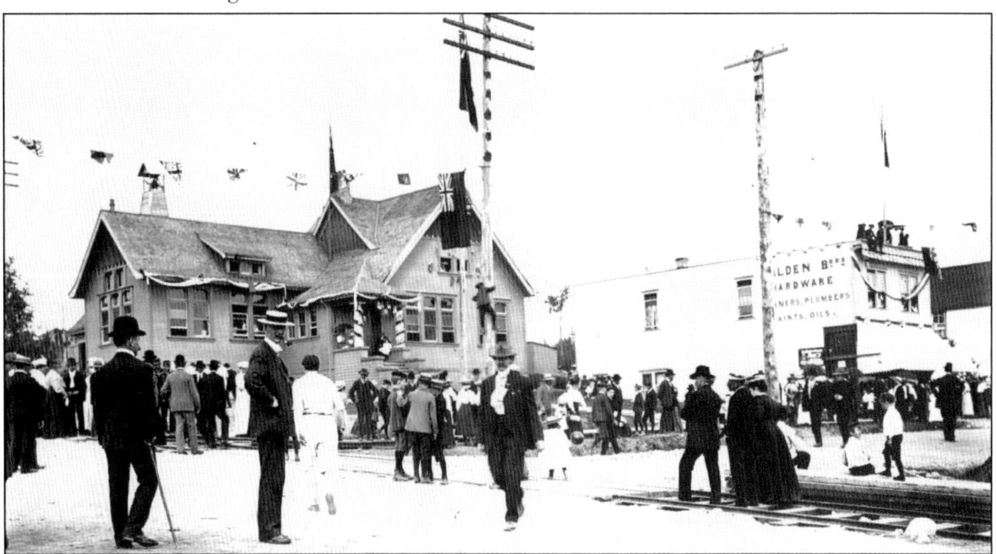

A crowd of people are present to mark Dominion Day celebrations in 1906 at the decorated District municipal hall (which one year later would become the first city hall) located on Lonsdale Avenue at First Street. The building was built in 1903 and became the first city hall from 1907 to 1912, when it was sold to the federal government for the post office. Walden Brothers Hardware store can be seen on the right.

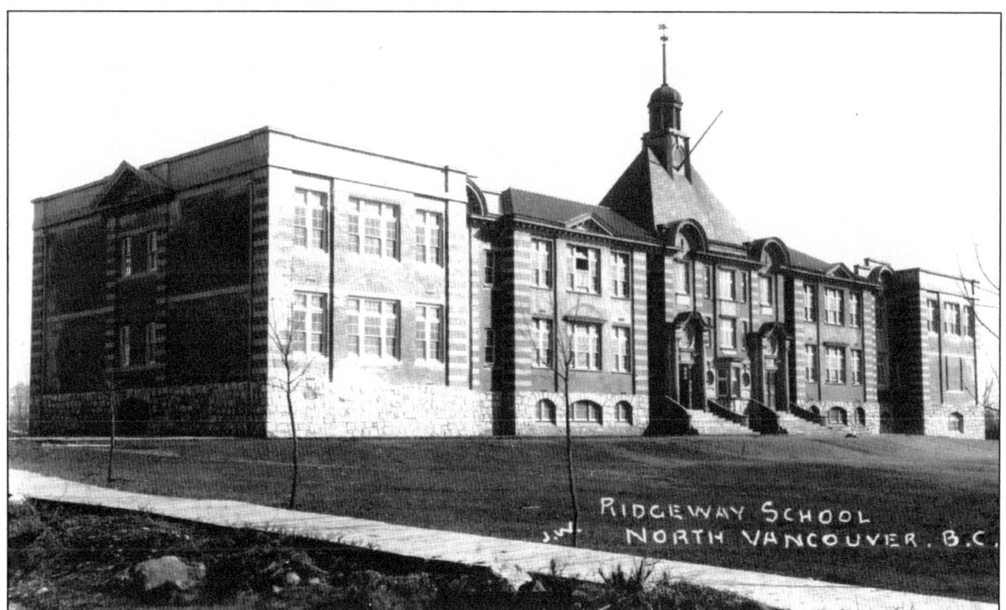

An example of optimism in the early years of the 20th century is Ridgeway School, a heritage legacy, built in 1912. In the 1919 photograph below, Ridgeway students in Miss Fraser's classroom include John Baker, John Barton, James Beckwith, Agatha Blackstock, Emily Buckholz, Margaret Cardinal, Raymond Croake, Robert Doherty, Thomas Doherty, Edna Edington, Doris Garling, Wesley Gibbon, Edward Grey, Robert Hale, Stewart Hale, Donald Haslet, James Hay, Borga Magnusson, Henrietta MacAffee, Elizabeth MacRae, Alan McColl, Janet McPhail, Gladys Paine, Samuel Palmer, Cyril Rathbone, May Robinson, Catherine Ross, James Stuart, Charles Thompson, Arthur Tinmouth, Willie White, Archibald Williams, Delia Wilkinson, George Wilson, Katie Whythyman, and Arthur Wootan.

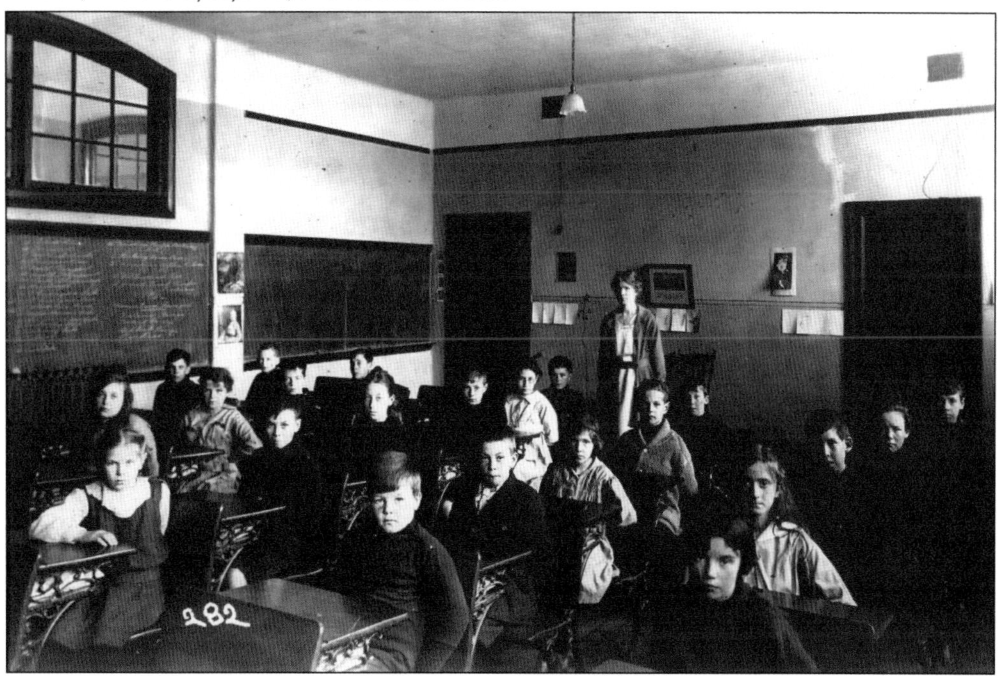

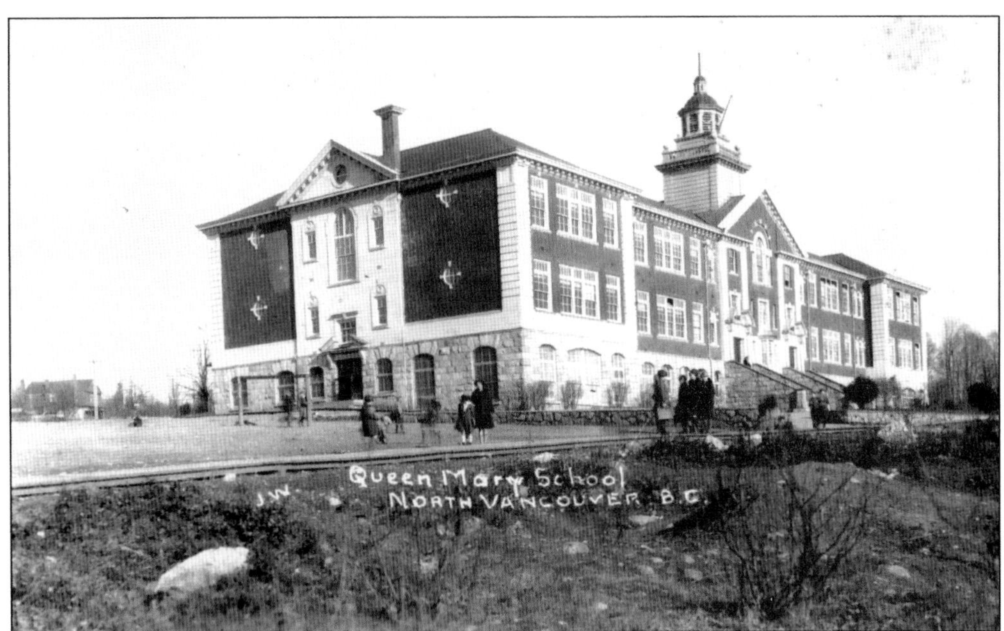

Another statement of confidence was projected when the construction of Queen Mary School, an architectural landmark shown in this 1920s photograph, began at 230 West Keith Road in 1914. The student population was increasing and the original Central School was overcrowded. The school opened for the 1915–1916 school year and accommodated all students from Central School, which then became the city hall. In the photograph below, taken around 1941, masked students, including Leonara Hutchinson at the centre in the dark dress and light sweater, participate in a gas drill as part of World War II preparedness.

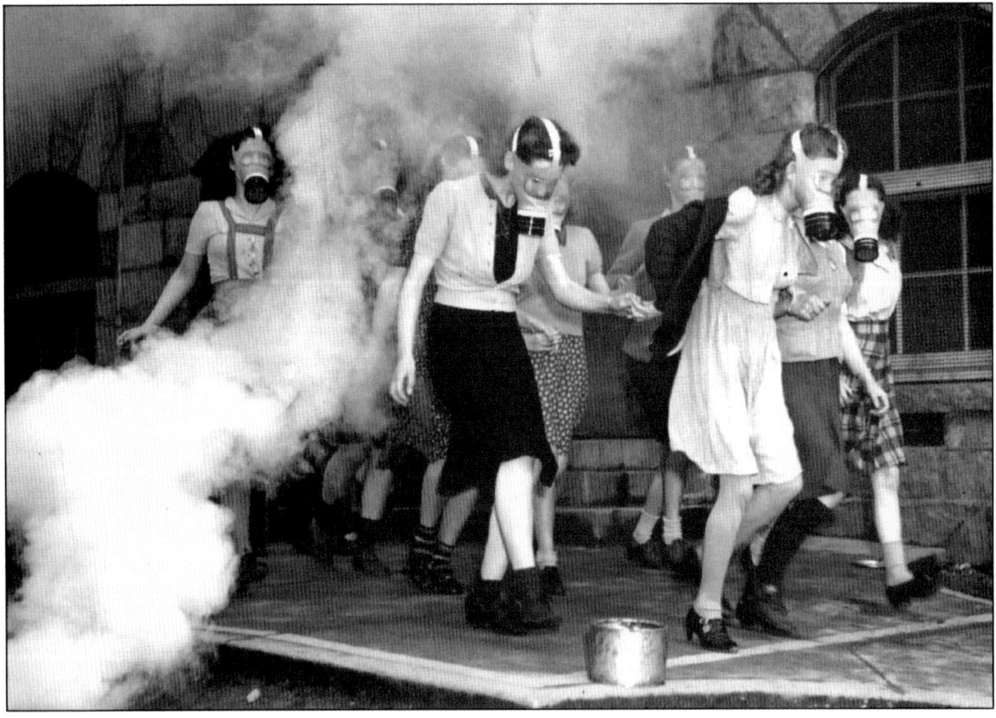

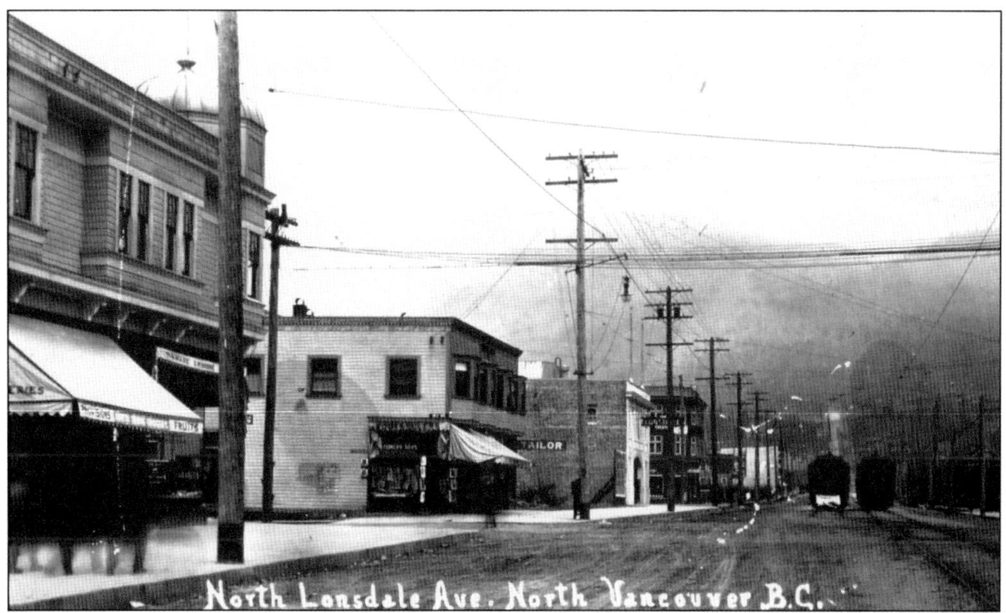

This postcard photograph, taken around 1912, shows the west side of Lonsdale Avenue at Fifteenth Street. Books are on display behind the window at the Booksellers bookstore that also sold stationery and toys. Awnings that would have sheltered pedestrians from rain are also visible. A large sign identifies a tailor's shop and to the right is Lonsdale Theatre. To the extreme left the awning for North Shore Grocery as well as a tinware store can be seen below the turret of the Lonsdale Block. Two streetcars, one of them on a passing track, are visible on Lonsdale.

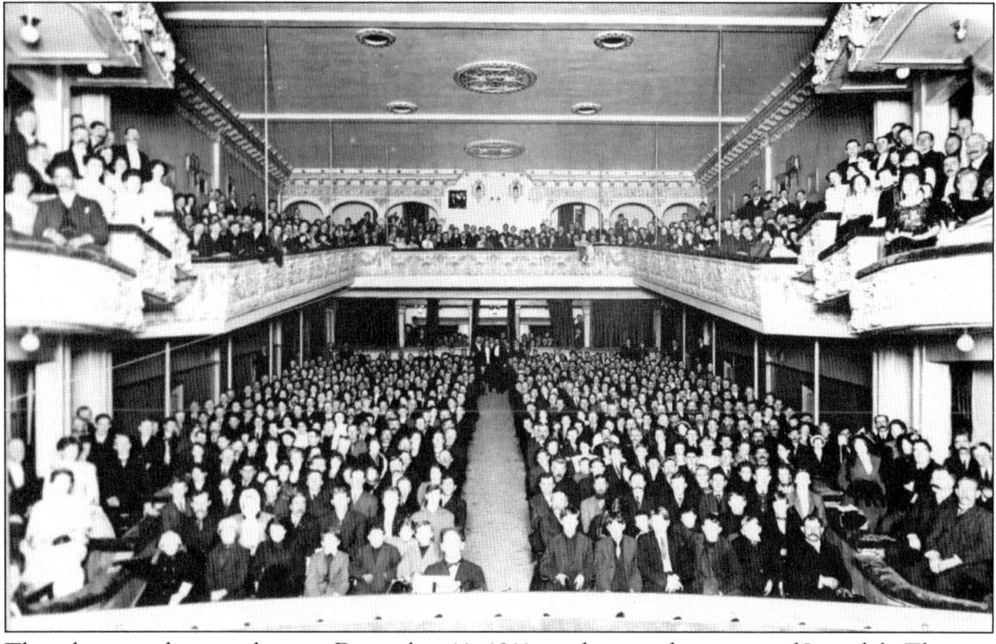

This photograph was taken on December 11, 1911, at the grand opening of Lonsdale Theatre. It was a full house as enthusiastic North Vancouver residents, wearing their evening outfits, packed the theatre knowing they could now go to watch a musical or theatrical show in their own neighbourhood.

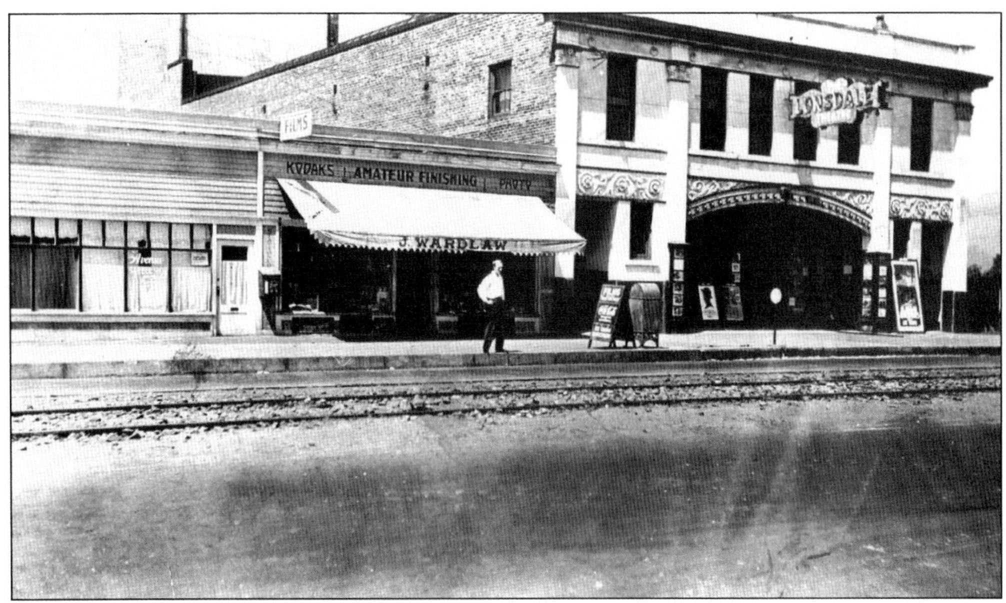

One of the shows at Lonsdale Theatre in this photograph taken in the 1920s is a Charlie Chaplin film, as evidenced by a sidewalk theatre sign. Avenue Barber shop and J. Wardlaw photographer also operated in the same 1500 block of Lonsdale Avenue. Jack Wardlaw also worked at the North Vancouver Ship Repairs in the early 1940s.

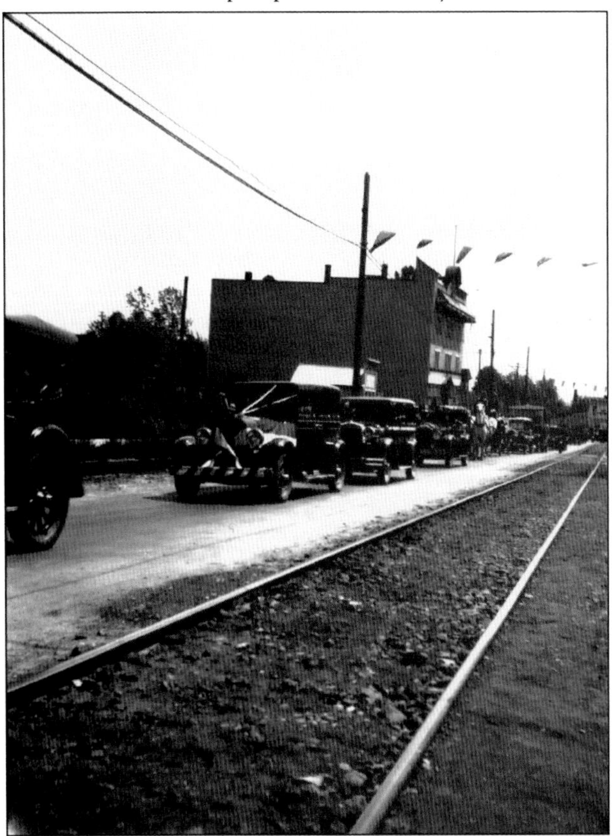

In this May 24, 1930, Victoria Day photograph, cars and horses were paraded on Lonsdale Avenue. The Masonic temple, built in 1910, in the 1100 block on the left, contained the North Vancouver Lutheran Church, a political party office, and a business school.

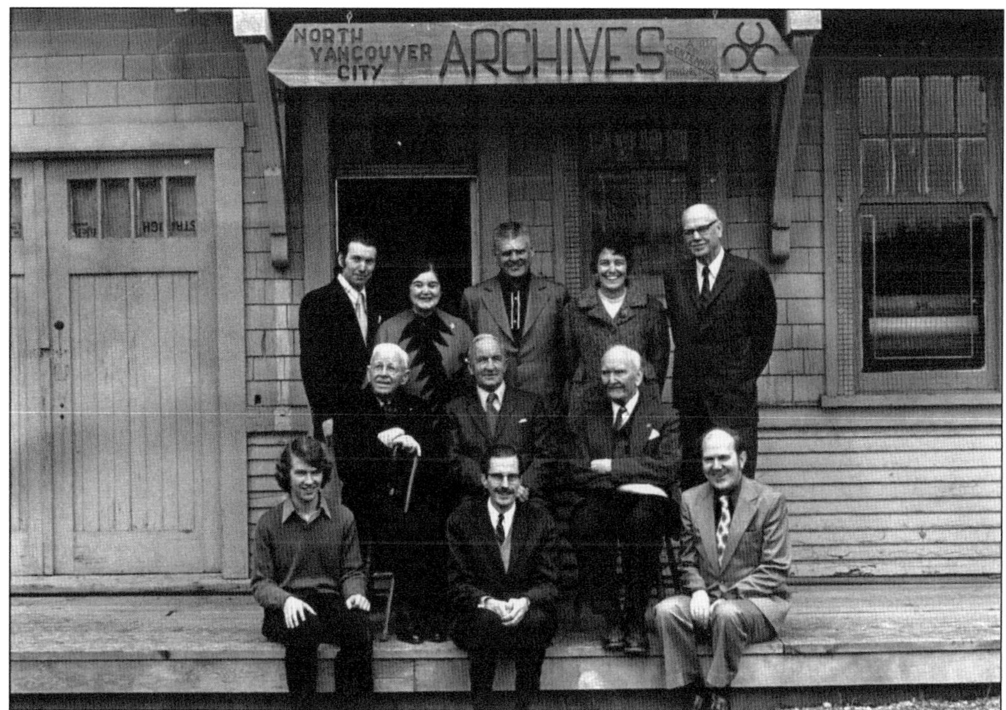

The North Shore Museum and Archives Committee members pose in front of the small museum situated in the PGE Station at Mahon Park on April 21, 1974. Committee members are, from left to right, (first row) Donald Bourdon, Bill Baker, and Ed Raymond; (second row) Rodger Burnes, Thomas Diplock, and Walter Draycott; (third row) John Maxwell, Alice Burritt, Jack Loucks, Anna Sumpton, and Don Langford. The photograph below shows an early automobile with a North Shore Museum sign in a parade around 1975 on Lonsdale Avenue at East Nineteenth Street. The Irwin & Billings Real Estate office can be seen in the background.

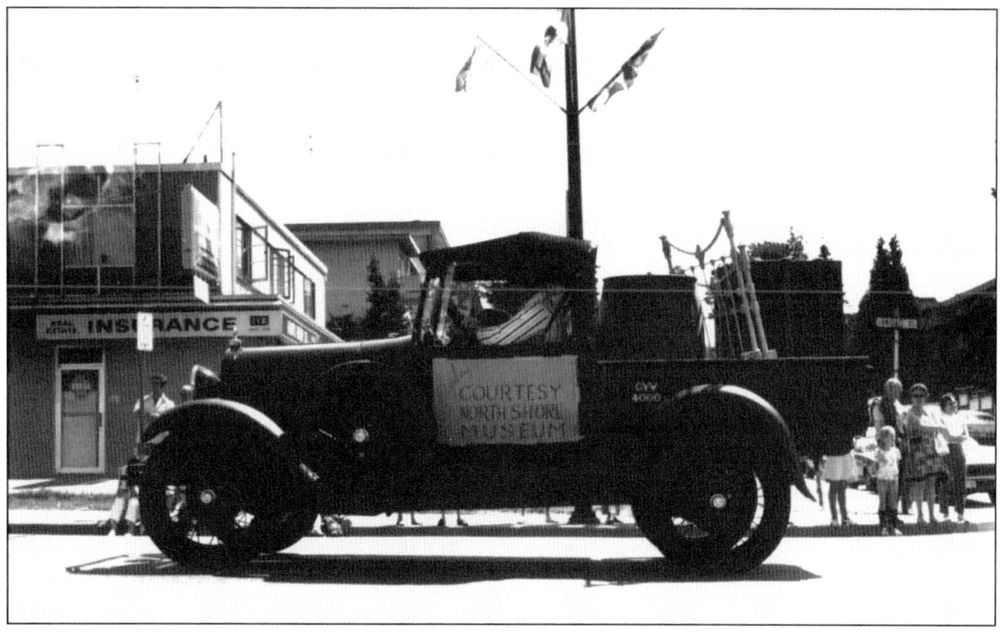

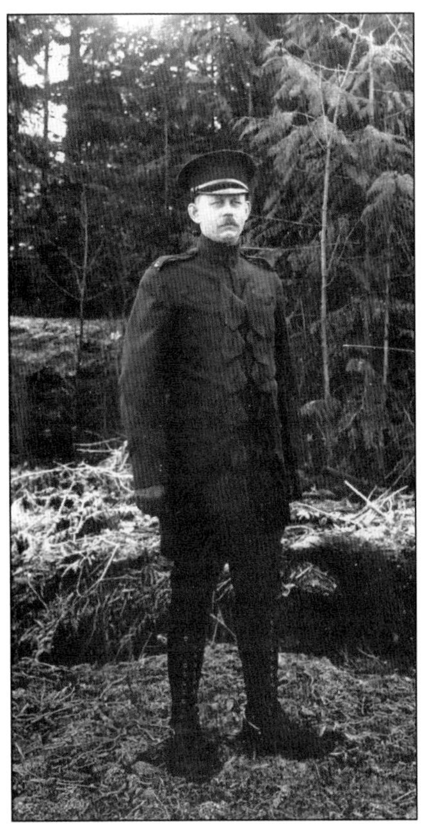

This *c.* 1909 photograph was taken of Major P. G. Tofft, who was the first police chief of the District of North Vancouver. The City of North Vancouver also had its own police force, which was replaced in 1934 with a provincial force and was again replaced with the Royal Canadian Mounted Police (RCMP) in 1950. The 1912 photograph below shows police commissioners and the force in front of the city hall. In the front row from left to right are unidentified, Alderman C. F. Foreman, unidentified, Mayor William McNeish, and Commissioner John B. Paine. Police Chief Arthur Davies is in the second row, fourth from the left.

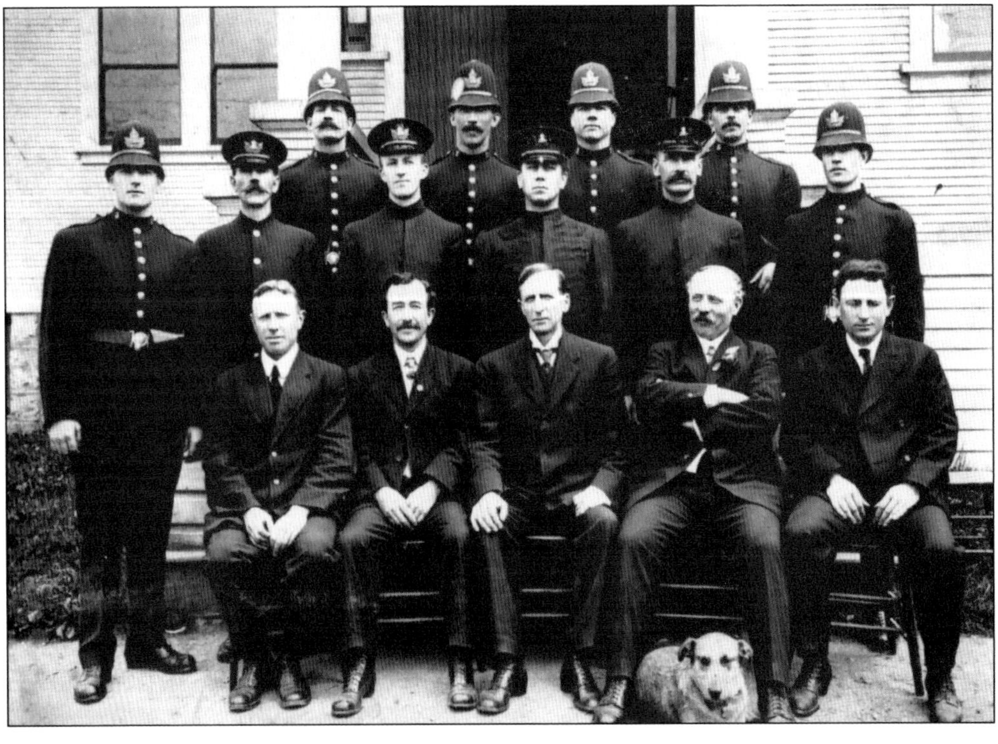

An unidentified City of North Vancouver policeman stands in front of streetcar No. 153 at the foot of Lonsdale Avenue sometime after 1912. Streetcar No. 153 is in the possession of the North Vancouver Museum and Archives, and is being restored.

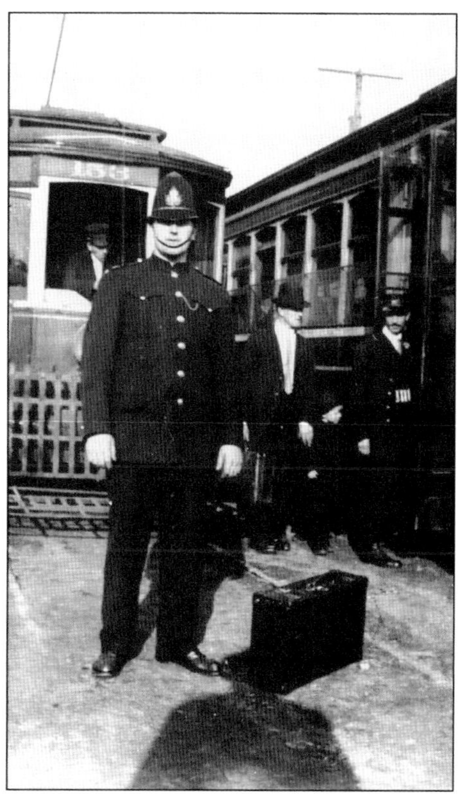

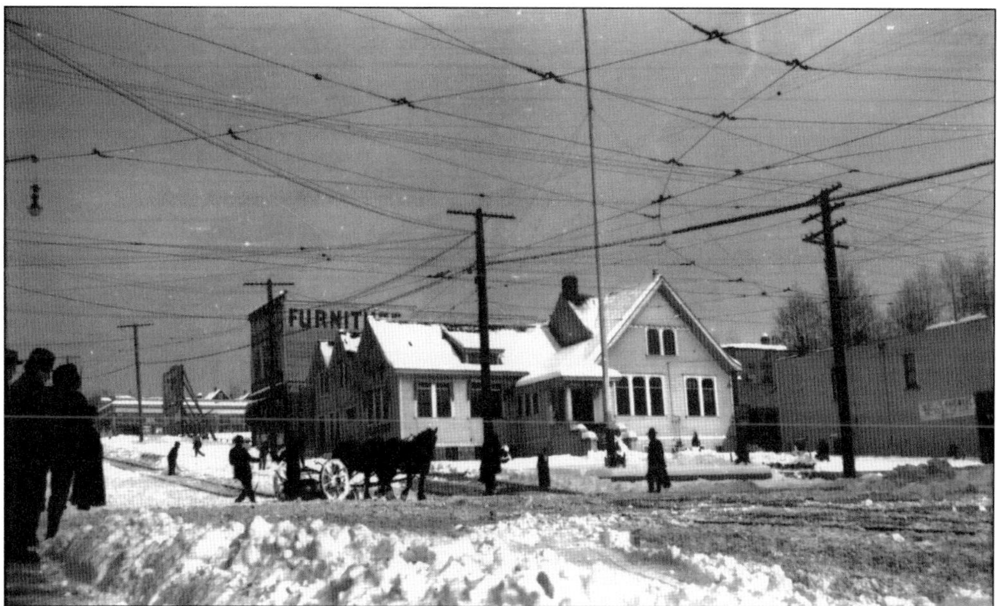

Two men are operating a horse-drawn snow plough in the winter of 1916 at the intersection of Lonsdale Avenue and First Street. The post office building can be seen on the northeast corner. A furniture store is situated behind the post office, and Buell's Hardware store can be seen to the right. The city hall was relocated to the Central School building (now home to the North Vancouver Museum galleries) in 1915.

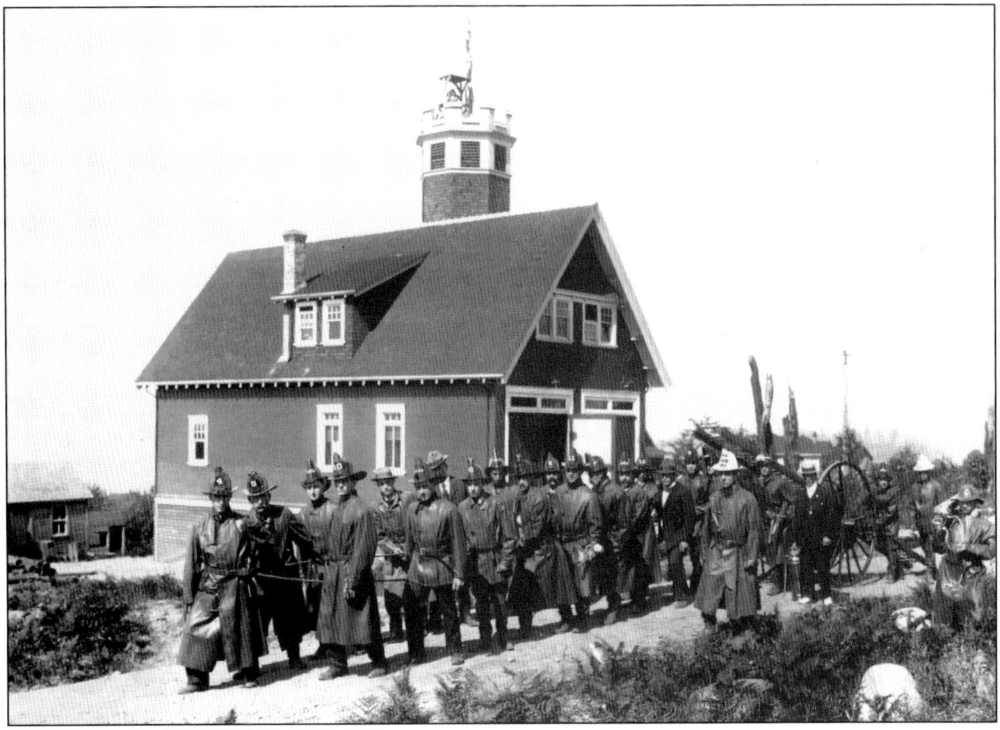

Volunteer firefighters are pulling the hose reel outside No. 1 Firehall on Fourth Street and St. Georges Avenue around 1908. Thomas Kennedy, who was one of the early fire chiefs, is situated at the back, seventh from the left, wearing a soft hat.

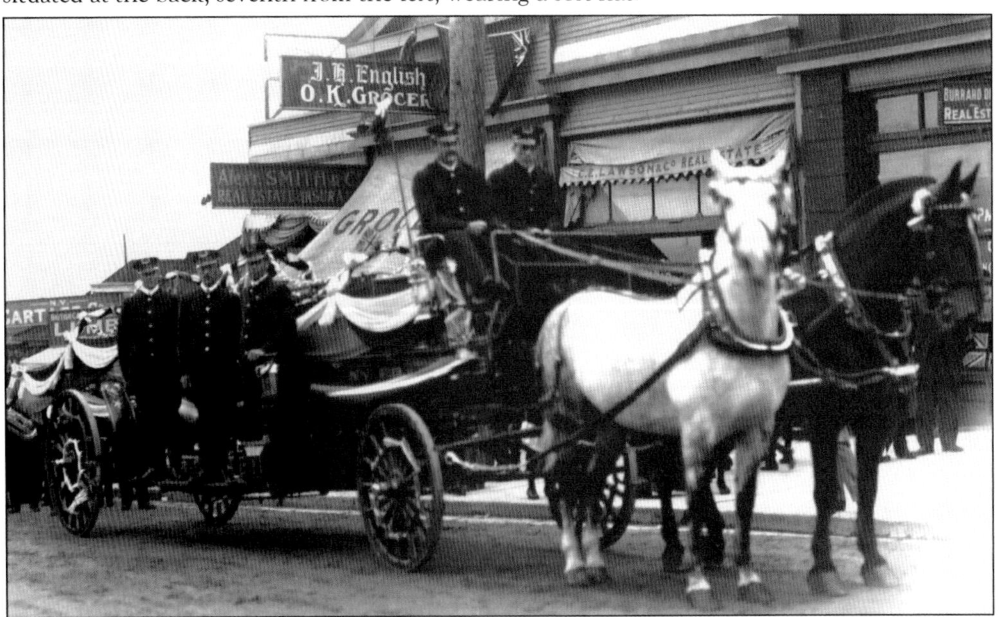

A decorated fire wagon with firemen and horses participates in a parade on Lonsdale Avenue just below Esplanade. Four businesses situated behind the fire wagon in this photograph, taken between 1910 and 1920, are (from left to right) North Vancouver Cartage, Alexander Smith Real Estate, J. H. English OK Grocery, and C. E. Lawson Real Estate. The firemen are unidentified.

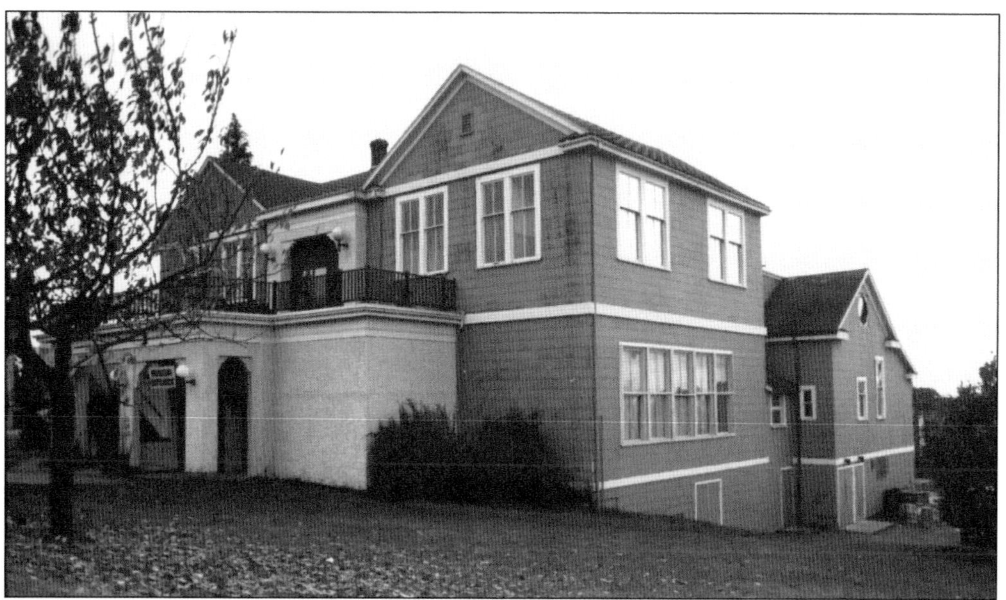

This building, at 209 West Fourth Street, currently houses the Presentation House Arts Centre, containing the North Vancouver Museum, a photography art gallery, and a theatre. It was previously the city hall and was originally built in 1902 as Central School. The building caught fire in 1975, resulting in extensive damage to the council chambers.

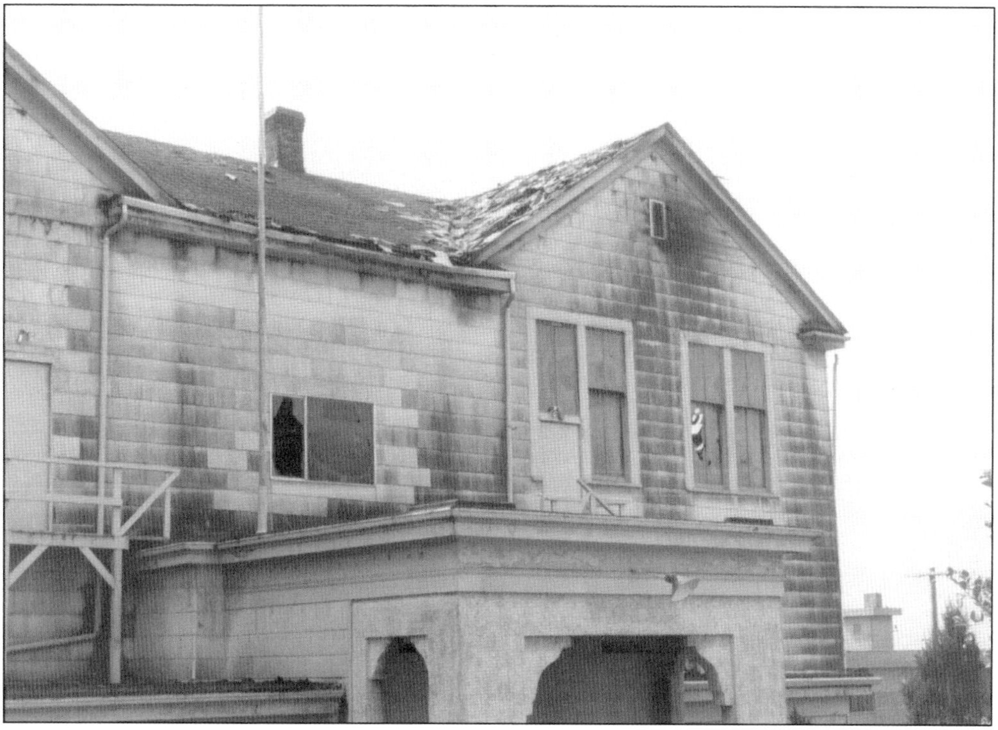

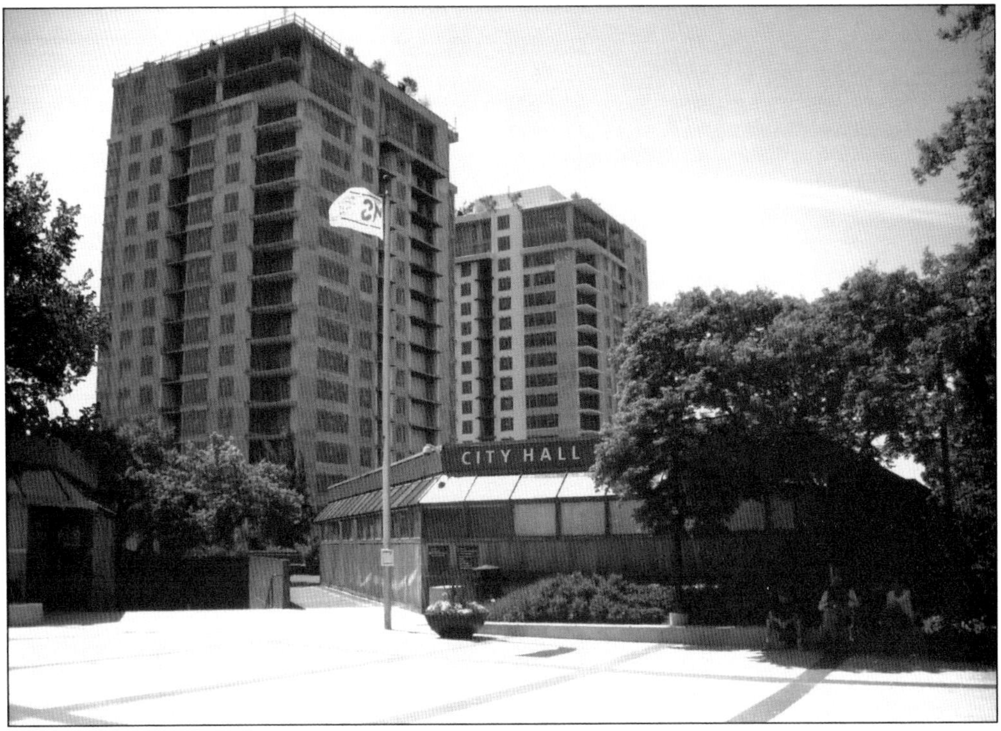

North Vancouver City Library's move from its old location on the extreme left above to its new location across the civic centre in 2008, shown in the 2009 photograph below, was funded by permitting the construction of high-density high-rises, on Thirteenth Street and Chesterfield, seen behind the city hall building.

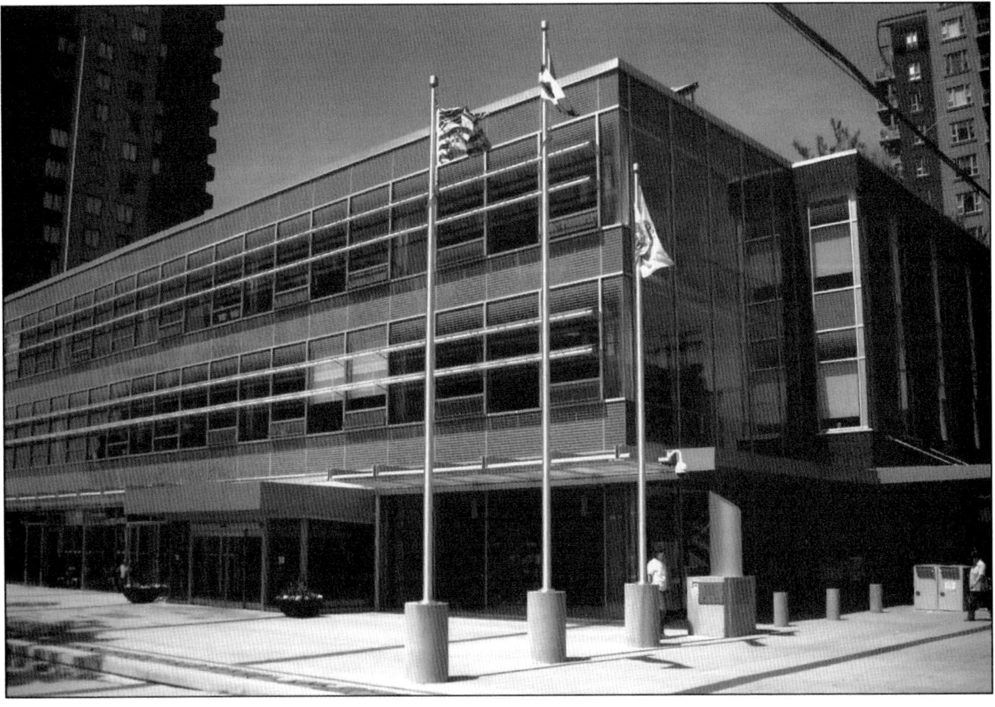

Six

Tents, Houses, Hotels, and High-Rises

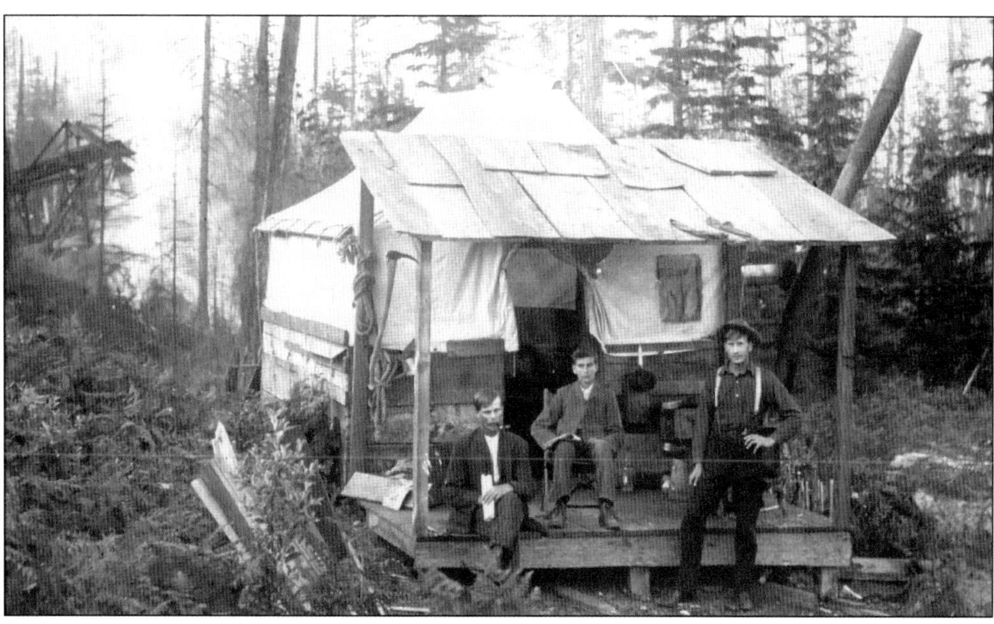

In the early part of the last century, many settlers arriving in North Vancouver bought a parcel of land, cleared the land, and built their own home. While doing so, depending on their financial means, families often lived in hotels or tents for months and sometimes for years. While furnished canvas tents were available to rent for $2 a month, a room at the Hotel North Vancouver cost approximately $2 a day! This photograph shows the exterior of a typical tent in the middle of a wooded area somewhere in North Vancouver.

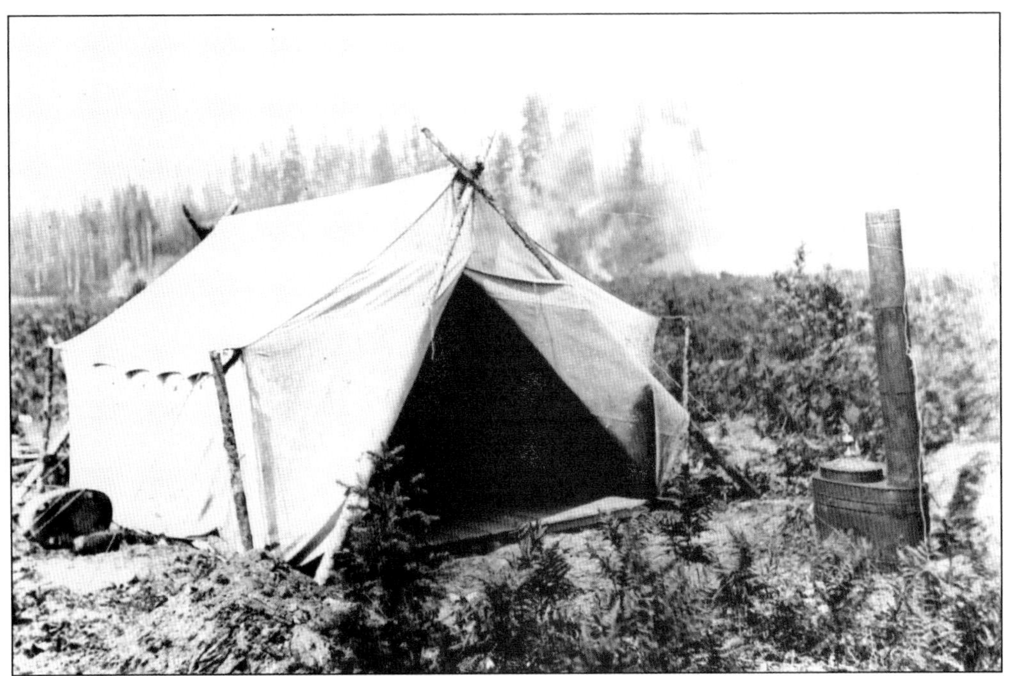

This 1910 photograph shows a tent belonging to someone by the initials of J. R. His stove can be seen to the right of the tent.

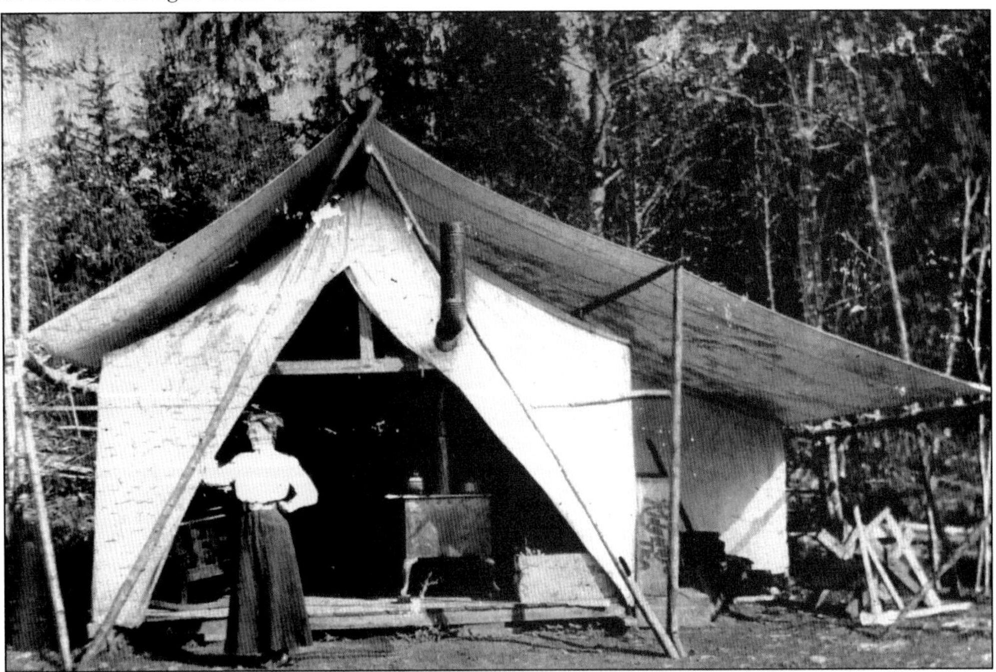

Evelyn Elliott stands in front of her tent in 1911. The Elliotts' tent was at the end of the Capilano streetcar line. Their stove apparently kept them warm and comfortable during cold winter days and they were able to use the facilities in Mr. Smith's store near their lot. Albert Elliott took the streetcar and then the ferry to go to work in Vancouver as a bookbinder. Previously, he and his business partner Fred Baglow operated Elliott & Baglow Photographers.

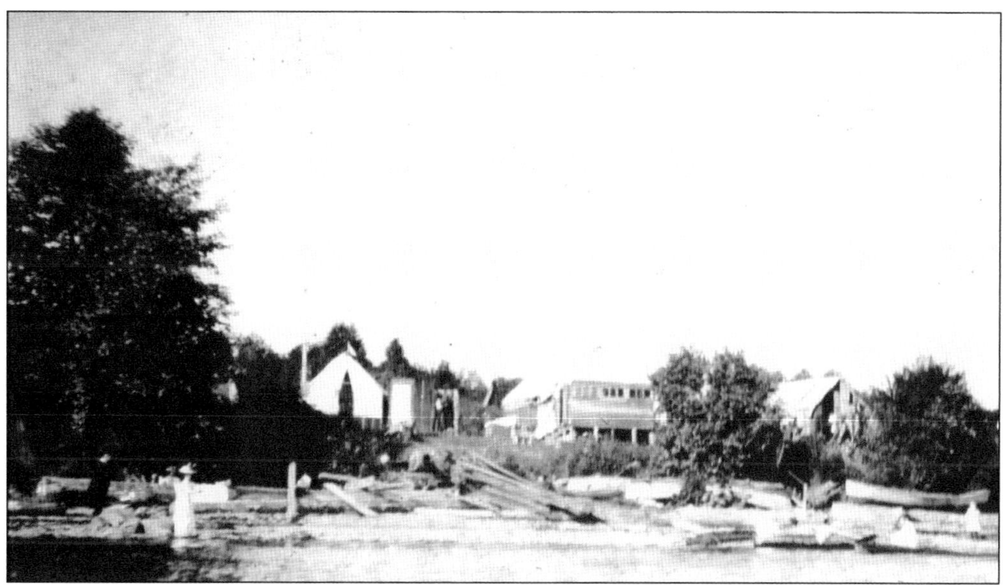

A 1908 campground shows multiple tents on the waterfront. Rowboats or canoes can be seen near the shore.

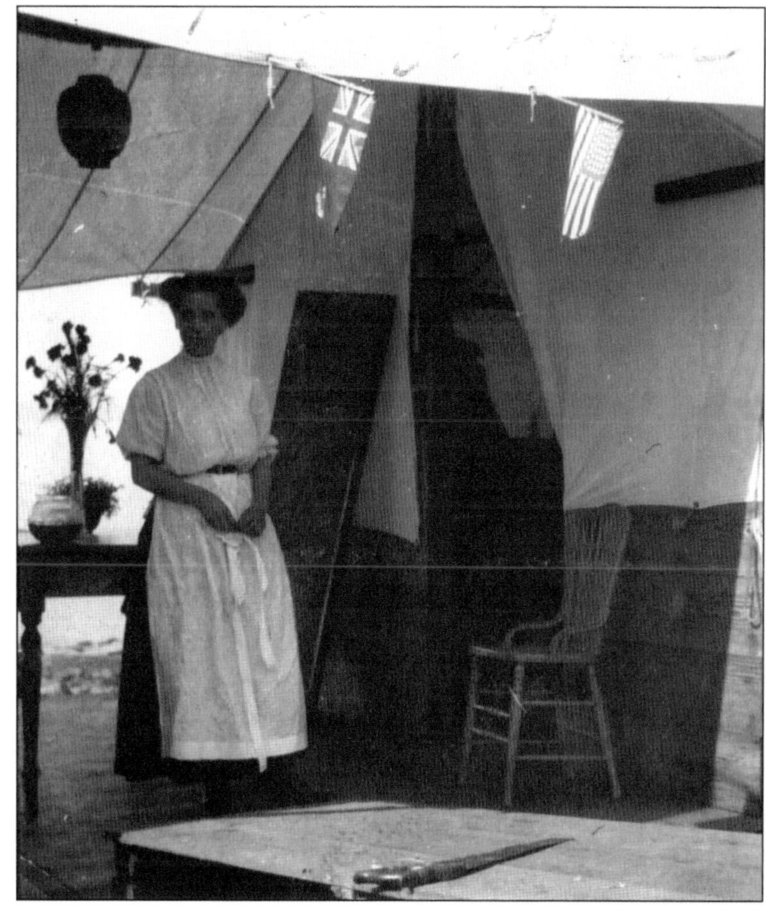

Situated on a waterfront campground to the west of the Hotel North Vancouver, Mabel Bisset stands in front of her tent home in about 1910.

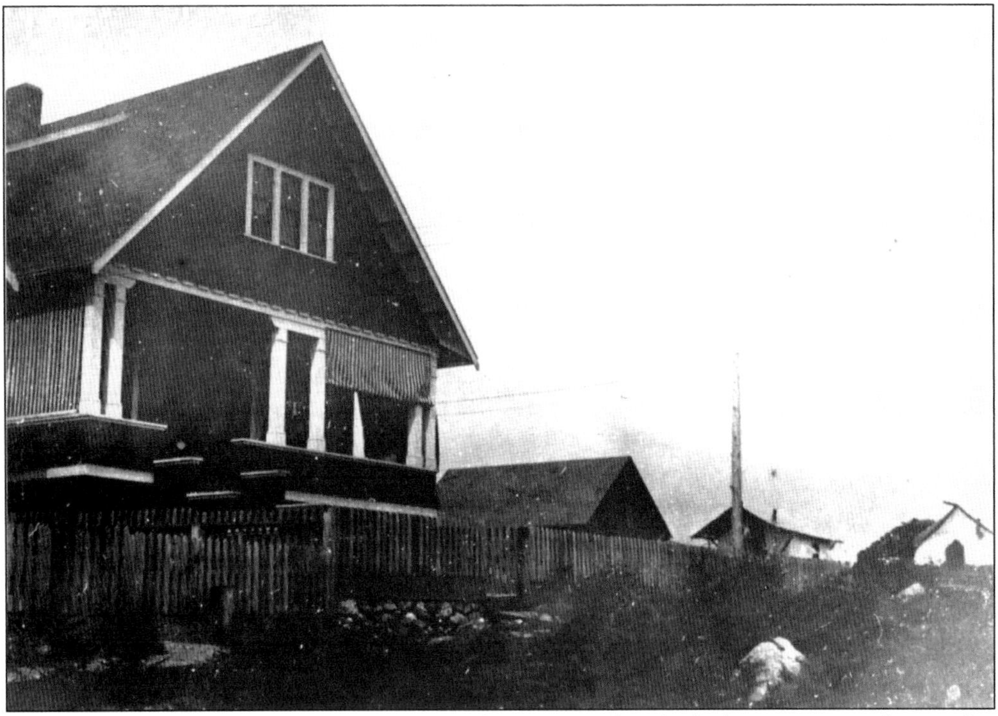

To the right of this house on 458 East Seventh Street, a close look shows a tent with a roof as well as a tent with a ridge pole.

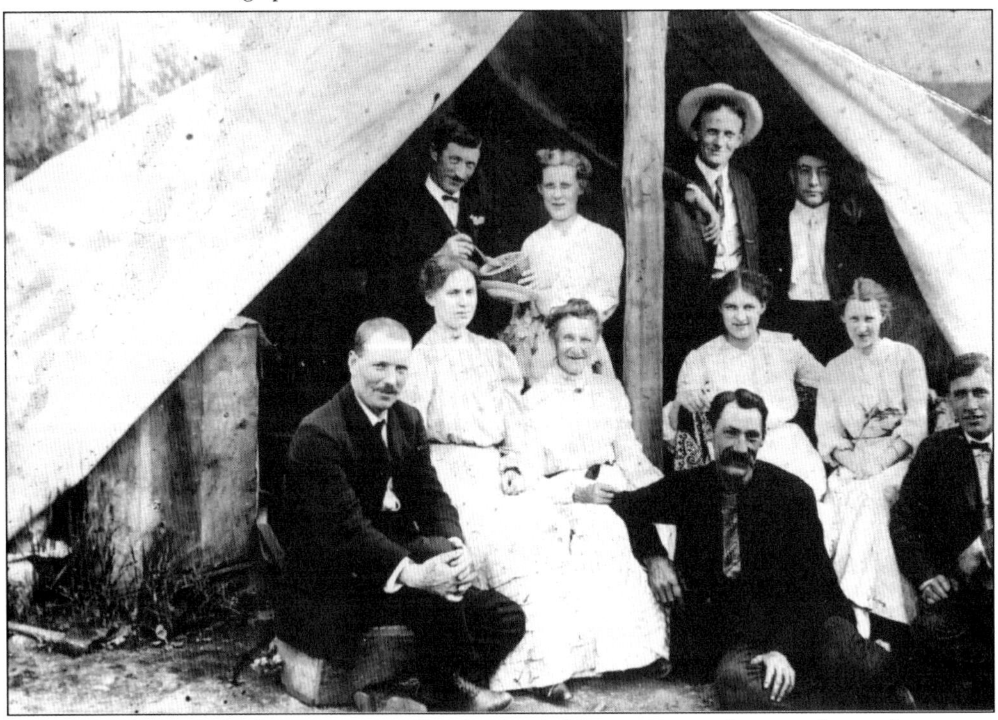

This 1905 photograph shows a group of early North Vancouver residents in front of a tent at 125 East Fourth Street.

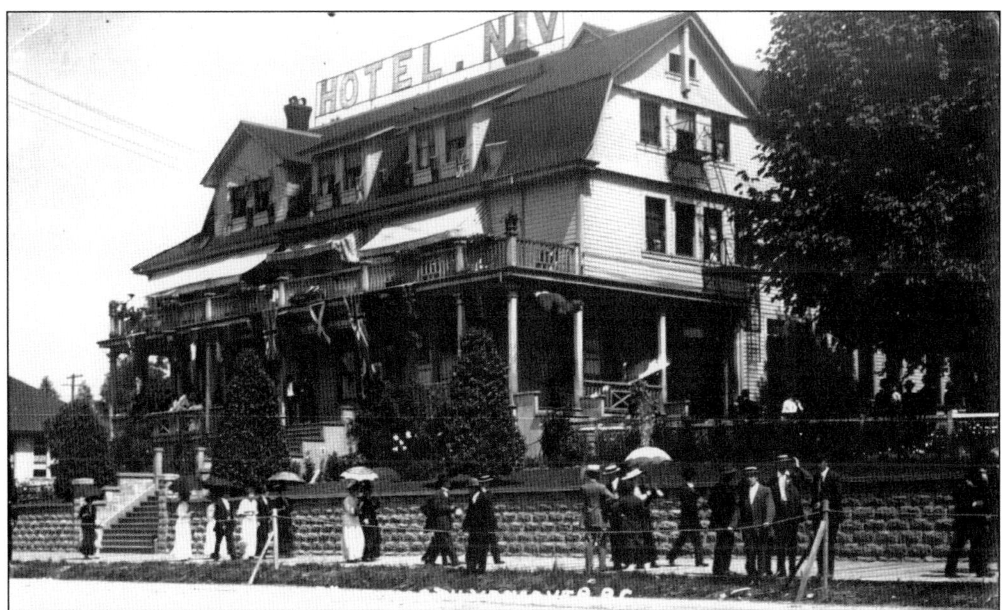

Pedestrians take a leisurely walk on the wooden sidewalk in front of the Hotel North Vancouver. Ladies are carrying parasols on what seems to be a sunny day. The date of this postcard's photograph is placed between 1905 and 1915.

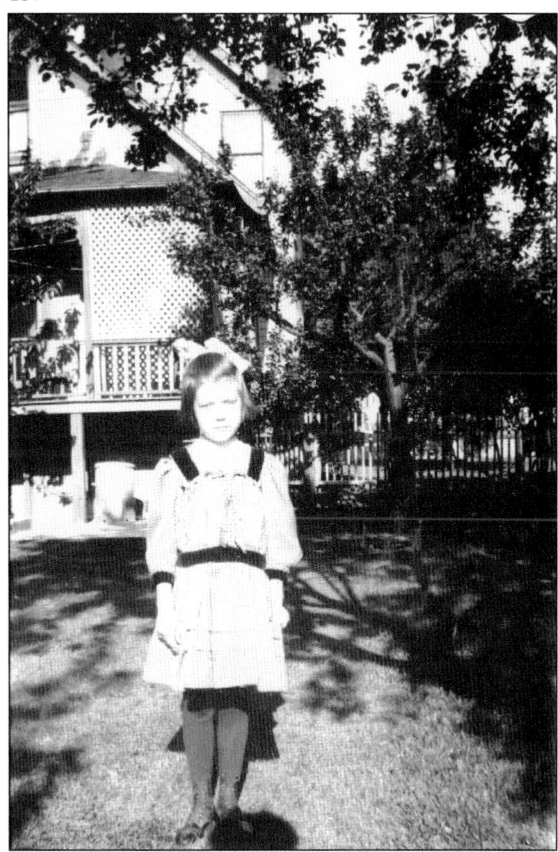

Hotelier Pete Larson's daughter, Alma Larson, stands on the grounds of the Hotel North Vancouver around 1908.

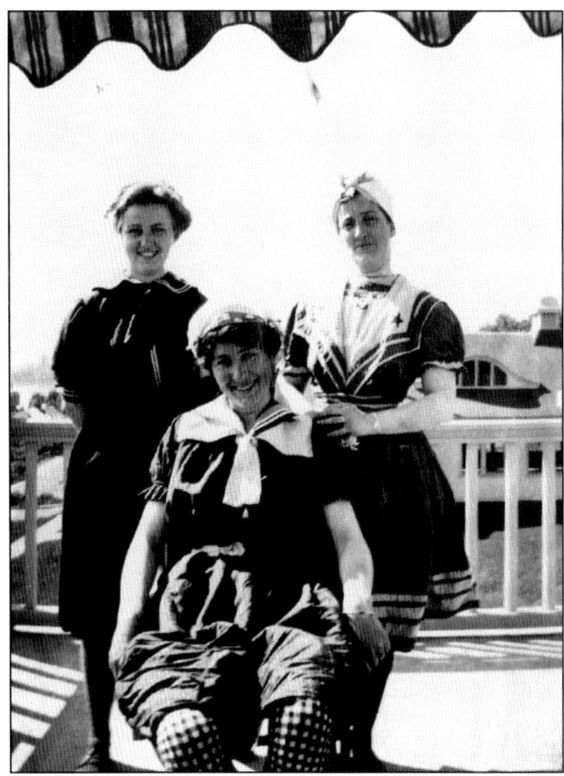

Olga Larson, Lillian Liersch, and Emma Stephens are all in smiles wearing their bathing suits around 1910. They are standing on the second-floor balcony of the Hotel North Vancouver, situated on Esplanade, across the street from the beach. In those days, the beach was much closer to Esplanade than the current shoreline.

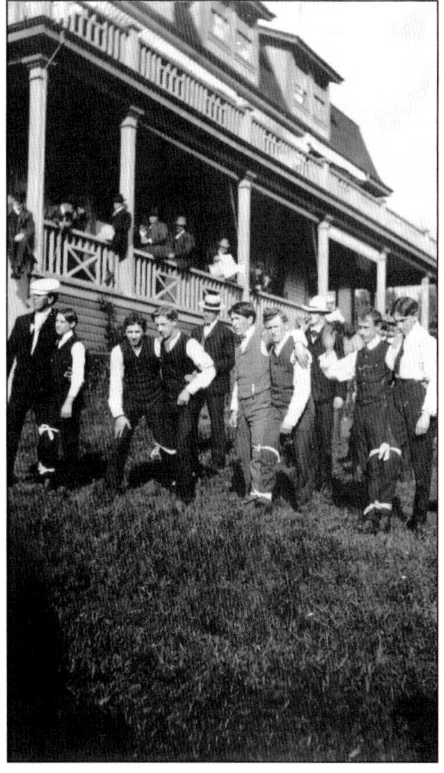

With several people watching from the veranda of the Hotel North Vancouver, young men are set to start a three-legged race. The grounds also acted as a community park and picnic area as, unlike most other areas in North Vancouver, the grassy settings were ideal for such events.

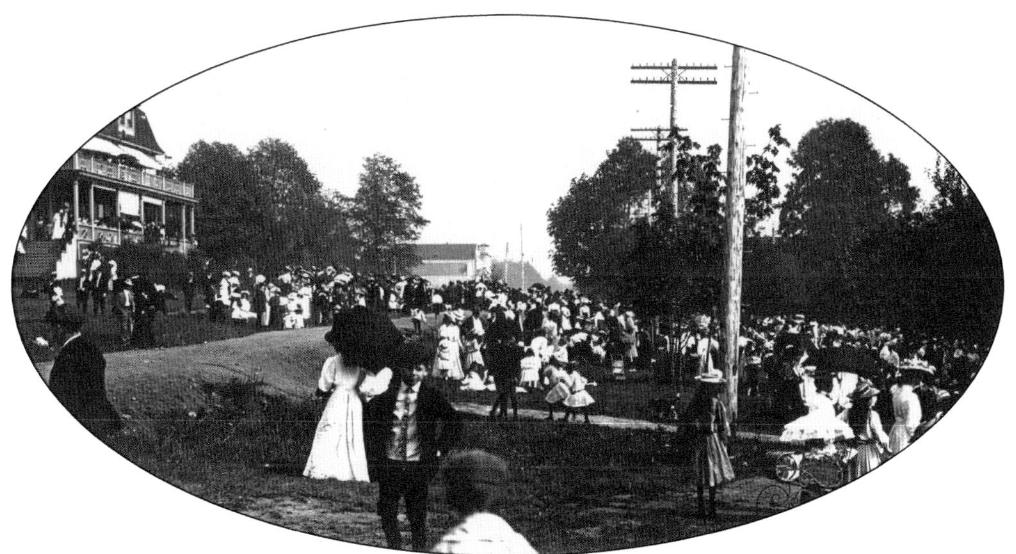

A large crowd of visitors and picnickers gathers in front of the Hotel North Vancouver and on both sides of West Esplanade. This photograph was taken around 1905.

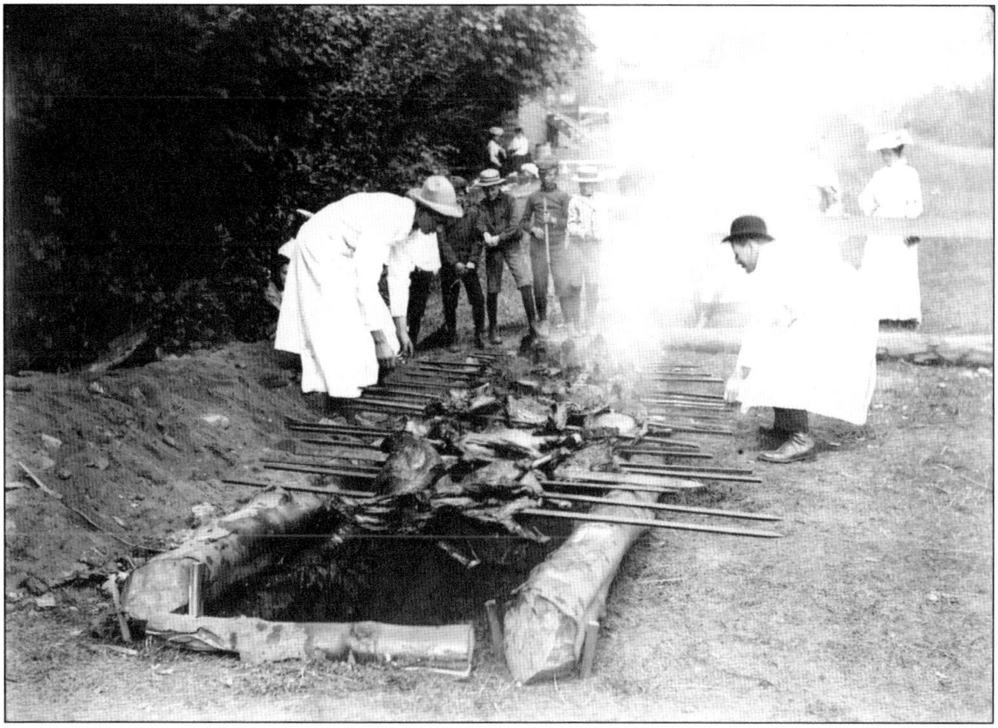

This outdoor barbecue was assembled on the grounds of the Hotel North Vancouver for the July 1, 1906, Dominion Day celebrations. Cooks turn the meat as young men watch the fire pit. In 1906 North Vancouver celebrated Dominion Day with full force after Vancouver withdrew its promotion. Visitors from Vancouver enjoyed a ferry trip to the event and packed North Vancouver on Dominion Day.

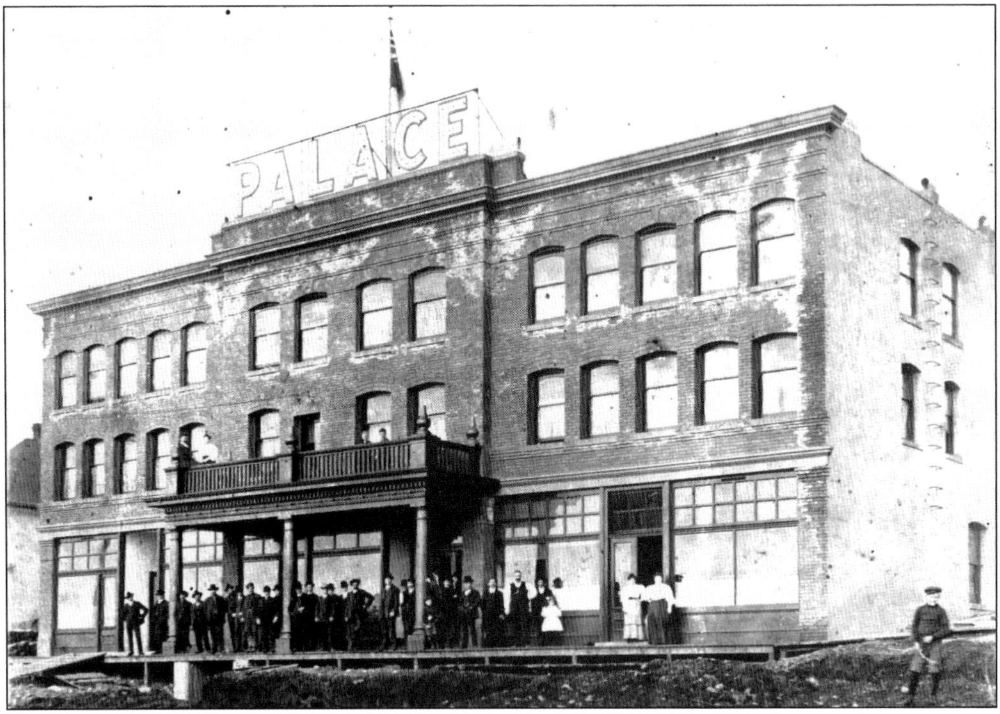

The opening of the Palace Hotel in 1906 on East Second Street was a notable event in North Vancouver. The hotel was a three-storey structure and featured a striking redbrick siding on its street side. The man standing fifth from the right is owner Lorenzo Reda. The child to his left is his daughter Theresa, and the two women to his left are Caroline Andruss (hotel coproprietor) and Angelina Reda.

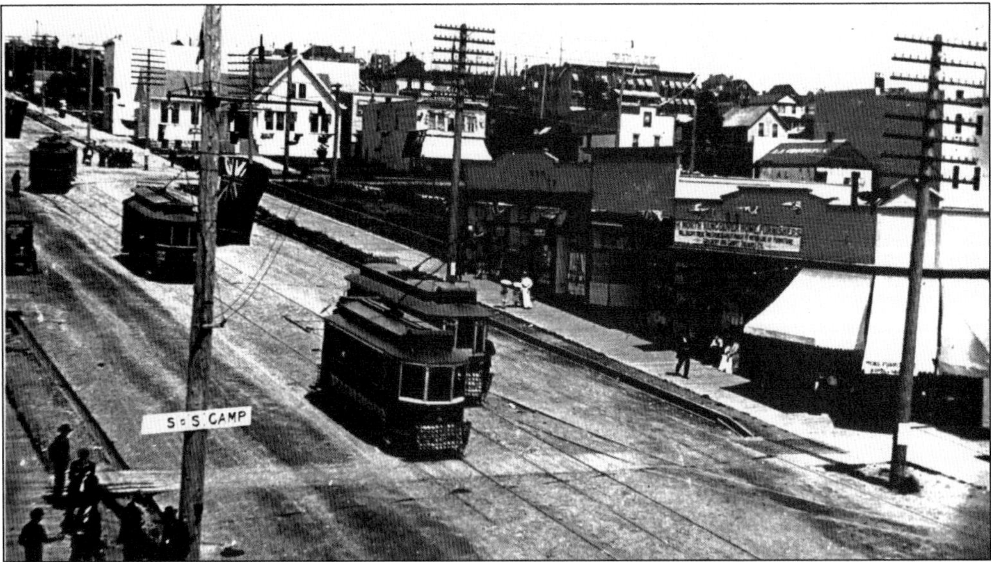

This 1908 photograph shows the Palace Hotel and its large sign in the distance in relation to Lower Lonsdale Avenue. The city hall is on Lonsdale and First Street and the North Vancouver Home Furnishers store is on the east side of Lonsdale with a couple of people sitting in front. Streetcars run up and down Lonsdale Avenue.

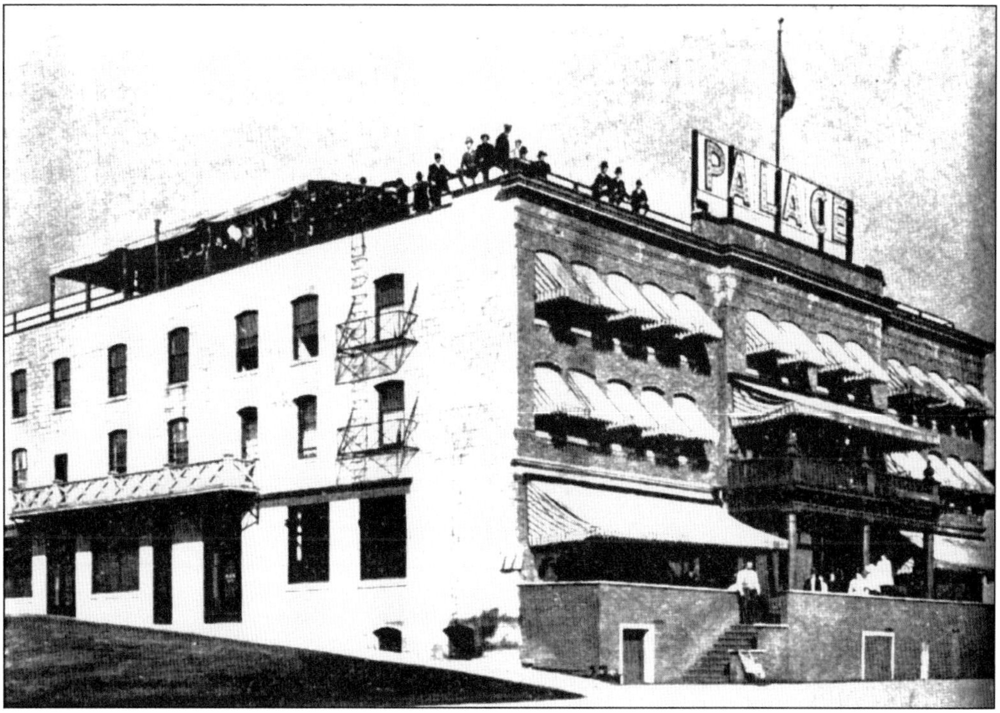

The Palace Hotel featured a rooftop garden, the first in the Province. A crowd of people is on the garden rooftop, which offered spectacular views of the mountains, Burrard Inlet, the city of Vancouver, and beyond.

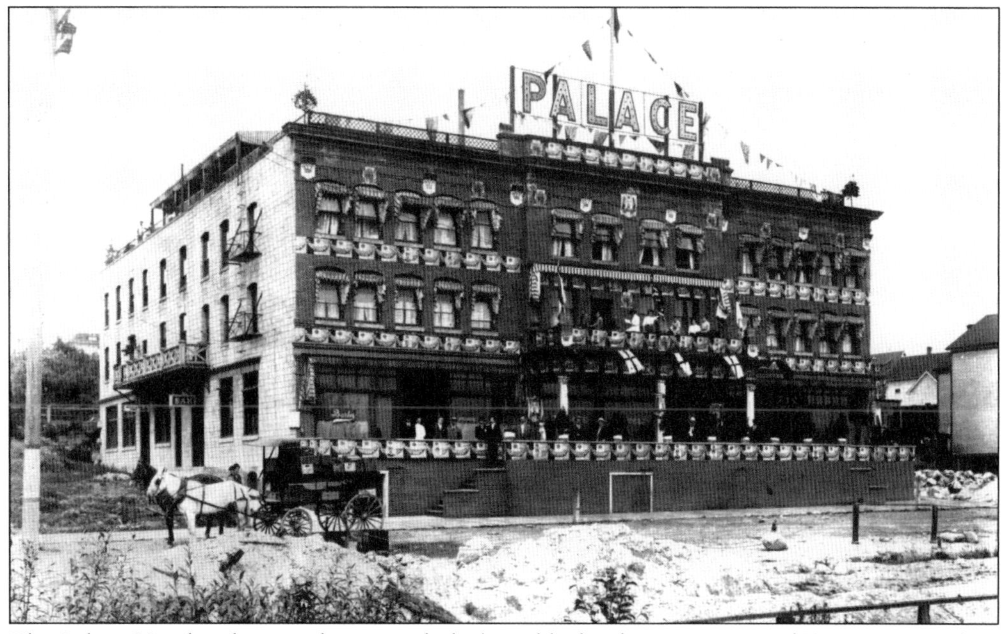

The Palace Hotel is decorated spectacularly (possibly for the coronation of King George V) in this 1911 photograph. Horses and buggies are carrying goods. The bar as well as the billiard and pool entrance can be seen on the west side of the hotel. Chinese cooks and laundrymen employed by the hotel lived in a dwelling to the right of the hotel.

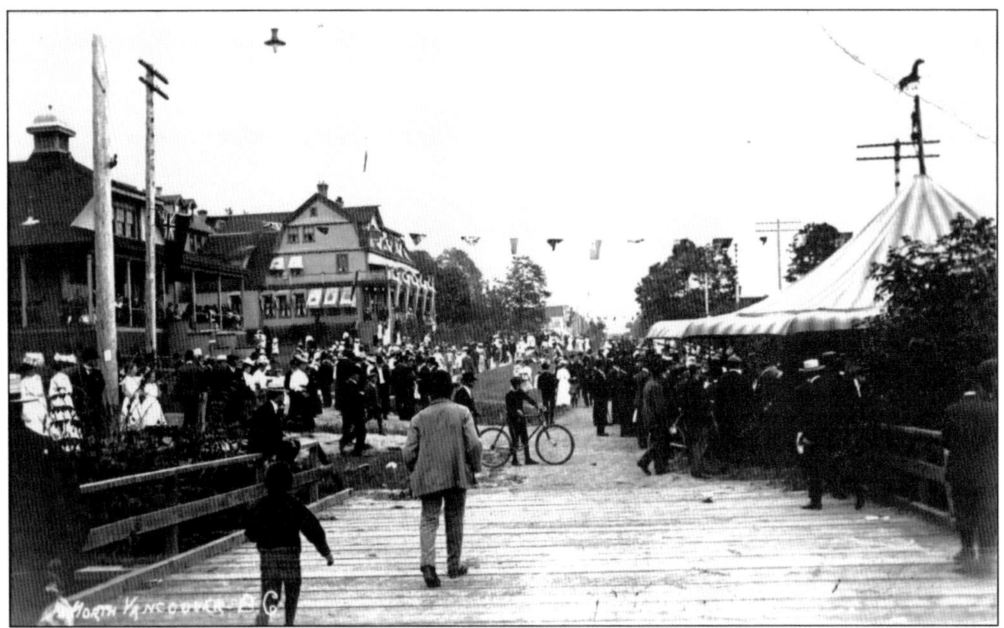

A large crowd of visitors and residents can be seen on Esplanade on Dominion Day, July 1, 1907. The year 1907 was the 40th anniversary of confederation, as well as the incorporation of the city. Thousands took advantage of extra ferry runs and events in Lower Lonsdale. Organized events and activities included sailing, swimming, athletics (track and field), barbecues and band concerts, a boxing match, and dancing in the Hotel North Vancouver pavilion.

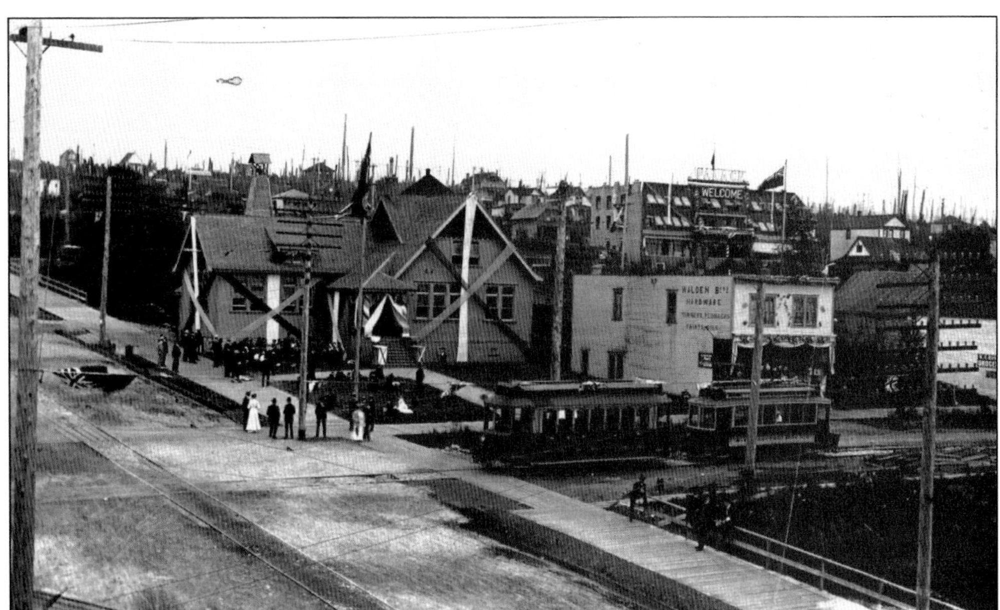

A crowd has assembled in 1907 in front of a decorated North Vancouver City Hall at Lonsdale Avenue and East First Street. The city hall is decorated for both Dominion Day and the City Incorporation Celebration. Walden Brothers hardware is to the right. The Palace Hotel with a Welcome sign is further back and also decorated. Streetcars are approaching Lonsdale Avenue from First Street.

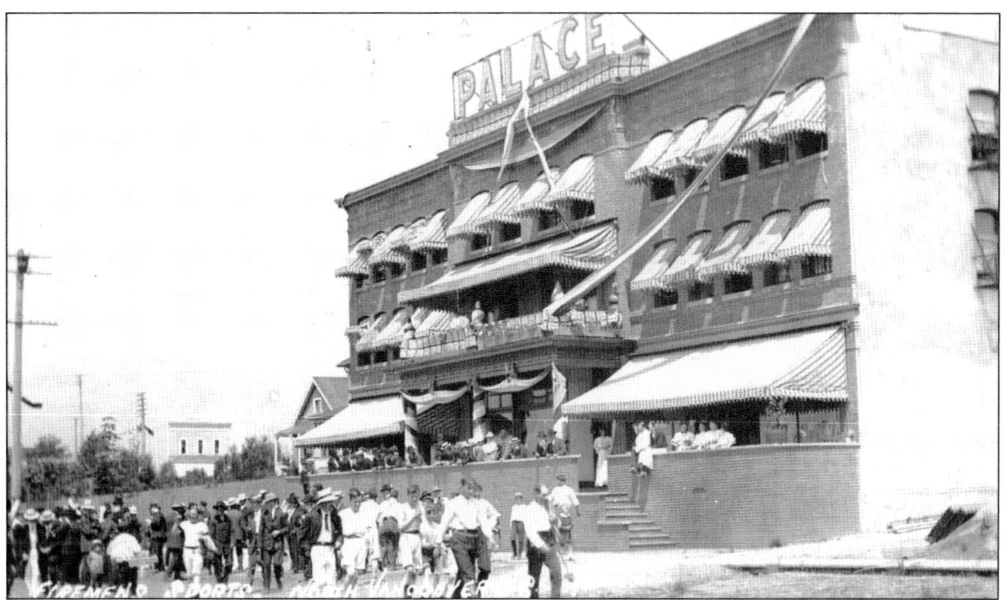

A Dominion Day crowd assembles in front of a decorated Palace Hotel on July 1, 1908. In 1989 the Palace/Olympic hotel building was demolished as the land value was, by then, very high. A residential tower, named the Olympic, was built in its place.

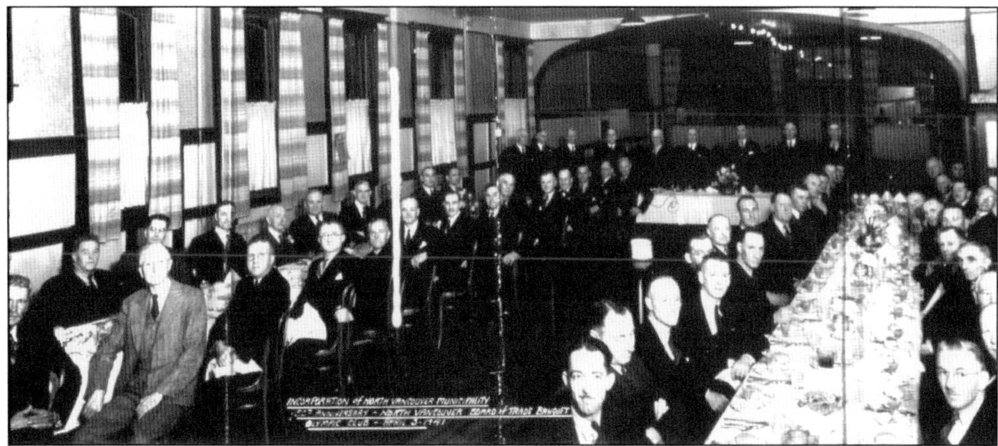

At the time this April 1941 photograph was taken, the Palace Hotel had become the Olympic Hotel. A board of trade banquet is held to celebrate the 50th anniversary of the incorporation of the District of North Vancouver municipality, from which the City seceded in 1907. The fact that this celebration occurred on City grounds shows that Lonsdale Avenue continued to be a community hub for both the City and the District for some time.

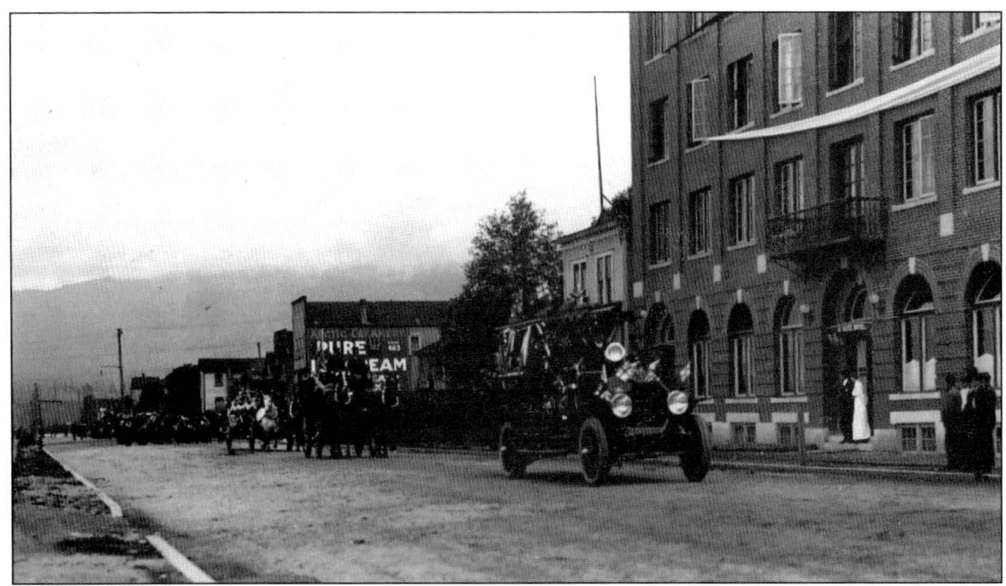

This *c.* 1913 photograph shows the St. Alice Hotel on the right, which was built in 1911–1912. Fire equipment and a band are in a parade on West Second Street. The Arctic Creamery can be seen in the background. Similar to the Palace Hotel, it was a brick–faced building, although only five stories high.

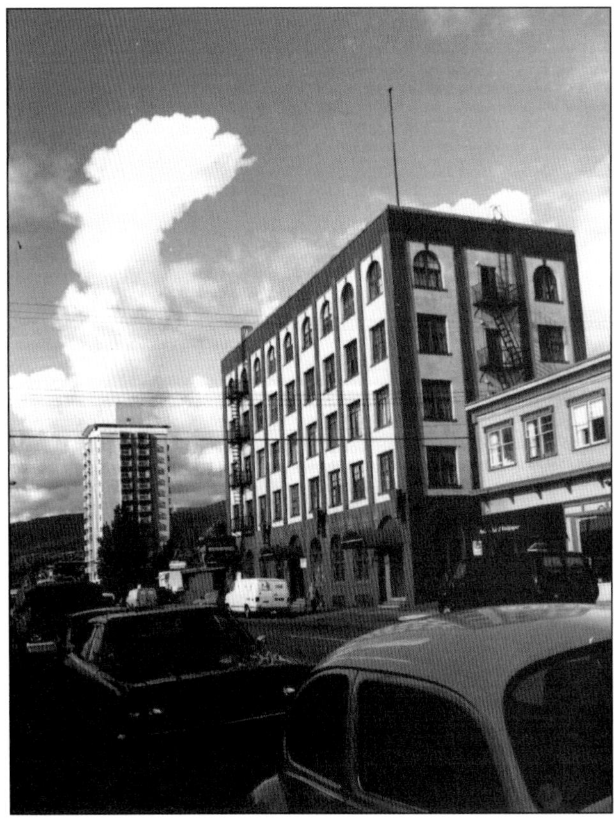

This photograph shows the St. Alice Hotel on November 3, 1981. By then, it was a residential building with many of its occupants deriving their income from pensions or social assistance. It is hard to imagine that there was a period when Lower Lonsdale was not a desirable place to live. A residential tower to the west of the old hotel is a harbinger of change coming to the Lonsdale neighbourhood. Heritage advocates did not succeed in preserving the St. Alice, which was demolished in 1989, and in its place a residential tower named the Observatory was built.

The Observatory, a 30-story building higher than any other building in the Lonsdale neighbourhood and indeed the North Shore, was built on the site of the St. Alice Hotel. In this 1990 photograph, the Observatory rises above all other buildings. When it was built, it also blocked many people's views. The Barraclough block on Lonsdale Avenue and Second Street, which used to house the Great Outdoor retail store, offers a relative measure to the scale of the Observatory.

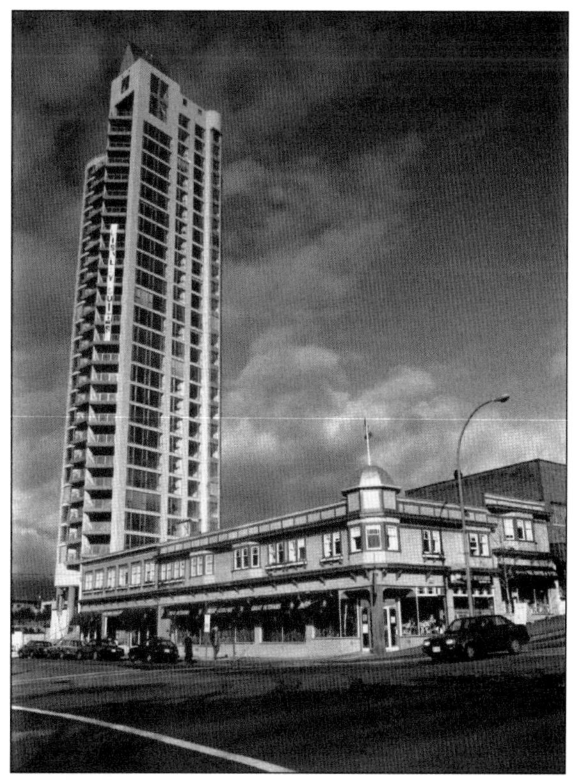

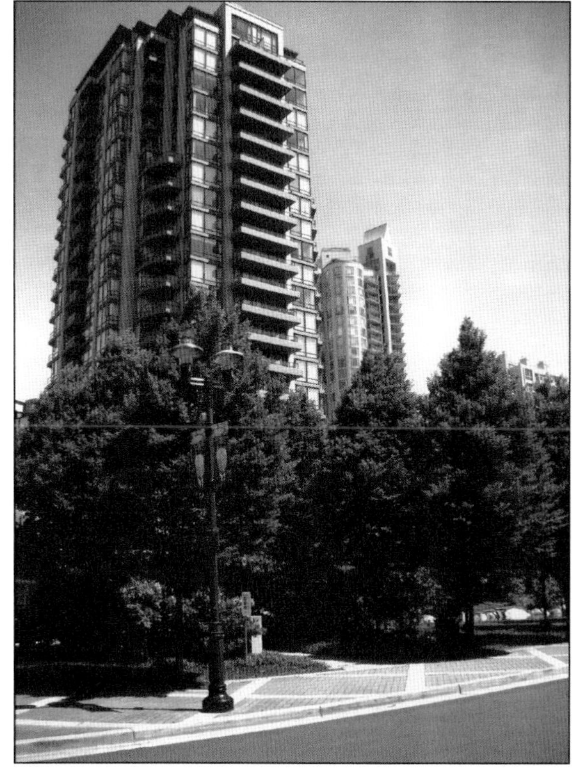

Jack Loucks Court, a small neighbourhood pedestrian park, in the midst of the high-density core of Lower Lonsdale on West First Street, is named after longtime mayor John Edwin (Jack) Loucks. Loucks was an elementary school teacher in North Vancouver and served as an elementary school principal for the last 21 years of his teaching career. He was elected mayor of the City of North Vancouver in 1977 and remained mayor until retirement in 1999.

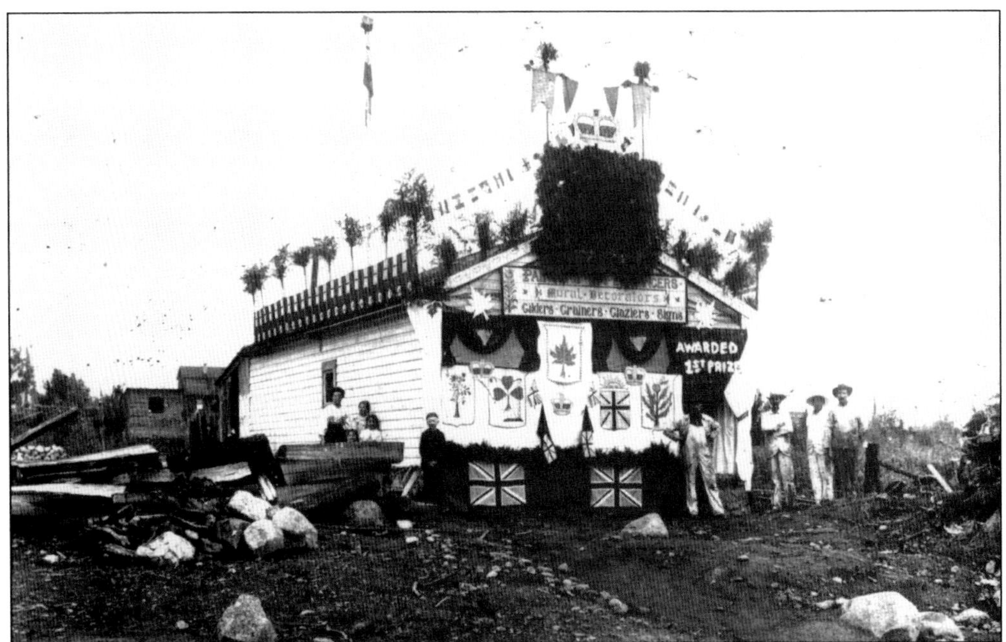

People standing in front of the decorated house of W. T. Grahame, at 1232 Lonsdale Avenue, are (from left to right) Mrs. Grahame, daughters, son Murdie, James Grahame, Walter Grahame, and workmen. This house was awarded first prize for the best decorated house on July 1, 1907.

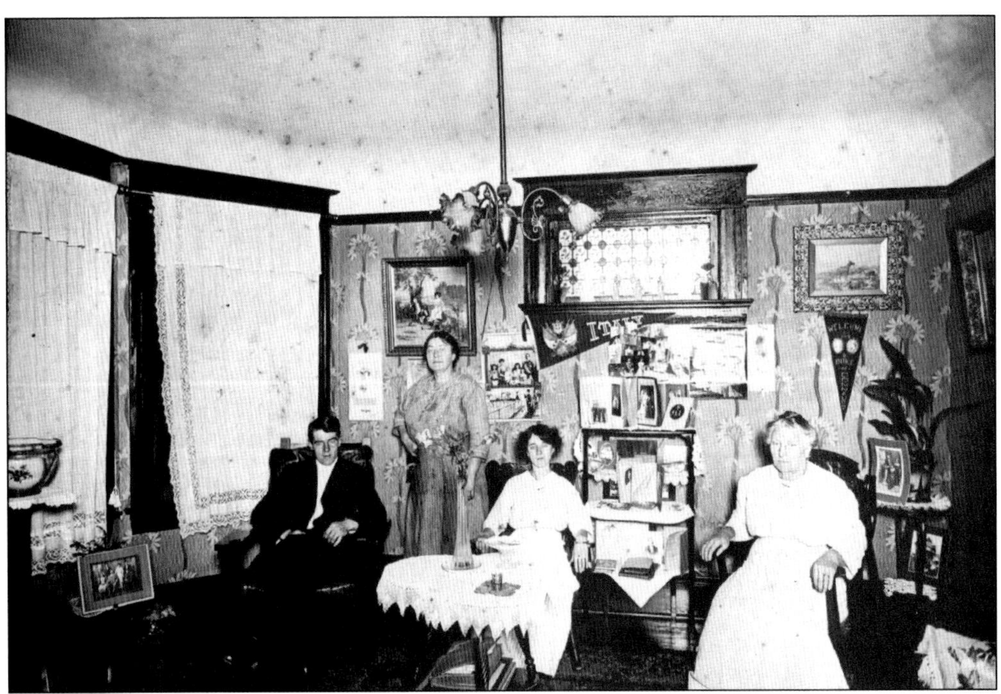

This interior view of the house at 204 West Fourth Street, around 1912, includes (from left to right) an unidentified man, Carolina Andruss, an unidentified woman, and Angelina Andruss. Carolina Andruss, together with Lorenzo Reda, launched the Palace Hotel. A photograph of Lorenzo Reda and family is placed on the table at left.

Antonio Bosco stands here with his wife Rose. They lived in the house behind them, which was built around 1910 by Antonio at 798 East Thirteenth Street, about a year before this photograph was taken.

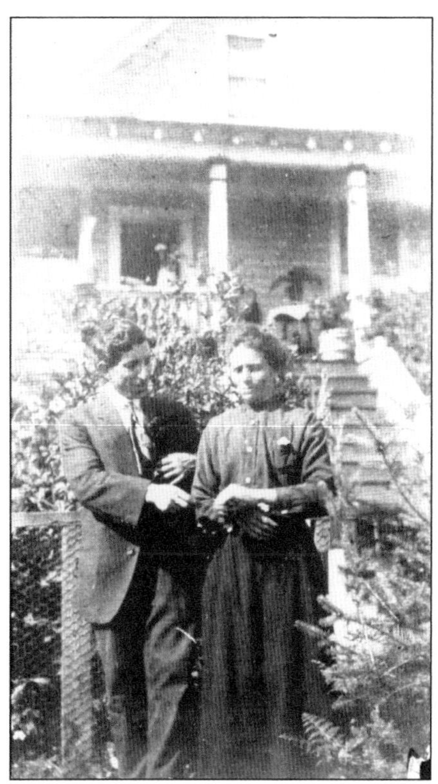

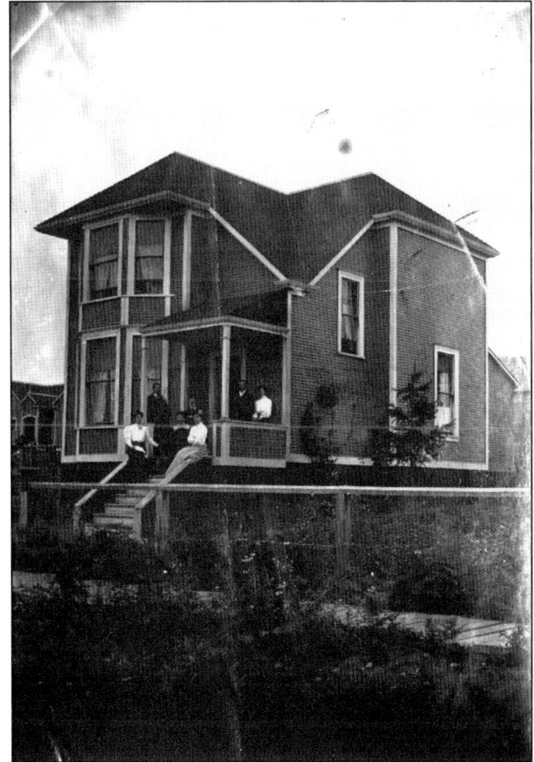

This house, built in 1908 at 176 West Third Street, belonged to Charles and Alice Nye. The man and woman at right are believed to be the Nyes. After Charles's death, Alice Nye had elderly boarders here.

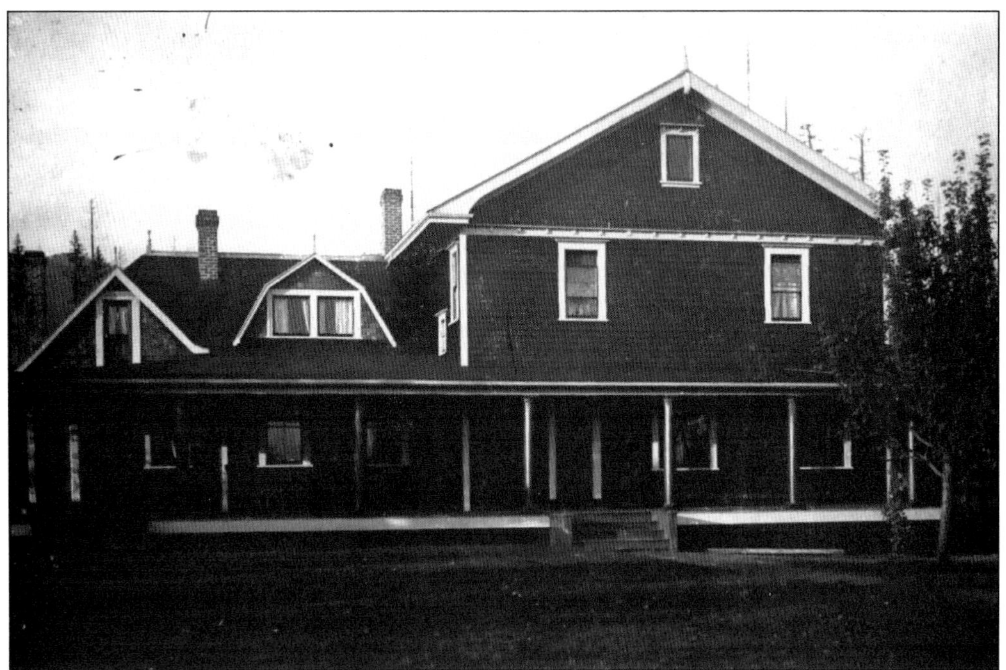

This house belonged to Arthur Bramah Diplock, the founder of the Western Corporation. His business associates were J. C. Keith, A. E. Kealy, piano dealer William Montelius, bookseller W. Sarel, and Lawyer A. D. Taylor. The Western Corporation offered a broad range of real estate related services during the real estate boom years.

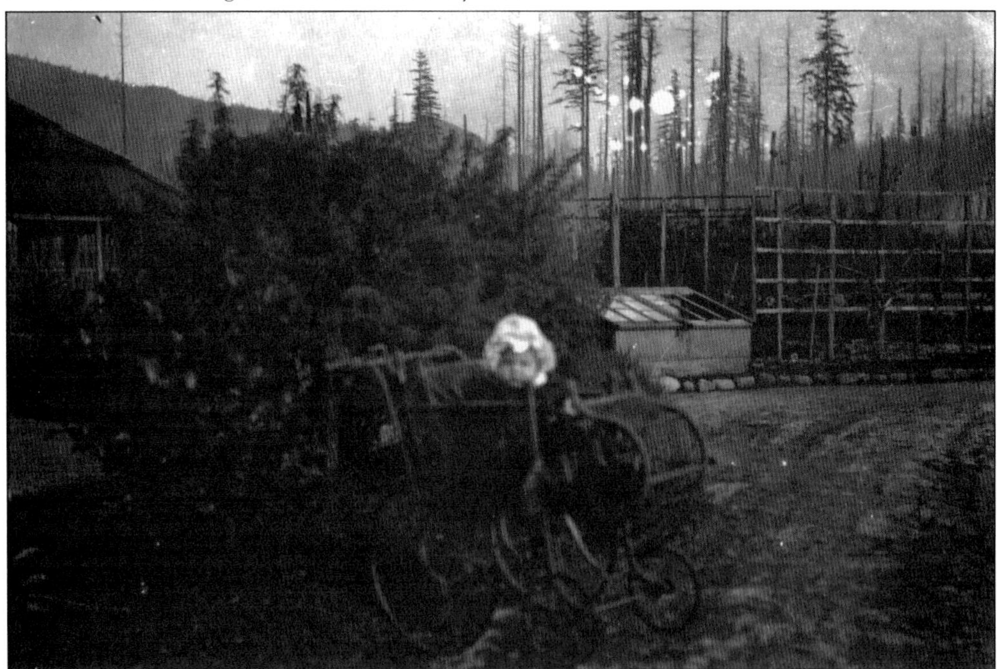

This 1917 photograph shows Arthur Diplock's daughter in a baby carriage at the Diplock home. Arthur Diplock was among the original five residents who arrived in the area near Fifteenth Street and Lonsdale Avenue in the late 1890s.

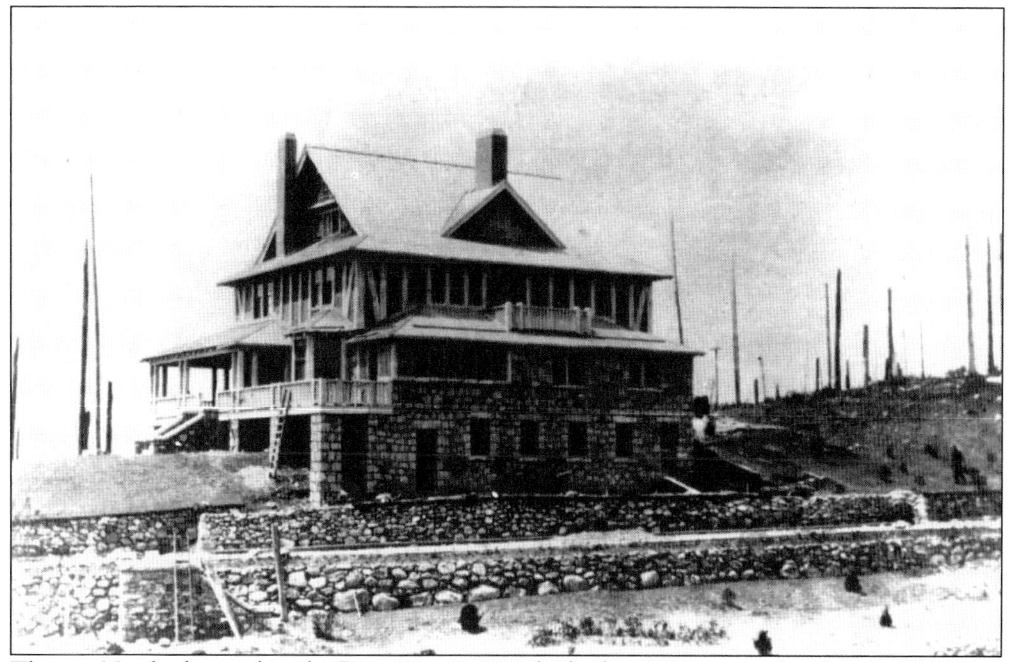

Thomas Nye had served in the Boer War. In 1912 he built a 6000-square-foot home at 230 East Carisbrooke at the top of Lonsdale Avenue that may have bankrupted him. The house later became the Kingsley School. The newly built house is shown here after a forest fire on Grouse Mountain.

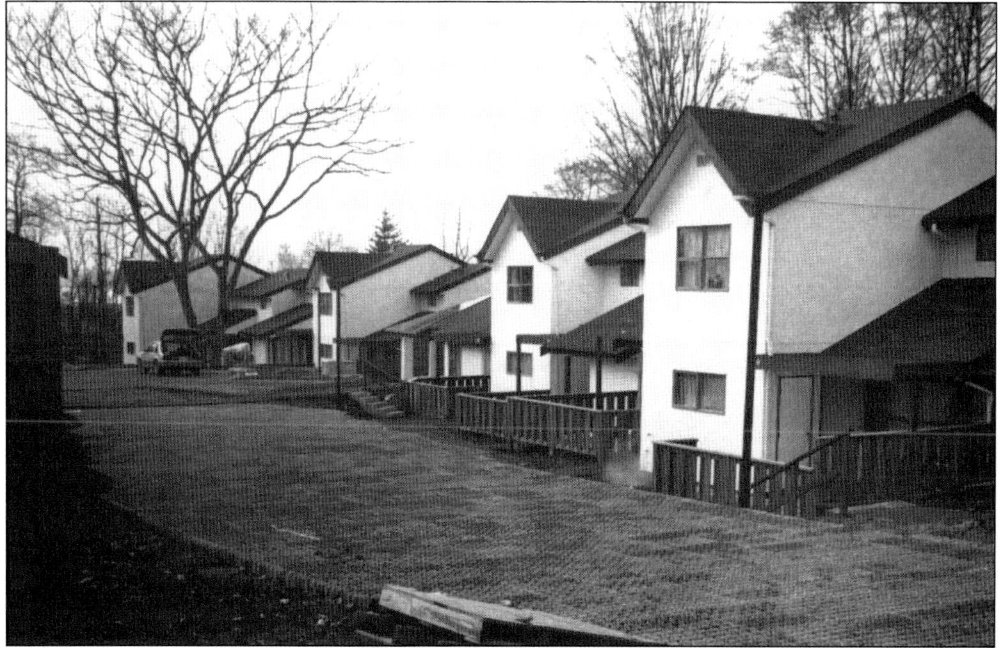

In the 1980s townhomes became popular with those who wanted to live in a house but could not afford one or did not want a large lawn to cut. The Walnut Gardens Townhouses in the 600 block of West Keith Road is an example of many townhomes built throughout the 1980s and 1990s.

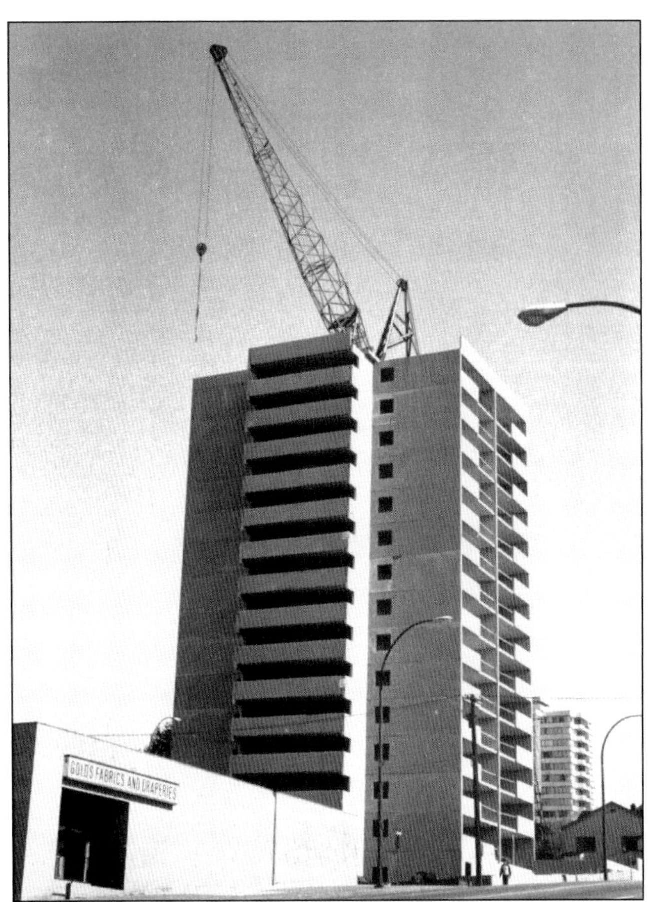

Construction of an apartment building at 110 West Fourth Street, around 1980, was a sign of things to come. The below May 31, 2009, photograph, taken on Chesterfield below Esplanade, shows the Lower Lonsdale boom of high-rises, with Central Lonsdale high-rises visible at the top of Chesterfield.

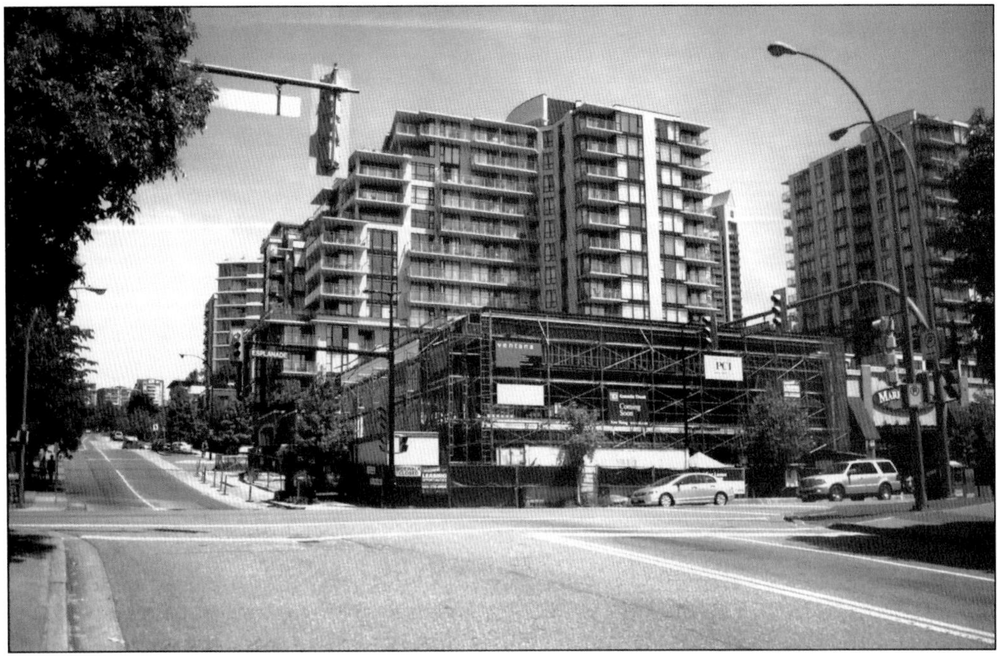

Seven

Living in the Neighbourhood

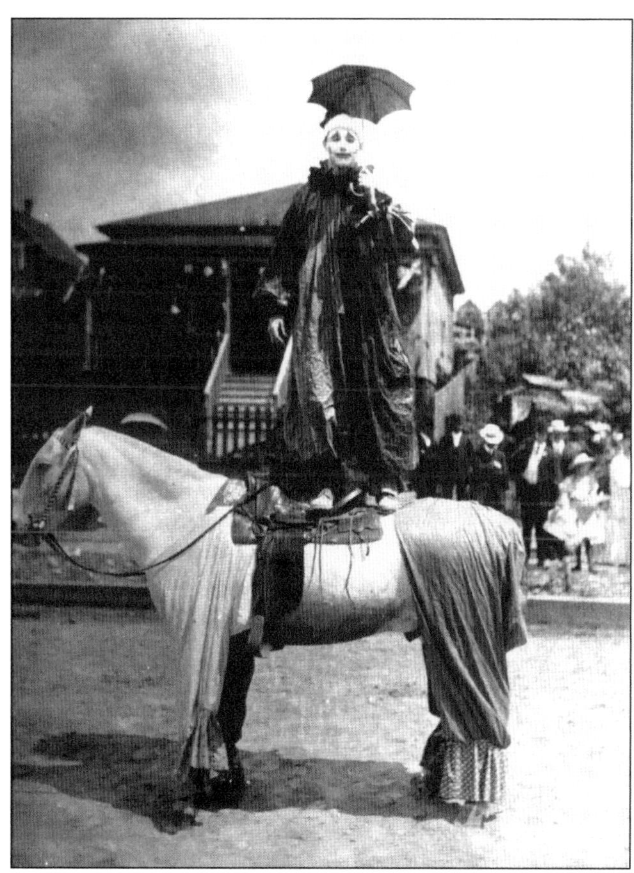

The Lonsdale neighbourhood has been full of life and activity since the early days. On July 1, around 1910, Stanley Huff dressed as clown for the Dominion Day parade and stood on horse Kinney-Johnny for this photograph opportunity.

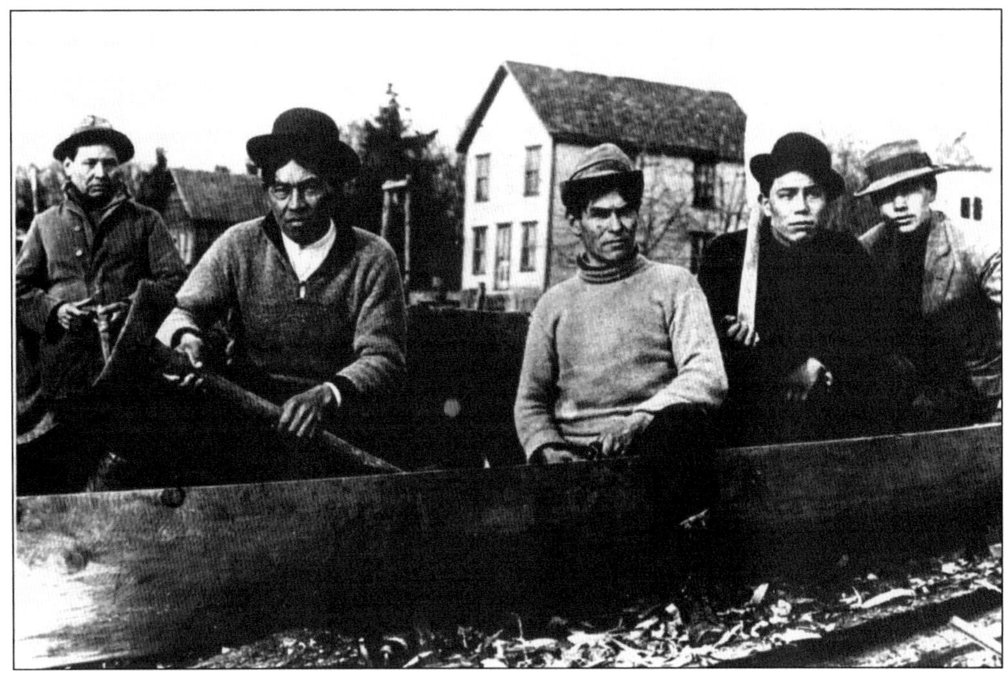

In this photograph, taken around 1912, a newly carved canoe is presented by five Squamish men identified as Dan Katies, Noel Julian, Willie Baker, Steven Antone, and an unidentified man. Houses on the Mission Reserve are visible in the background.

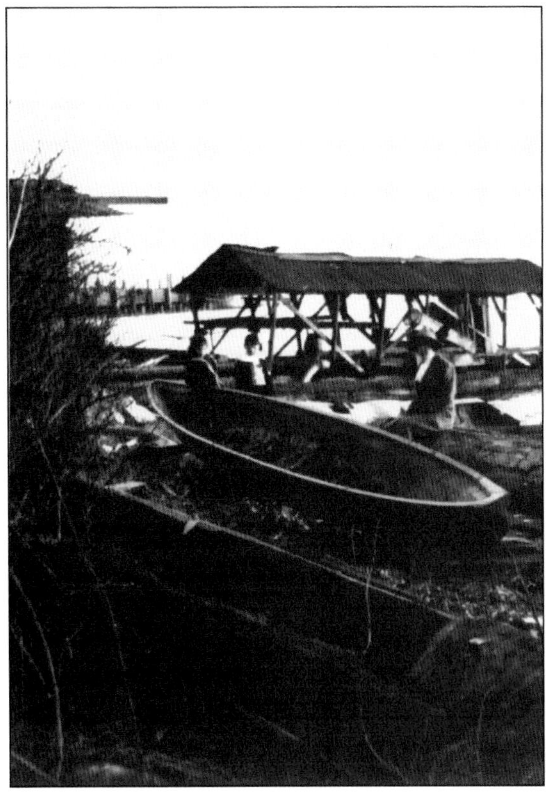

This dugout canoe was built in 1909 at the Mission Reserve. The woman at right became the first wife of Fred Mills in 1913; he arrived in British Columbia from eastern Canada in 1906. He was an active member of the Vancouver Mountaineering Club on the North Shore.

Camel Mountain has two distinctive summits, and one is shown here, called the Crown. A Vancouver Mountaineering Club hiking party led by Fred Mills included Hewton, Lyttleton, and Miskin on October 6, 1908. Crown lies northwest of Grouse Mountain in North Vancouver. Crown was accessible from Grouse Mountain, which in turn was reachable from the top of Lonsdale.

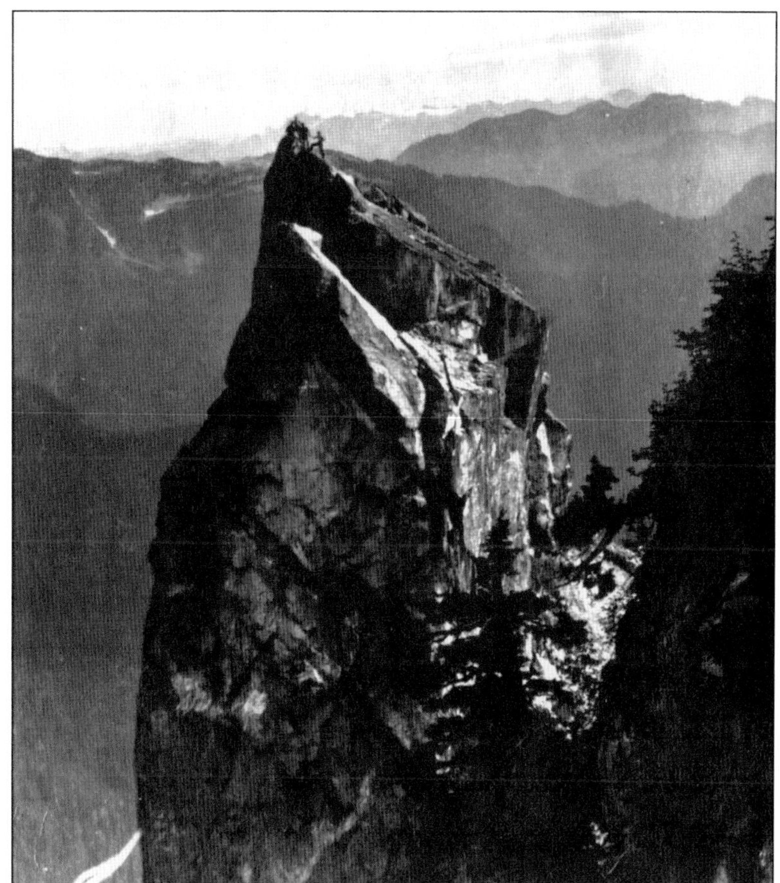

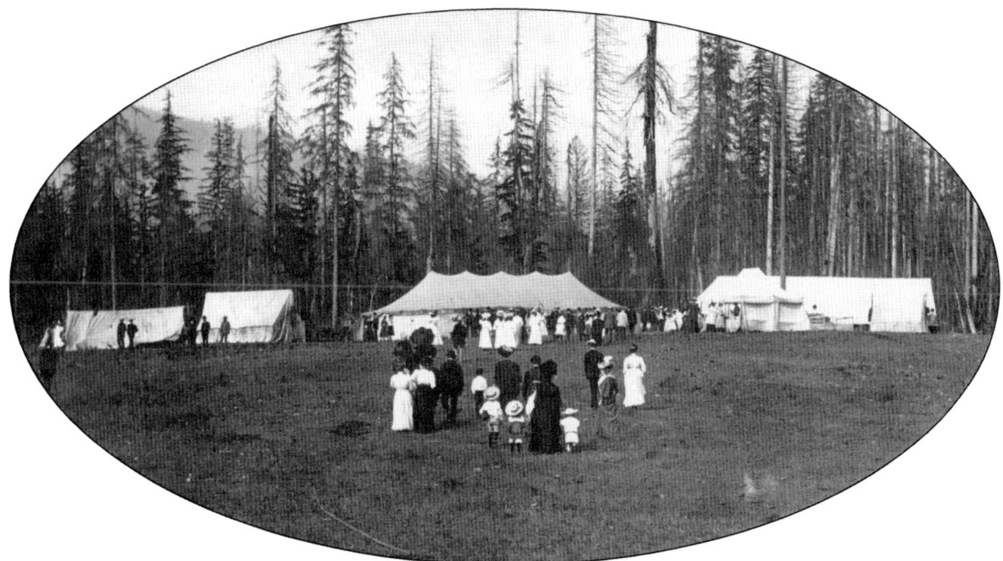

Tents were used for gatherings and social events, as seen in this *c.* 1906 photograph. The location of this gathering is at the Twenty-third and Lonsdale Avenue Horticultural Grounds.

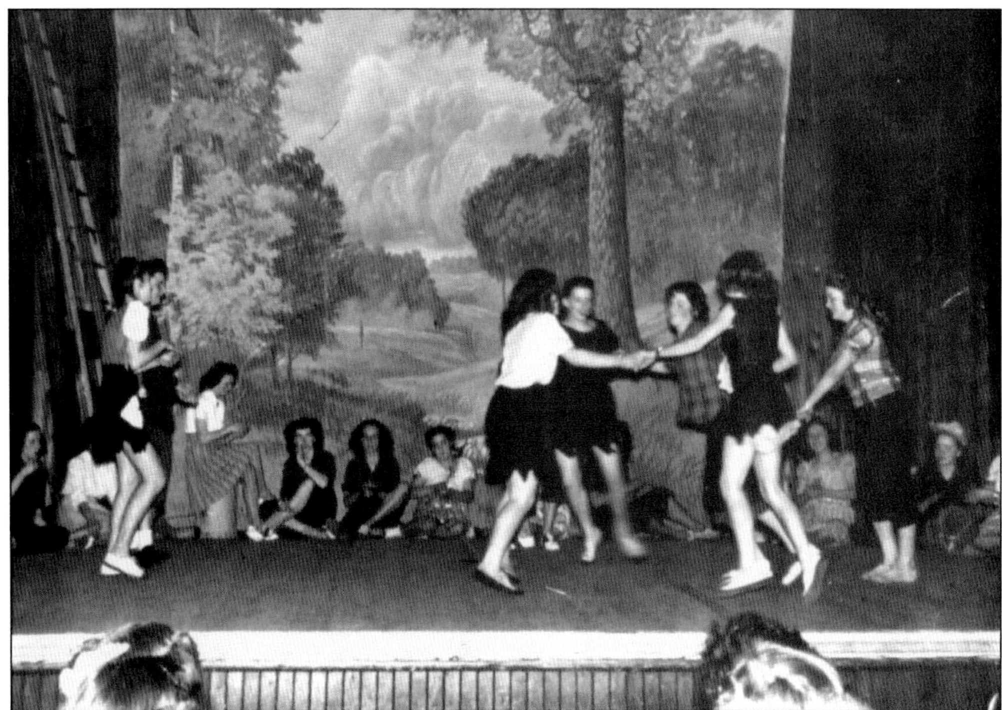

North Vancouver High School Girls' Athletic Club performs a square dance at the Horticultural Hall on the 27th or 28th of March 1947. The photograph below shows the Horticultural Hall in 1910, which for decades was an essential centre for holding various exhibits, club meetings, and community gatherings.

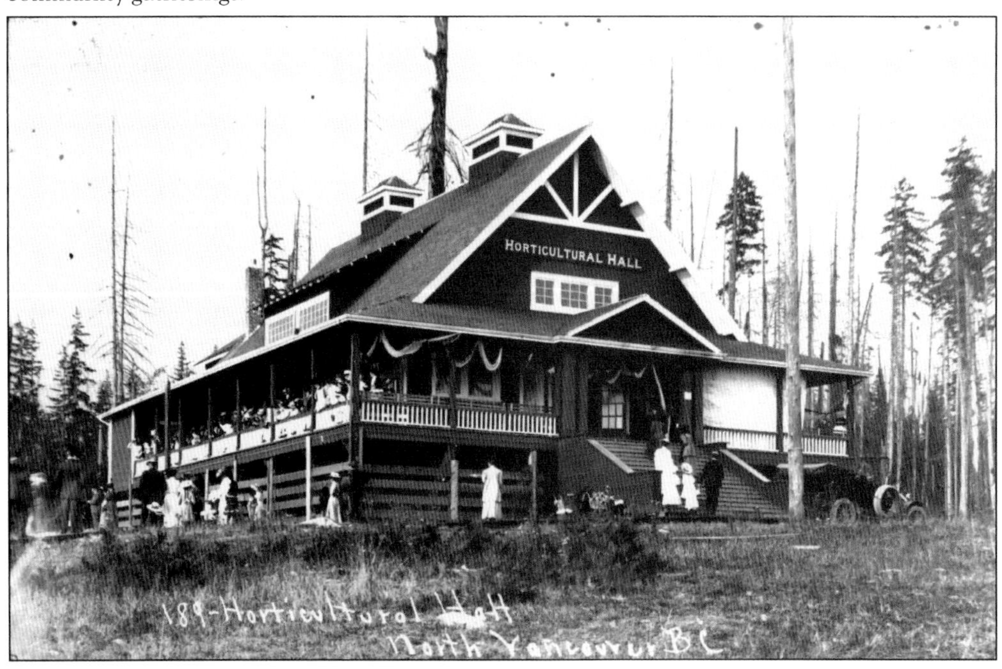

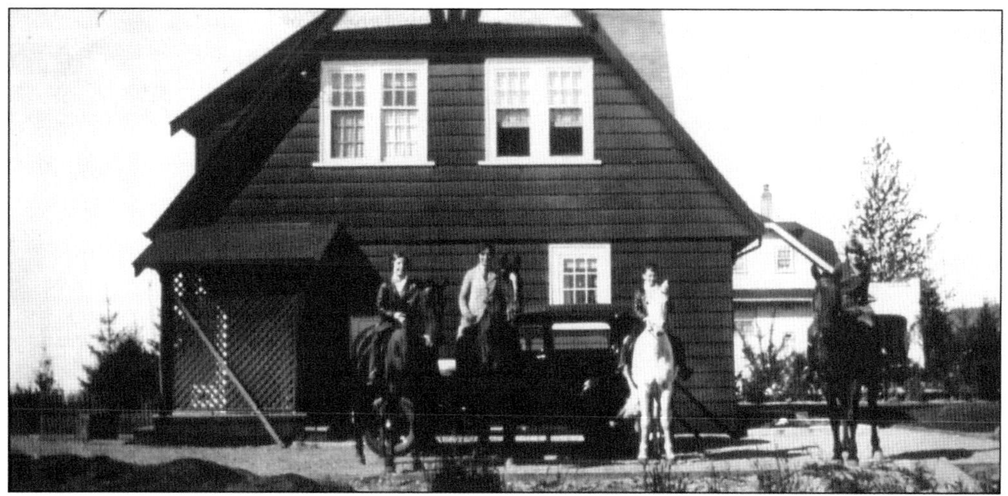

Long after the introduction of cars, horseback riding was popular with some people in North Vancouver, as apparent in this 1932 photograph taken at 1473 West Keith Road. Riders are identified as (from left to right) Pat Humphreys, Mrs. Meredith, Sandy Paton, and Betty Hargreaves.

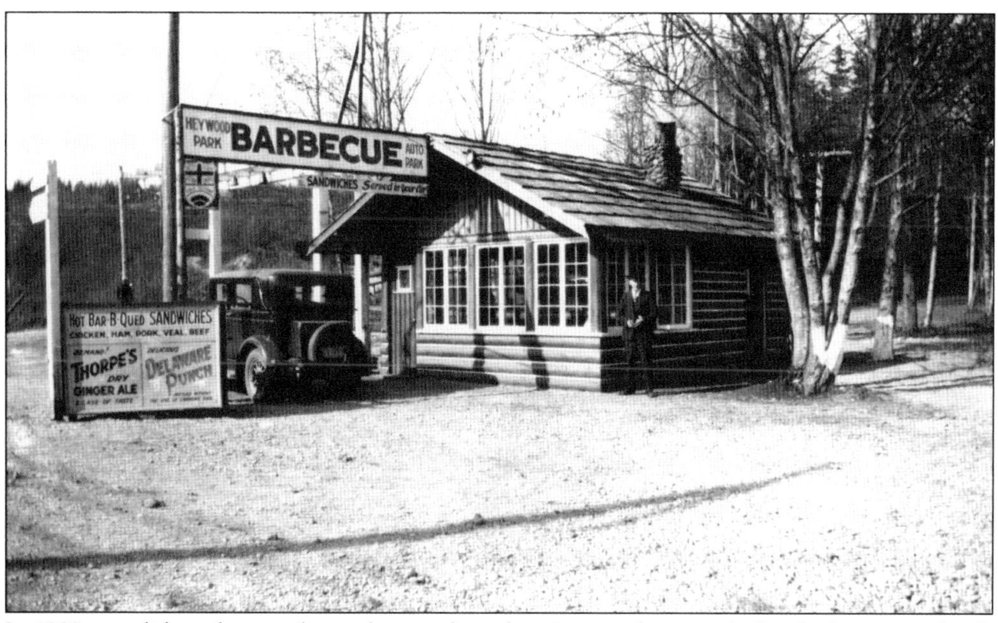

In 1929, one did not have to leave the comfort of one's car to be served a hot barbecue sandwich or a "Delicious Delaware Punch" at Heywood Park Barbecue on Marine Drive and West Keith Road.

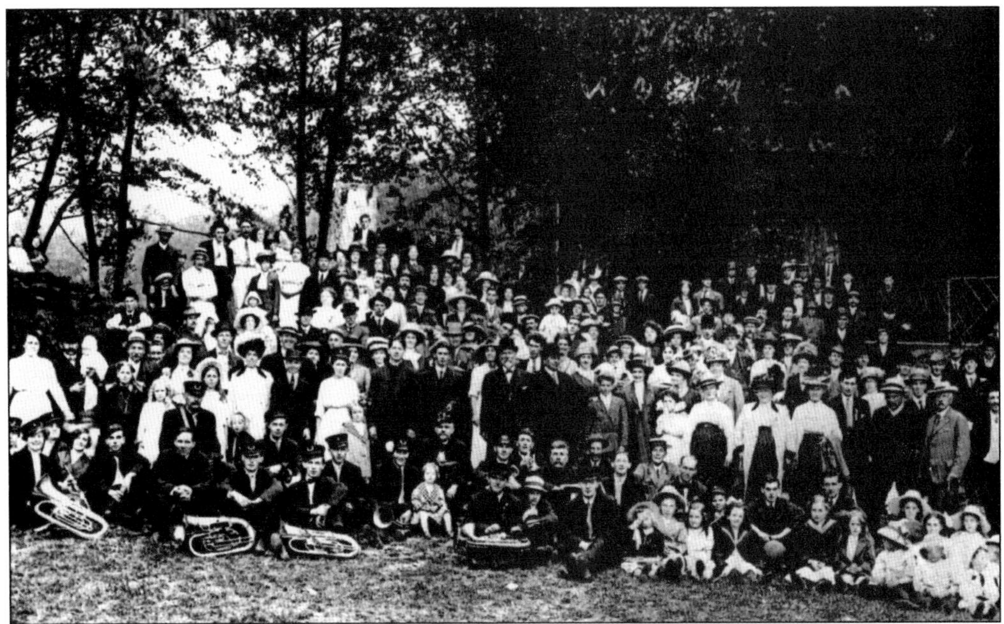

Wallace Shipyard employees and their families are present at an annual picnic. Andy Wallace, Wallace Shipyards founder, has been identified as being among the joyful crowd. Wallace Shipyards offered unprecedented employment opportunities to men and later, during World War II, to as many as 1000 women.

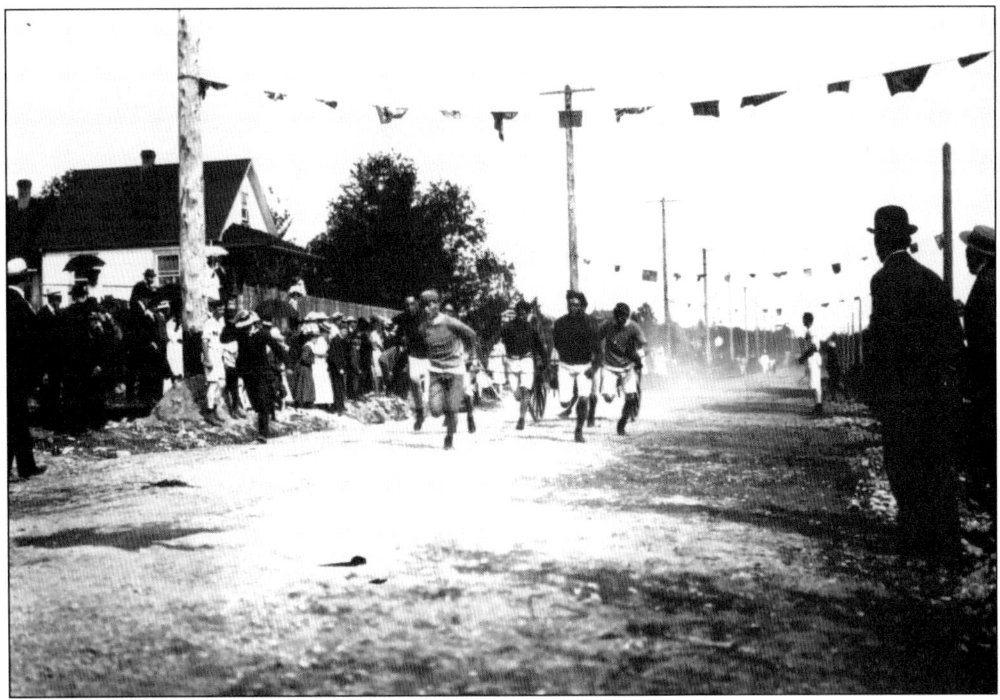

The First Nations team speeds ahead in a hose reel race, watched by a crowd on the 200 block of East First Street.

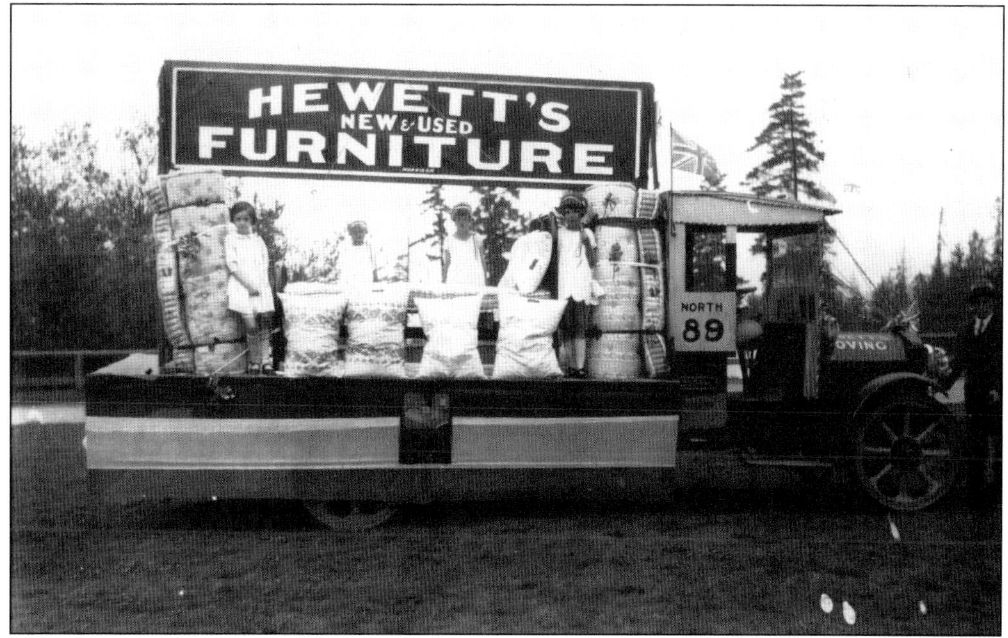

A decorated Hewett's Home Furniture truck in Mahon Park won the first prize at a parade, around 1929. Bunty Hewett stands at the right.

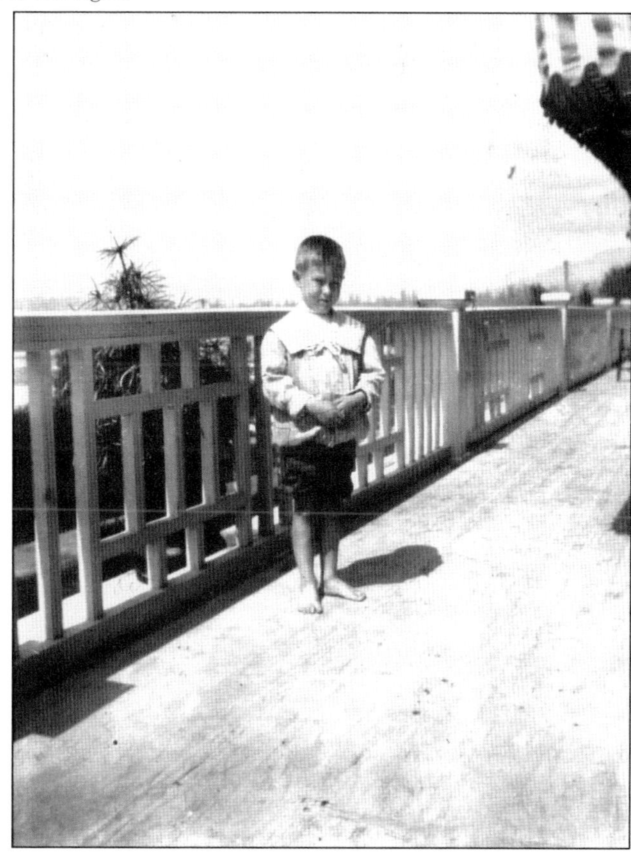

John Liersch stands on the veranda of the Hotel North Vancouver. He and his mother lived in the hotel from 1911 until 1914. Later on he attended North Vancouver High School.

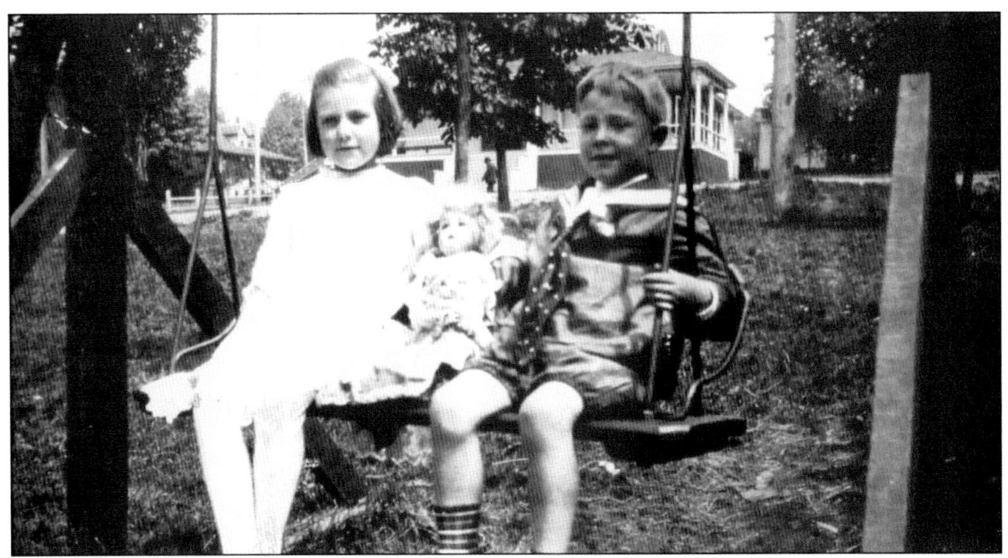

John Liersch and Pete Larson's daughter, Alma Larson, play on garden swing at Hotel North Vancouver.

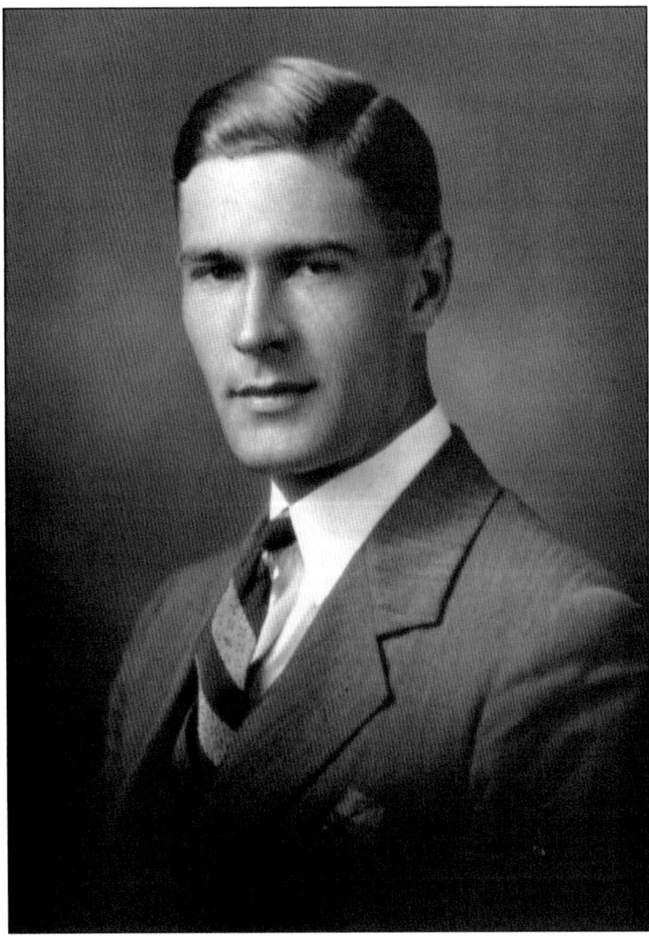

John Liersch went on to graduate with a forestry degree from the University of British Columbia. He later served on the University of British Columbia Board of Governors and was head of its Forestry Department. He was a recipient of the Order of Canada for his work in education.

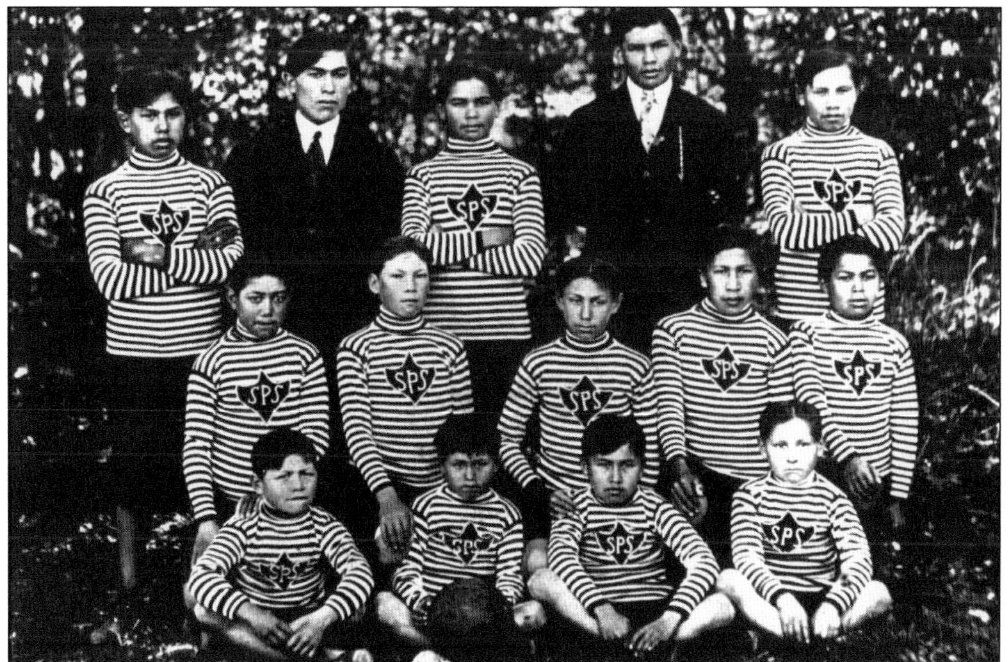

This 1908 photograph is of the St. Paul's Indian Residential School soccer team. The school was located north of the Mission Reserve, run by French-speaking nuns teaching English to Squamish-speaking children. The members of this soccer team are identified as, from left to right, (first row) Issa Joe, Jack Andrew, Dennis Paull, and Andy Paull; (second row) Isadore Pierre, Albert Campbell, Albert Julian, Frank Baker, and Ernest Isaac; (third row) Alexander Domnick, Felix Thomas, Alfred George, Henry George, and David Thomas.

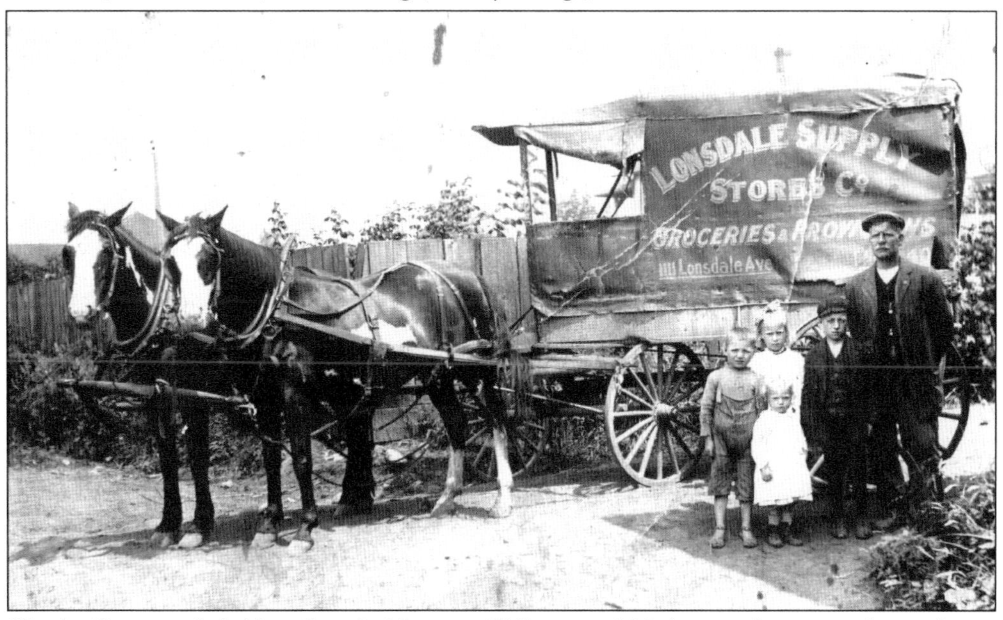

Charles Ritter and children Joseph, Victoria, William, and Violet stand next to a horse-drawn delivery wagon that says "Lonsdale Supply Stores Co.—Groceries and Provisions" on the side in this *c.* 1913 photograph.

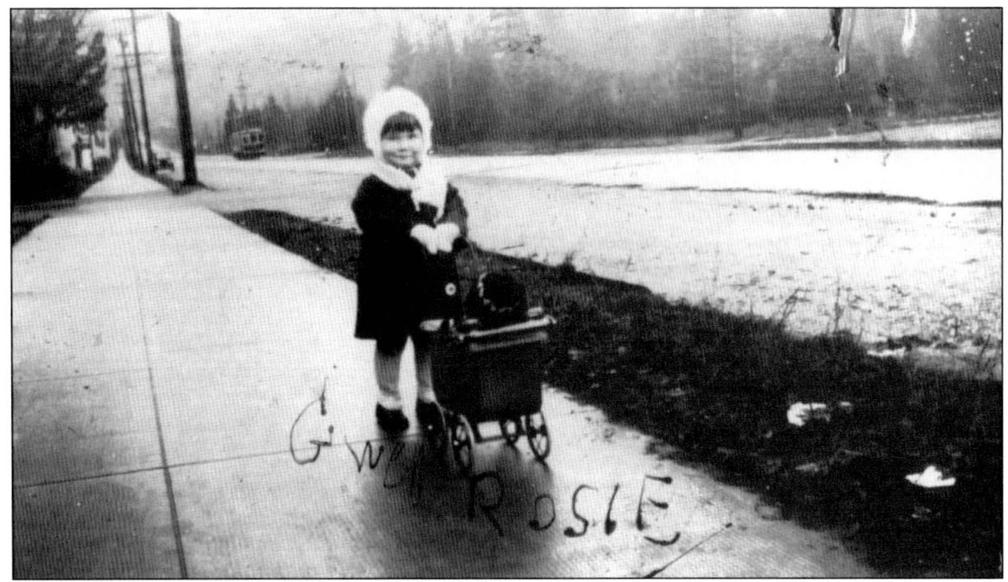

Gwen Jones is shown in the above photograph taken in 1933 with her doll and buggy on the 1700 block of Lonsdale Avenue. Twenty-eight years later, in January 1961, a grown Gwen Weaver (née Jones), stands on the same block with her child.

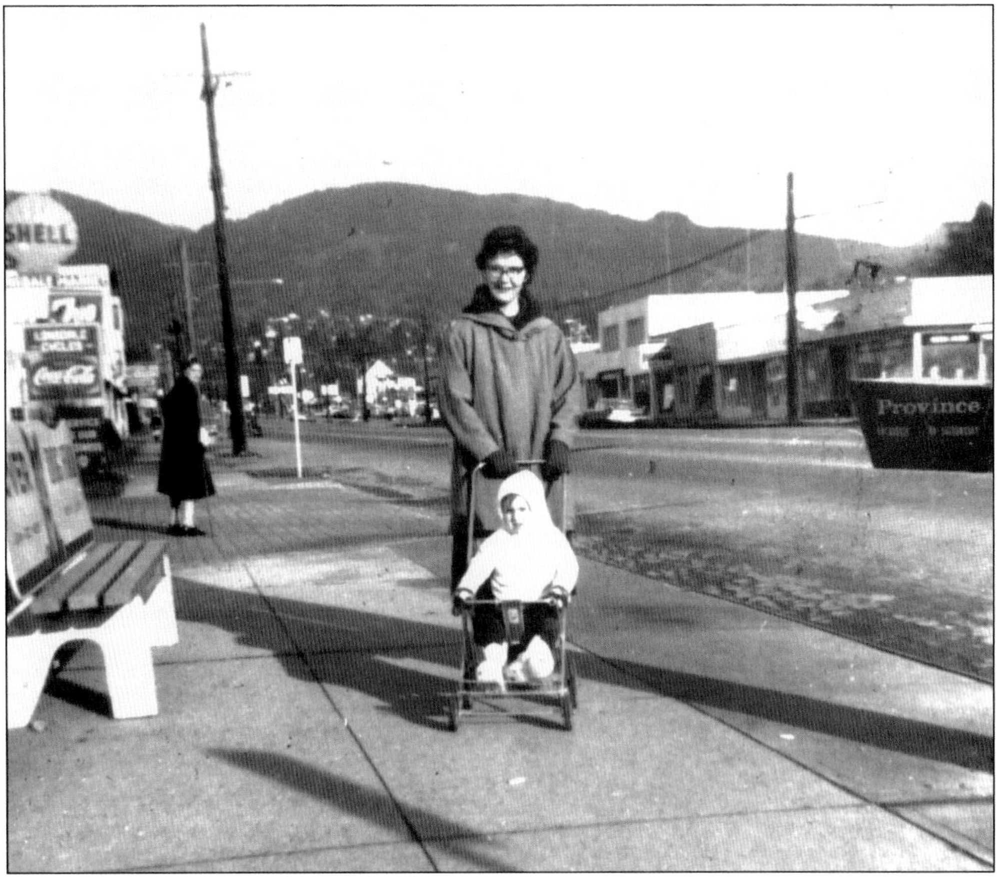

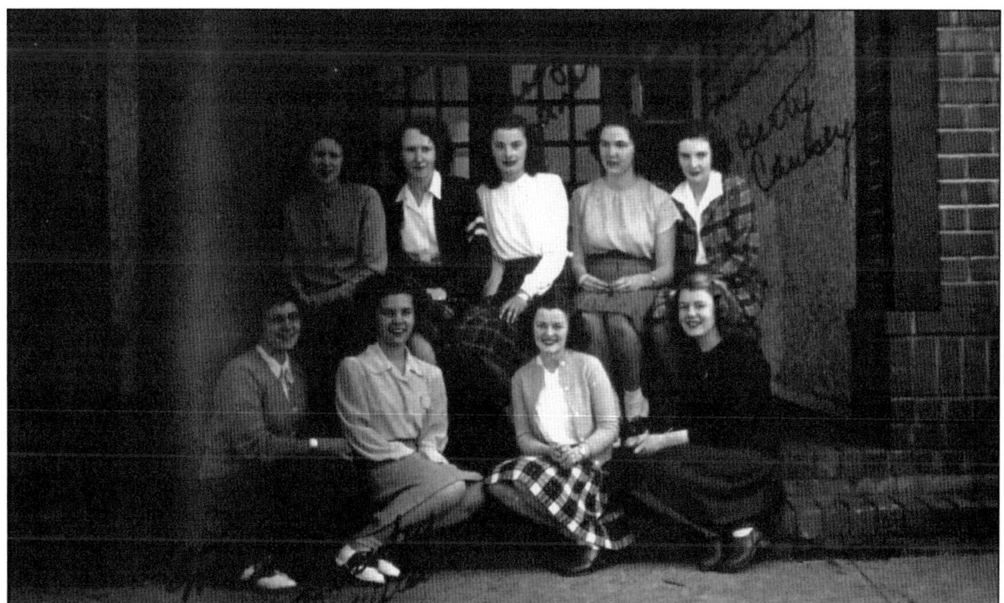

Gwen Jones is among her North Vancouver High School classmates (back row, second from right) in this 1943 photograph. Students in the class of 1947 are, from left to right, (first row) Kaye McNamee, Beverley Wilson, Helen Mathieson, and Jean Sandy; (second row) Doreen Leonard, Margaret Bartley, Mary Frances Daniel, Gwen Jones, and Betty Cawsey.

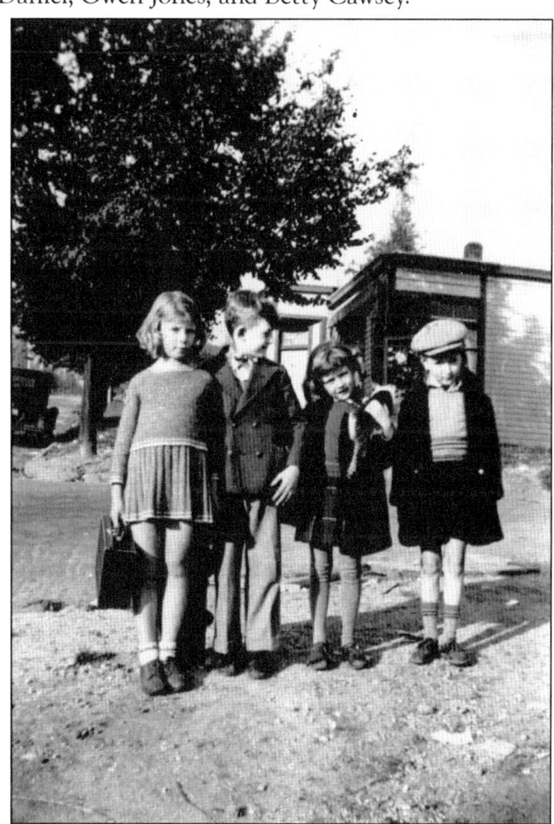

Children standing near Windsor Confectionery and Grocery at the northeast corner of Lonsdale Avenue and Windsor Road in 1938 are (from left to right) Margaret Coe, Ian Morrison, Bev Morrison, and Eric (whose last name is unidentified).

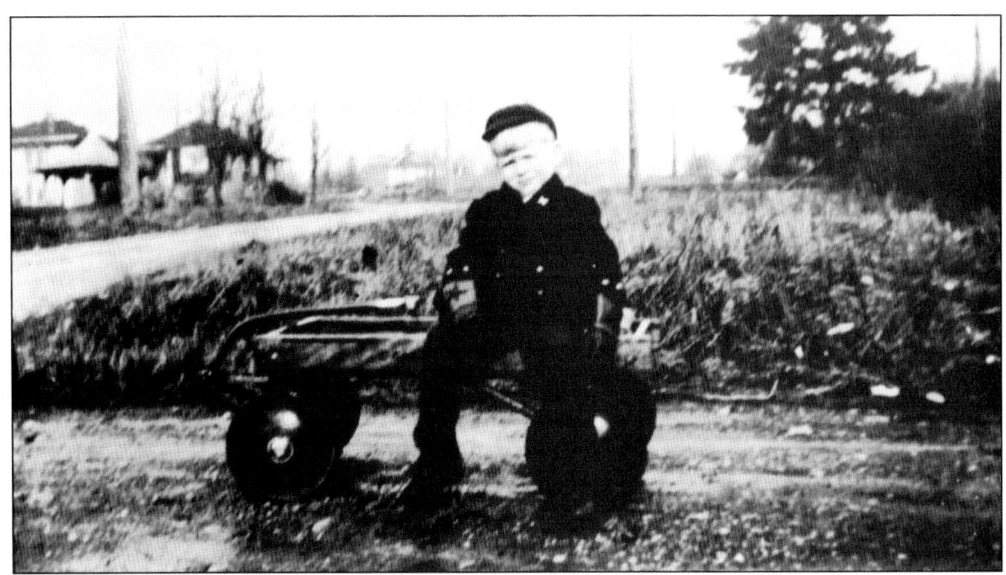

A young Bob Nicholson sits on a CCM Bikewagon, around 1934. Behind him one can see the 1600 block of Lonsdale Avenue. The wagon is in the North Vancouver Museum Collection.

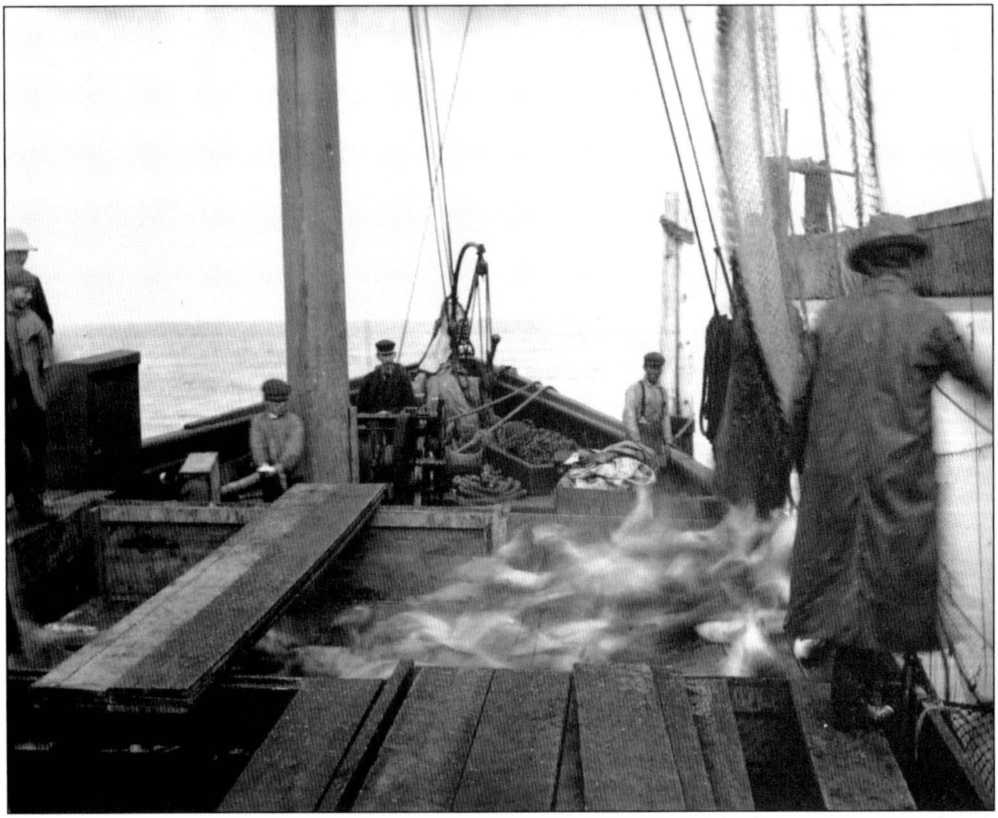

Fishing was a reliable means to earn a living in days when fish stocks had not yet been depleted. Local fishermen unload fish onto the fishing boat *Selkirk* in 1903.

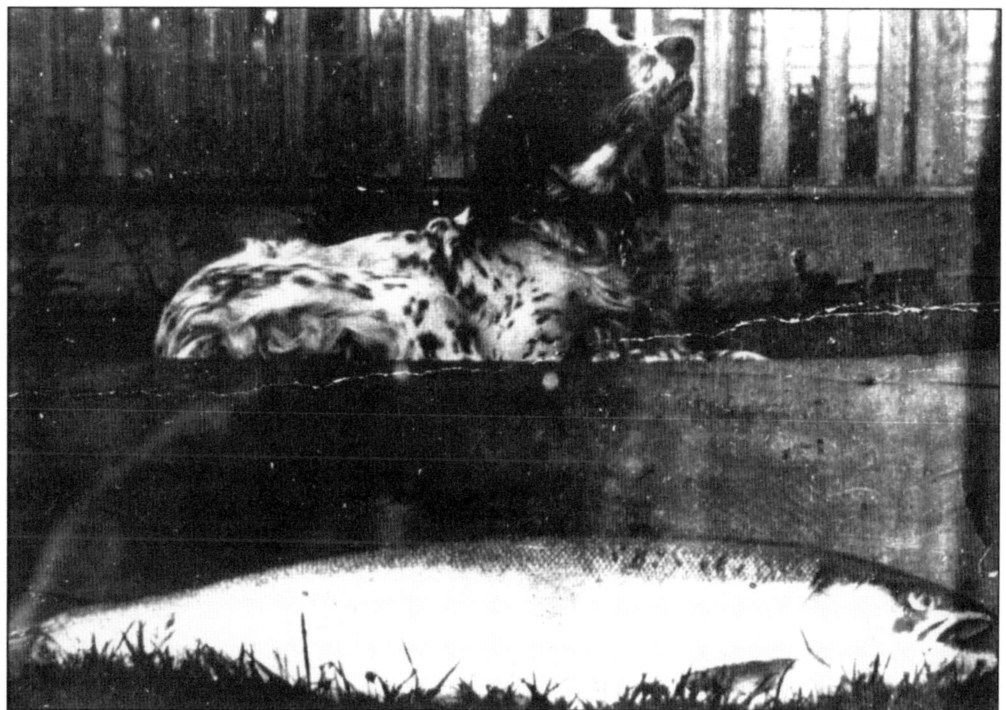

Not only were fish in abundance, some were also quite large in those days, like this one caught in the Capilano River, which is longer than the dog in the background.

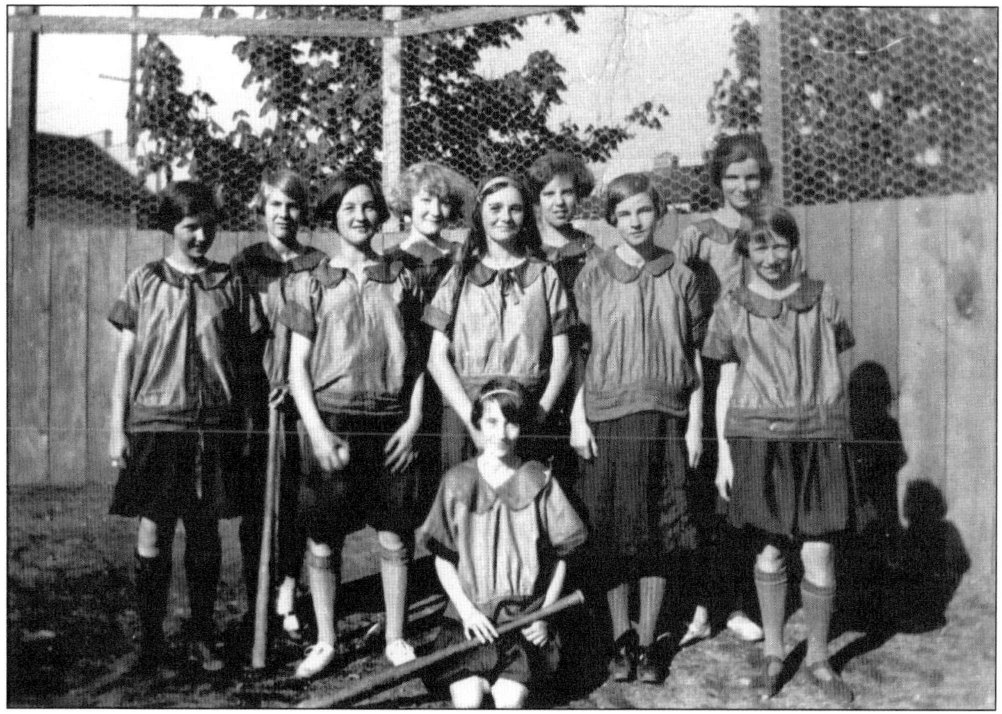

The Lonsdale School junior girls baseball team members stand together on the school grounds in 1926. Some of the girls are wearing sports bloomers.

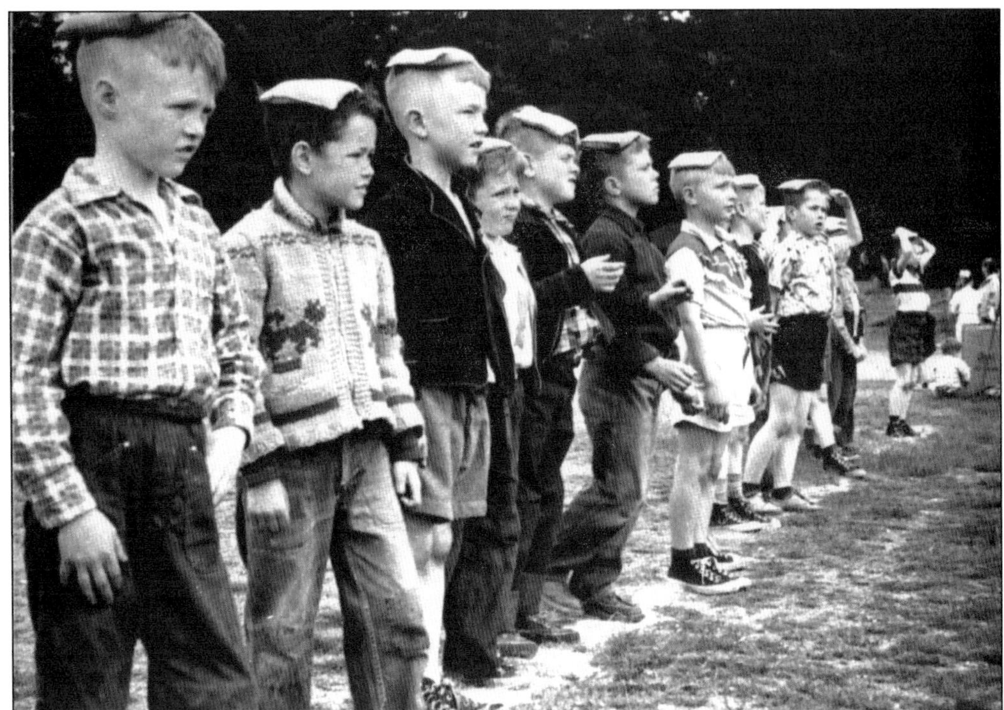

Grade two boys participate in the bean bag races in the Lonsdale School Sports Day in 1955, including Robert Grant, David Matthews, Kenny Watland, Ted Sebastian, Keith Kirkness, Stuart Lawson, Doug Botting, and Kenny Hadden.

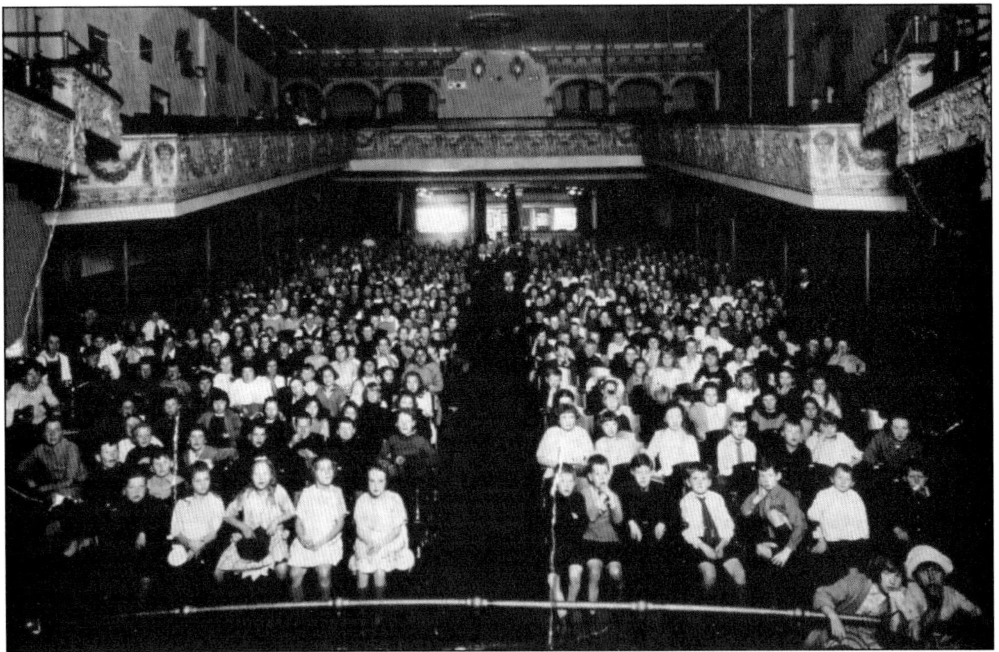

Fire prevention awareness was a key safety measure in the 1920s. Schoolchildren watch demonstrations provided by the City of North Vancouver Fire Department on Fire Prevention Day at Lonsdale Theatre.

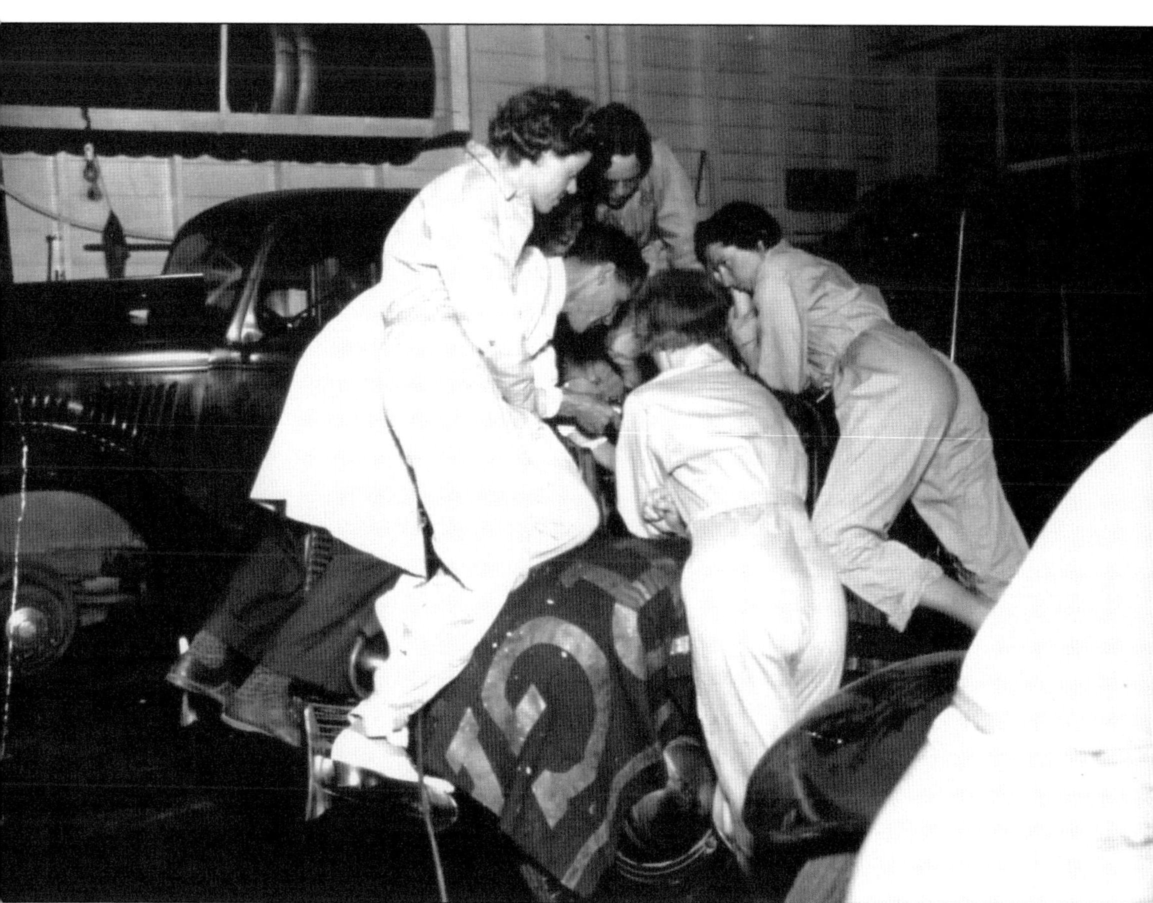

These women are learning basic automobile mechanics from Dave Bonar at McMillan Motors, which was located at Lonsdale Avenue and East Third Street. In this 1940 picture are Mollie Nye at left and Joyce Loutet at right.

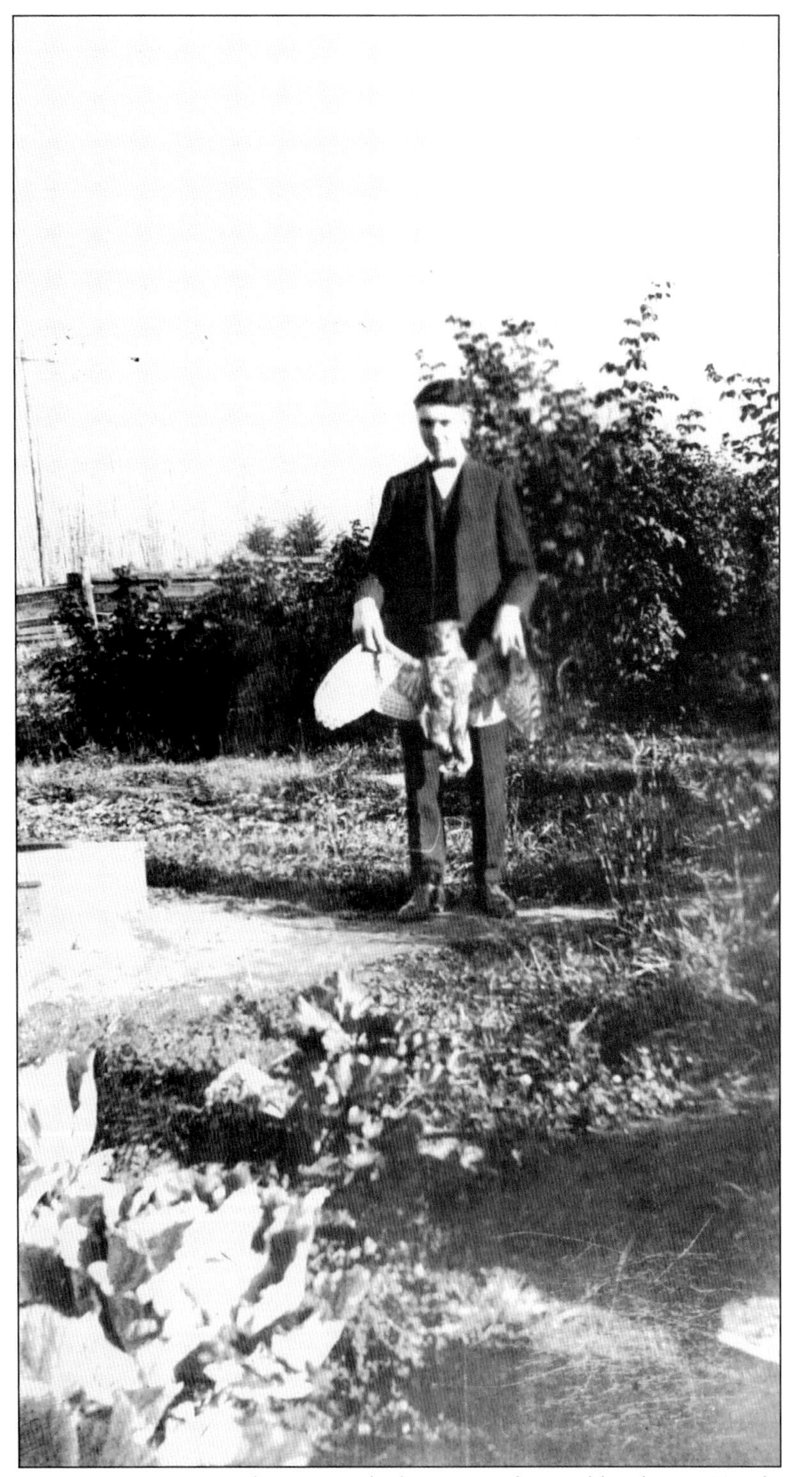

John Lentsmann, 19 or so years of age, spreads the wings of an owl he shot in North Vancouver in about 1922. The owl was apparently causing problems in his mother's chicken yard.

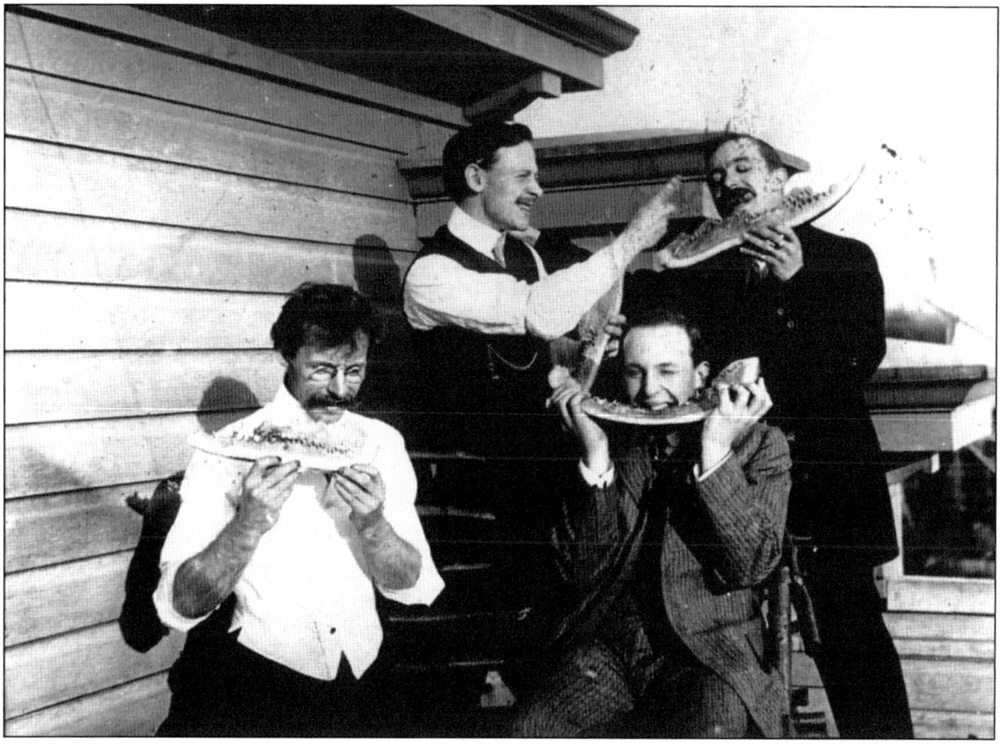

Photographer Albert Elliott (front, left) and business partner Fred Baglow (top, left) are having a pleasurable time eating watermelons on the roof outside the Elliott & Baglow studio. Fred Baglow was hard of hearing, but his good speech enabled him to deal with customers. The second photograph shows the studio sign and skylight in the Junction Block on Lonsdale Avenue at West Esplanade.

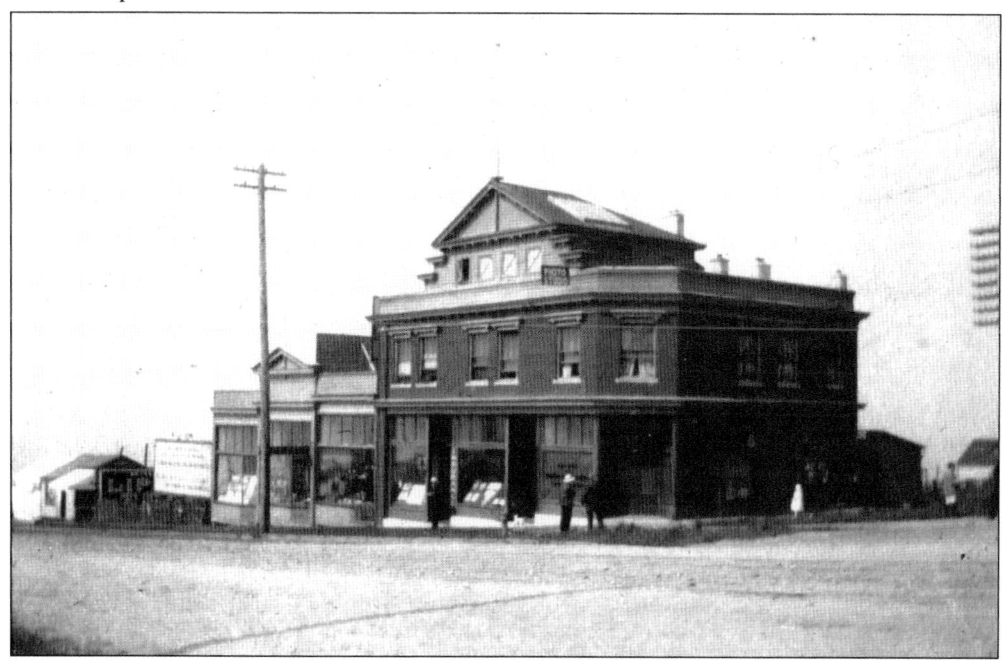

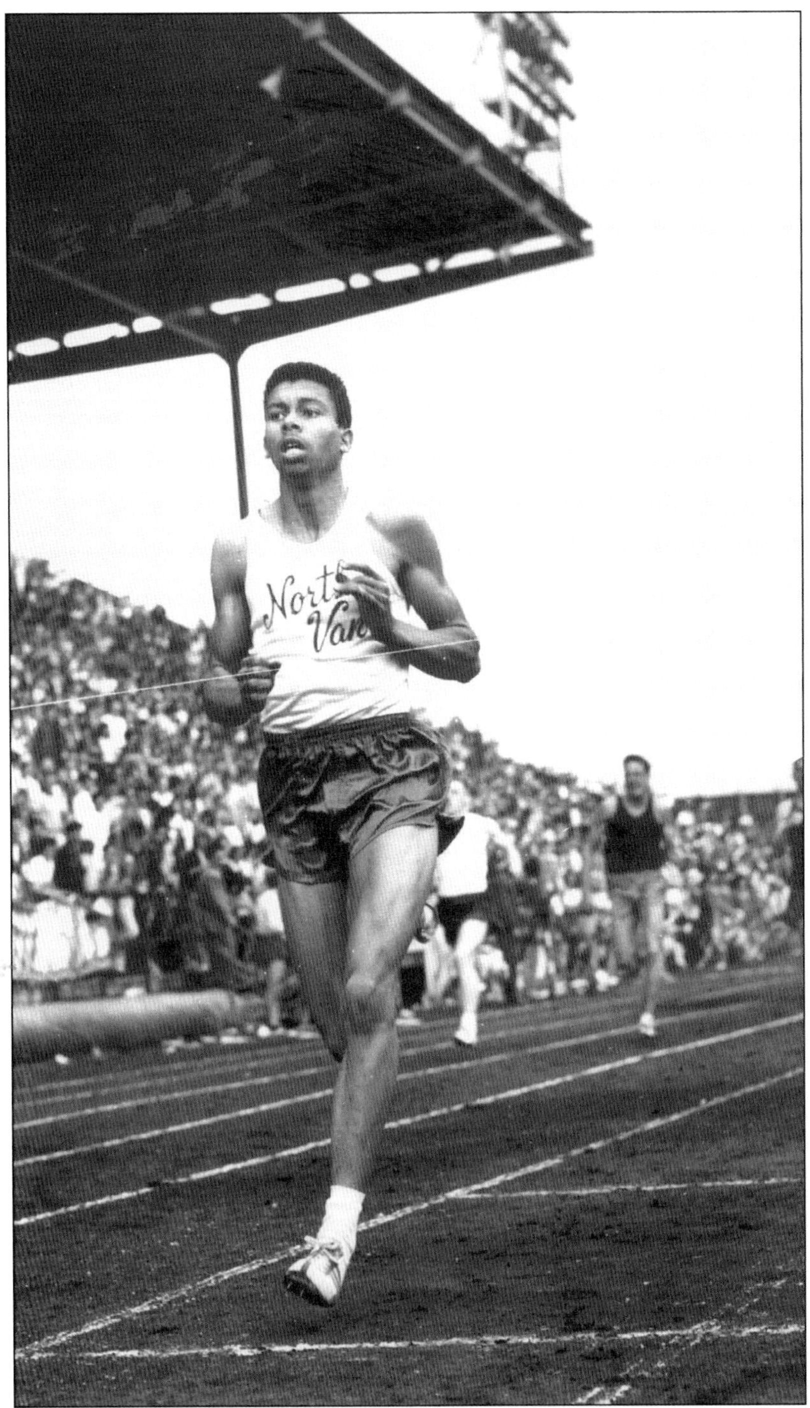

This photograph captures Harry Jerome of North Vancouver High School breaking Percy Williams's 220-yard record in May 1959. On July 15–16, 1966, he tied the world record in the men's 100 yards at 9.1 seconds in Edmonton. "Hurricane Harry" also had an impressive combined time of 29.5 seconds for back to back 100 and 220 yards. There is a statue of Jerome in Stanley Park and a recreation centre is named after him at Lonsdale Avenue and Twenty-third Street.

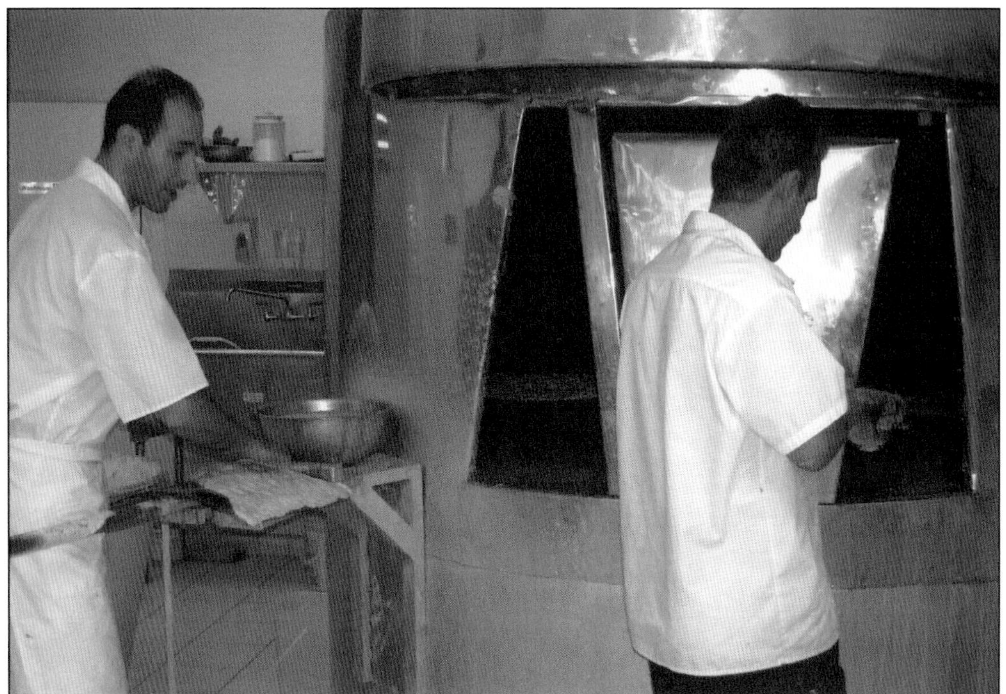

Since the late 1970s, thousands of Iranians have chosen North Vancouver as their home. Lonsdale neighbourhood's many Iranian bakeries, grocery stores, and other businesses are a reflection of this choice. For example, Naan Hut, a traditional Iranian bakery on 137 West Seventeenth Street, brings a bread-baking tradition, several thousand years old, to North Vancouver's Lonsdale neighbourhood. Kaumars Khanipoyani (left) skilfully prepares and places the dough in the oven while Reza Mohammadi retrieves the very hot naan, called sangak. *Sangak* means "pebbles" in Farsi and traditionally the bread was cooked on small river stones.

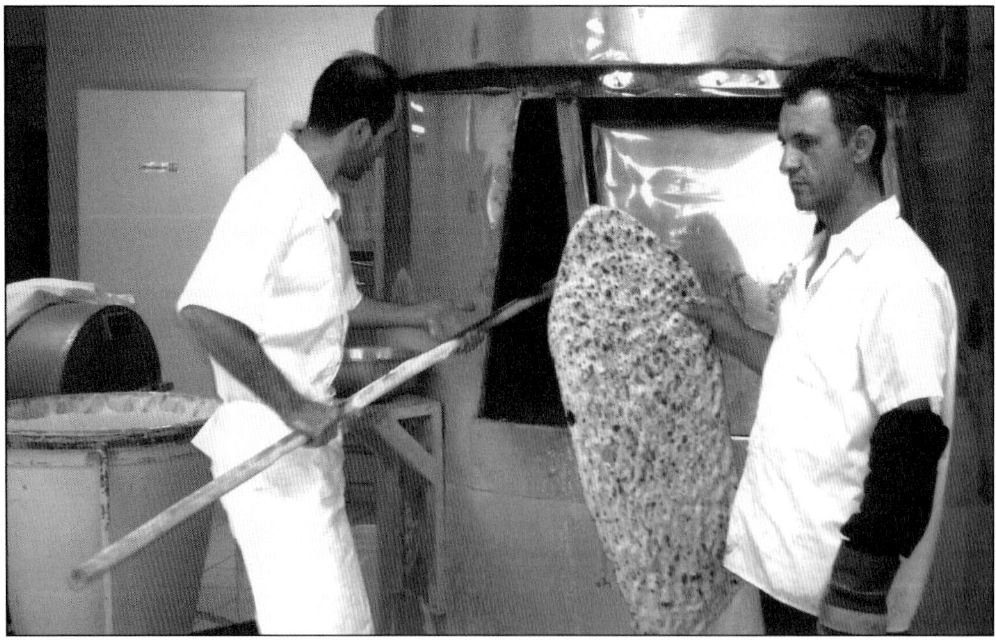

About the North Vancouver Museum & Archives

Founded in 1972, the North Vancouver Museum & Archives (NVMA) is the community's most important custodian of history and heritage. It operates two major public facilities, a museum in the City of North Vancouver and an archives in the District of North Vancouver. NVMA is governed by the North Vancouver Museum & Archives Commission, an agency whose members are appointed by the mayors and councils of the City and the District. The Friends of the North Vancouver Museum & Archives Society, a membership organization, is a registered charity dedicated to helping the NVMA achieve its goals.

Using historical photographs and locally significant artifacts, the museum galleries (209 West Fourth Street, North Vancouver) tell stories of the people and events that have shaped North Vancouver. A permanent exhibit animates the story of the community's rise from an isolated logging town to today's dynamic urban community.

North Vancouver's archives is located in an elegant historic building in Lynn Valley (3203 Institute Road, North Vancouver) known as the Community History Centre. Built in 1920 as Lynn Valley Elementary School, the building was retrofitted in 2005–2006 to serve as the administrative headquarters for NVMA. Located on the centre's second floor, the archives contains extensive municipal, business, and personal records, historical photographs, maps and plans, books, and documents relating to North Vancouver. These materials—a rich resource for tracing local history and genealogy—may be consulted in a public research room. For more information visit www.northvanmuseum.ca.